SPORTS IN LITERATURE

Henry B. Chapin

Wilmington College

A McKAY ENGLISH AND HUMANITIES SERIES BOOK

David McKay Company, Inc.   *New York*

Sports in Literature
COPYRIGHT © 1976 BY
David McKay Company, Inc.
All rights reserved, including the right to reproduce
this book, or parts thereof, in any form, except for
the inclusion of brief quotations in a review.

Manufactured in the United States of America
Design by Carol Basen

To Helen—
for being a sport about it all,
with love

Library of Congress Cataloging in Publication Data

Main entry under title:

Sports in literature.

(McKay English and humanities series)
Bibliography: p.
1. Sports—Literary collections. 2. American
literature—20th century. 3. English literature
—20th century. I. Chapin, Henry B.
PS509. S65S6   813'.5'080355   76-8235
ISBN 0-679-30301-4

ACKNOWLEDGMENTS

"The Dumb Football Player," Copyright © 1933, 1961 James Thurber. From *University Days*, in *My Life and Hard Times*, published by Harper & Row. Originally printed in *The New Yorker*.

"The Sleeper." From *Stand Up, Friend, With Me*, by Edward Field, copyright © 1963. Reprinted by permission of Grove Press, Inc.

"The Football Game." Reprinted from *The Young Manhood of Studs Lonigan* by James T. Farrell by permission of the publisher, Vanguard Press, Inc. Copyright, 1934, by Vanguard Press, Inc. Copyright © renewed 1961 by James T. Farrell.

"High School Football Days." Reprinted by permission of Coward, McCann & Geoghegan, Inc. from *Vanity of Duluoz* by Jack Kerouac.

"The Eighty-Yard Run." Copyright 1940 and renewed 1968 by Irwin Shaw. Reprinted from *Selected Short Stories of Irwin Shaw*, by permission of Random House, Inc.

"The Footballer in the Small Room." George Braziller, Inc.—from *The Pocket Mirror*, Poems by Janet Frame; reprinted with the permission of the publisher. Copyright © 1967 by Janet Frame.

"In the beginning was the," Lillian Morrison. Reprinted by permission of the author from *Sprints and Distances*, T. Y. Crowell Co., Inc. Copyright © by Lillian Morrison.

"Autumn Begins in Martins Ferry, Ohio." Copyright © 1962 by James Wright. Reprinted from *Collected Poems* by James Wright, by permission of Wesleyan University Press.

"A Mad Fight Song for William S. Carpenter, 1966." Copyright © 1972 by James Wright. Reprinted from *Collected Poems* by James Wright, by permission of Wesleyan University Press.

"The Bee." Copyright © 1966 by James Dickey. Reprinted from *Poems 1957–1967* by James Dickey, by permission of Wesleyan University Press.

"The First Black Student." From *End Zone*, Don DeLillo, pp. 3–22. Copyright © 1972 by Don DeLillo. Reprinted by permission of Houghton Mifflin Company.

"The Basketball Game." Excerpted from *The Last Picture Show* by Larry McMurtry. Copyright © 1966 by Larry McMurtry. Used with permission of The Dial Press.

"Ex-Basketball Player." Copyright © 1957 by John Updike. Originally appeared in *The New Yorker*, and reprinted by permission of Harper & Row, Publishers, Inc.

"The Double Play." Copyright © 1961 by Robert Wallace, and reprinted by permission of the author.

"Hometown Piece for Messrs. Alston and Reese." From *The Complete Poems of Marianne Moore*. Copyright © 1959 by Marianne Moore. Reprinted by permission of The Viking Press, Inc.

"Polo Grounds." From *Collected Poems of Rolfe Humphries*, copyright © 1965 by Indiana University Press. Reprinted by permission of the publisher.

From *The Carpentered Hen and Other Tame Creatures* by John Updike: "Tao in the Yankee Stadium Bleachers." Copyright © 1956 by John Updike. Originally appeared in *The New Yorker*, and reprinted by permission of Harper & Row, Publishers, Inc.

"Cobb Would Have Caught It." Robert Fitzgerald, *In The Rose Of Time*. Copyright 1943 by Robert Fitzgerald. Reprinted by permission of New Directions Publishing Corporation.

"The Base Stealer." Copyright © 1948 by Robert Francis. Reprinted from *The Orb Weaver*, by Robert Francis, by permission of Wesleyan University Press.

"Pitcher." Copyright © 1953 by Robert Francis. Reprinted from *The Orb Weaver*, by Robert Francis, by permission of Wesleyan University Press.

"Dream of a Baseball Star." Gregory Corso, *The Happy Birthday of Death*. Copyright

PREFACE

This anthology began in a course called Sports in Literature, which I have been teaching at Wilmington College. I was able to develop this course because of my vocation as a teacher of literature and my lifelong avocation as a sports fan and, in a small way, participant.

Because of my twin concerns, I have often noticed the mutual hostility between those students (and teachers, too, at times) who have felt strongly allied to either the worlds of literature or of sport. Stereotypically, the "sissy poet" and the "dumb jock" have all too often scrutinized each other with loathing at worst and boredom at best. This conflict between mind and body runs deeply in one strain of our Western culture and is the source of both intellectual snobbery and anti-intellectualism. The conflict also contradicts the Greek concept of the unity of mind and body, a unity that I prefer to stress. Consequently, I have tried to demolish the stereotypes of the "sissy" and the "jock."

What is at stake here is nothing less than our ideal of what a human being ought to be. The question, with respect to sports, becomes, "What is the ideal of manliness?" In this way, life is enormously simplified by disregarding half of humanity. For men, growing up in America too often means being encouraged to be tough and insensitive. As an example, I can remember being ridiculed for enjoying opera when I was in college. This inculcation of cloddishness clearly has great implications for women as well as men, and the division of sensibility into the tough vs. the sensitive is part of the *mal*aise. Though the pun may be unpardonable, it still suggests some of our contemporary trouble. As a partial antidote, I have included in this volume a significant selection of women's writings on sport. Consequently, it should be apparent that neither sport nor this book should be thought of as being for men only.

Sport and literature (or any art, for that matter) need not and should not conflict. As a teacher, I have found myself using sports analogies to make literature accessible to students accustomed to thinking of it as one of the more unpleasant hurdles in their race toward a degree. For instance, I think of the effect of Shelley's

"Ozymandias" as a result of so many meanings being forced to fit into just fourteen lines. In the same way, Muhammad Ali's "phantom punch," which so quickly dispatched Sonny Liston, gained its power from being forced to fit into a space so small that it was invisible to the naked eye. Restrictive form increases power.

I have also likened the verbal pyrotechnics of Gerard Manley Hopkins to the behind-the-back dribbling and other fancy moves of a Pete Maravich or a Nate Archibald. One may then go on to discuss that fancy and imagination are, despite Coleridge's strict distinctions, comparable, and a player with fancy moves may thus be said to move with imagination. The function of imagination as both a source and a result of literature may be discussed, and the class might even discuss when fancy moves are organically necessary and when they are mere rococo ornamentation.

Similarly, I have compared the massive power of a Dreiser novel to the force without finesse of, say, Bronco Nagurski or, should the students lack the proper historical sense, Larry Csonka or whatever bone-crushing athlete comes to mind.

To the teacher who is a sports fan, these analogies will readily come to one's aid, while to others they will seem corny. What is important is that resistance to literature be broken down by placing it in a familiar and more acceptable context. Using sports literature is one way to accomplish this aim. As more nontraditional students enter our schools, sports literature may be one way of reaching them and speaking to their condition.

The readings in this anthology have been collected with three somewhat different, though overlapping, audiences in mind: (1) students of sports and literature, (2) students of English composition, and (3) the general reader.

Interest in sports literature as a distinctive literary type is comparatively recent. There are some indications that this interest is beginning to spread across the nation's high schools and colleges. My correspondence suggests there is an underground network of teachers who have developed courses in this subject independently of one another.

The bad aspects of sports are obvious and known to all. One may cite the exploitation of players, the quasi-militaristic values that are often taught, the ridiculous salaries of the pros (and some college players!), the rah-rah chauvinism, and the corruption of recruiting as instances of what is wrong in sports.

On the other hand, one might also cite the positive values of concern for excellence, discipline, courage, cooperation, dedication, and *joie de vivre* which characterize the best in sports. I believe that all these qualities are important antidotes to a pervasive decadence afflicting some Americans.

The stories and poems in this anthology shed much light both on the positive and the negative sides of sport with an imaginative power that should help all students to understand these issues in depth. And, since sport is really a microcosm of society, understanding these issues should lead to a greater understanding of the world we live in.

The works included in *Sports in Literature* are of significant literary value. None of the pseudo literature that so often gets mixed up with sports (works like "Casey at the Bat" or locker-room inspirational verse) has been included. I gave thought to including some for purposes of comparison and contrast, but the possibility of a student eagerly defending "If you think you are beaten, you are" dissuaded me. However, I think that there is enough good reading here to inspire the student with delight and instruction.

I also believe that the general reader will find this book filled with pleasurable reading. If you love sports and love to read, the works gathered together here will sustain you for a very long time.

I am grateful to the many people who helped and encouraged me while the idea for this anthology was becoming a reality. I owe special thanks to the students in my first Sports in Literature class because of their enthusiasm. Along the way I was aided by John Baskin, Grace Butcher, Helga McCoy, Lew Marcuson, Bill Woods, Fred Raizk and Val McMurtrie. Wilmington gave me time, with a sabbatical leave, and money, granted by a committee headed by Alex MacNutt. Finally, Morris Freedman, mentor and friend, gave me the right advice at the right time.

CONTENTS

FOOTBALL

The image of the dumb jock especially haunts the game of football, and the selection from James Thurber is a humorous sketch of this stereotype. After chuckling over Thurber's brief piece, we might consider just how fair he is being. Conversely, Edward Field's poem "The Sleeper" poignantly explores the feelings of one who felt he was a sissy in boyhood. To what extent do these stereotypes coincide with reality?

James T. Farrell's memorable character, Studs Lonigan, uses football to prove his manhood; in so doing, he feels that everyone should envy him for being able to play a man's game. The intrinsic satisfaction that Studs derives from the game is not great, if one considers how much he is always aware of the crowd and needs it for stimulation. He is dependent upon the cheers of other people to validate his own deeds because of the insecurity of his ego.

Farrell also suggests that Studs, along with his teammates, is not terribly skillful at playing football and that, in such things as leaving his feet while tackling, he reveals himself as a novice. In fact, he is a showboat player without much ability, and the pursuit of excellence is not important to him. This discrepancy between the way Studs views himself and the way the reader views him creates an ironic context within which is revealed the essential brutality of this sandlot football game, epitomized by the vicious anti-Semitism and the dirty play.

This violence, which Farrell renders with considerable strength, takes place outside the rules of the game, and it is, therefore, an uncivilized encounter that violates the concept of sportsmanship. The difference between dirty play and sportsmanship is not always easy to discern, however, and most football games are in constant danger of falling into uncivilized chaos when something goes wrong. In its own way, therefore, football is a human attempt to impose order upon chaos, a job also performed by art. Seen in this light, football constructively channels aggression. It may even be what William James was searching for—a moral equivalent to war.

The selection by Jack Kerouac vigorously conveys the feeling of one season of high school football. The ethnic variety of working-class Massachusetts and the ups and downs of the season are vividly, though not very stylishly, told.

The piece is thinly veiled autobiography. For instance, Lu Libble is Lou Little, the famous Columbia coach. It is not so well known that Jack Kerouac was a good enough high school football player to get a college scholarship. It was at Columbia, however, that he met that other guru-to-be of the Beat Generation, Allen Ginsberg. The promising football career was soon diverted into literature and the Bohemian life.

Sport is ordinarily a youthful activity. What happens when success and acclaim occur so early in life that the recipient becomes unfit to live a more mature, adult life? Christian Darling, in the story by Irwin Shaw, finds it difficult to grow up after his early success, however modest, in football.

A clue to Darling's difficulty in his changing relationship with his wife, as evidenced by their differing attitudes toward modern art, his drinking, her calling him "Baby," and the moving scene when he plunges his arms, jacket and all, into the bathwater. All in all, "The Eighty-Yard Run" is a penetrating story about illusion and reality and the need of human beings to come to terms with them.

The very notion of football poetry may seem to be a contradiction in terms, conjuring up images of the Kansas Jayhawk Yell (whose strident rhythms actually inspired one poem by Vachel Lindsay) or inspirational verse designed to revive teams during halftime pep talks. But, on second thought, it is not really so surprising that one of the major American social rituals should interest poets.

For example, Janet Frame writes of the pain of football and Lillian Morrison of its patterned beauty. James Wright's poetry is characterized by a vivid imagination coupled with an affinity for the everyday life of people like the factory workers and high school football

heroes to be found in "Autumn Begins in Martins Ferry, Ohio."
Wright is also capable of making sharp social statements (though
they may be indirectly communicated) as in "A Mad Fight Song for
William S. Carpenter, 1966," which refers to one of the more insane
moments of the war in Vietnam.

James Dickey was a college football player and hurdler. His work
frequently displays rhetorical power and a fascination with power
itself as a theme. In "The Bee," he describes an incident in which a
child, stung by a bee, runs out into a car-choked highway and is in
mortal danger. The poet applies some old football lessons to save the
child. One might ask whether the poem is sentimental about the old
football experience or if it is fundamentally true. One might also ask
whether ex-football players are better equipped for decisive, heroic
action than those who have never played the game.

Finally, the selection from Don DeLillo's novel, *End Zone,* deals
with the black athlete who is put in the position of having to be the
Jackie Robinson of whatever team or school he plays for. That is to
say, the first black to play in any situation is expected to be extraordinary. Now that more and more blacks have become involved
in contemporary sport, the Jackie Robinson Syndrome has been
subtly replaced by the Superstar Syndrome—black players cannot
afford to be ordinary. This piece by DeLillo also contains a satirical
caricature of a coach's pep talk in which pieties are delightfully
mixed with vulgarities.

JAMES THURBER

THE DUMB FOOTBALL PLAYER

from *My Life and Hard Times*

Another course that I didn't like, but somehow managed
to pass, was economics. I went to that class straight from the botany
class, which didn't help me any in understanding either subject. I used
to get them mixed up. But not as mixed up as another student in my
economics class who came there direct from a physics laboratory. He

was a tackle on the football team, named Bolenciecwcz. At that time Ohio State University had one of the best football teams in the country, and Bolenciecwcz was one of its outstanding stars. In order to be eligible to play it was necessary for him to keep up in his studies, a very difficult matter, for while he was not dumber than an ox he was not any smarter. Most of his professors were lenient and helped him along. None gave him more hints, in answering questions, or asked him simpler ones than the economics professor, a thin, timid man named Bassum. One day when we were on the subject of transportation and distribution, it came Bolenciecwcz's turn to answer a question. "Name one means of transportation," the professor said to him. No light came into the big tackle's eyes. "Just any means of transportation," said the professor. Bolenciecwcz sat staring at him. "That is," pursued the professor, "any medium, agency, or method of going from one place to another." Bolenciecwcz had the look of a man who is being led into a trap. "You may choose among steam, horse-drawn, or electrically propelled vehicles," said the instructor. "I might suggest the one which we commonly take in making long journeys across land." There was a profound silence in which everybody stirred uneasily, including Bolenciecwcz and Mr. Bassum. Mr. Bassum abruptly broke this silence in an amazing manner. "Choo-choo-choo," he said, in a low voice, and turned instantly scarlet. He glanced appealingly around the room. All of us, of course, shared Mr. Bassum's desire that Bolenciecwcz should stay abreast of the class in economics, for the Illinois game, one of the hardest and most important of the season, was only a week off. "Toot, toot, too-tooooooot!" some student with a deep voice moaned, and we all looked encouragingly at Bolenciecwcz. Somebody else gave a fine imitation of a locomotive letting off steam. Mr. Bassum himself rounded off the little show. "Ding, dong, ding, dong," he said, hopefully. Bolenciecwcz was staring at the floor now, trying to think, his great brow furrowed, his huge hands rubbing together, his face red.

"How did you come to college this year, Mr. Bolenciecwcz?" asked the professor. "*Chuf*fa chuffa, *chuf*fa chuffa."

"M'father sent me," said the football player.

"What on?" asked Bassum.

"I git an 'lowance," said the tackle, in a low, husky voice, obviously embarrassed.

"No, no," said Bassum. "Name a means of transportation. What did you *ride* here on?"

"Train," said Bolenciecwcz.

"Quite right," said the professor. "Now, Mr. Nugent, will you tell us—"

EDWARD FIELD

THE SLEEPER

When I was the sissy of the block who nobody wanted on
    their team
Sonny Hugg persisted in believing that my small size was
    an asset
Not the liability and curse I felt it was
And he saw a use for my swift feet with which I ran away
    from fights.

He kept putting me into complicated football plays
Which would have been spectacular if they worked:
For instance, me getting clear in front and him shooting
    the ball over—
Or the sensation of the block, the Sleeper Play
In which I would lie down on the sidelines near the goal
As though resting and out of action, until the scrimmage
    began
And I would step onto the field, receive the long throw
And to the astonishment of all the tough guys in the world
Step over the goal line for a touchdown.

That was the theory anyway. In practice
I had the fatal flaw of not being able to catch
And usually had my fingers bend back and the breath
    knocked out of me

So the plays always failed, but Sonny kept on trying
Until he grew up out of my world into the glamorous
Varsity crowd, the popular kids of Lynbrook High.

But I always have this to thank him for:
That when I look back on childhood
(That four psychiatrists haven't been able to help me bear
    the thought of)
There is not much to be glad for
Besides his foolish and delicious faith
That, with all my oddities, there was a place in the world
    for me
If only he could find the special role.

JAMES T. FARRELL

THE FOOTBALL GAME

from *The Young Manhood of Studs Lonigan*

I

Watching himself in the mirror, Studs hitched up his football pants, carefully arranging the cotton hip pads around his sides. Wished he had better ones. Wouldn't be much protection from a boot in the ribs. He touched the schimmels under his blue jersey, and put on his black helmet. Every inch a football player!

He thought of himself going out to play with old street pants, a jersey, and football shoes. Dressed that way, tackling so hard he'd knock them cuckoo; jumping up ready to go on, no matter how hard he was slammed. No use to be senseless and play without sufficient padding. Only it was swell thinking of being reckless that way, having the crowd recognize such gameness.

He flexed and unflexed his arm muscles. Even with the drinking and carousing he'd done these last couple of years, he was still pretty hard and tough. He slapped his guts. They were hard enough, too, and there was no alderman yet, or not enough anyway to be noticed. And there never would be, because he'd take care of himself before that ever happened. He'd never have a paunch like his old man had. Iron Man Lonigan! The bigger they are, the harder they fall. He lit a cigarette and sat on the bed, thinking proudly of his body, good and strong, even if he was small; powerful football shoulders, good for fighting. And this afternoon he'd prove that it was a good body, and that there was heart and courage inside of it.

But there wouldn't be any girls out there for him to be playing for. Other guys had girls. Wished he had a girl, Lucy, a girl coming out only to see him play . . . Goofy! . . . But he still loved Lucy even if he hadn't seen her in about four years. And if she was coming out there to see him play, because she loved him, he would play much better, and instead of being in it just for the fun and the glory, and to show them all what he was made of, he'd be playing for her also. And he wanted to. Christ sake, he was getting like a clown, all mush inside. He tried to laugh at himself; it was forced.

Smells of the cooking Sunday dinner came tantalizingly from the kitchen. His mother came to the bedroom door, and said that she had a bite ready for him.

"I can't! I'm going to play football," he snapped in uncontrolled exasperation.

"I certainly don't think much of a game that deprives you of your food," she replied.

Jesus Christ! Couldn't she understand anything!

She nagged and persuaded. He got up, and walked towards the door, with her following, still wanting him to eat. He said that he couldn't play with a belly full of food, and as she dipped her hand in the holy water fount on the wall, and showered him, he slammed the door. The father, hearing him, called that he wouldn't have such vulgar language used around the home; but Studs was gone.

He went down the steps two and three at a time, thinking why they always had to be like that, never open to reason and sense, wanting you to do whatever they wished in everything. Felt like leaving home, and living in a room by himself; some day he'd have to, if they didn't keep from trying to run everything he did.

It was humid and sunless. He liked the click of his cleats on the sidewalk. He felt so good, and in such condition, that he had an impulse to run. He checked himself, and took his time. Studs Lonigan was going to use his noodle, and conserve his energy. He was a wise guy, and in everything in life he was going to be that way, always with a little stuff left in him for a pinch.

Jim Clayburn's dude father came along, dressed in snappy gray, wearing a derby, and tapping a cane on the sidewalk. With his gray bush of hair, his face looked soft, almost like a woman's. Must have been something of a sissy and teacher's pet in his own day at school, just as Jim had been. He bowed stiffly to Studs, and Studs nodded, hoping he noticed the football outfit. Jim was studying law now, clerking for a measly ten or fifteen bucks a week. Well, by the time Clayburn, with all his studying and kill-joy stuff was in the dough, Studs Lonigan would be running his old man's business, and be in the big dough too.

He saw Tubby Connell and Nate Klein flinging passes in the street in front of the poolroom. Nate muffed one, and Studs told him to get a bushel basket. He lit a cigarette and laughed at Nate's scenery; an old-fashioned square black helmet that must have come down from Walter Eckersall's day; tight green jersey with holes in the sleeves; pants so big that he swam in them; shoes turned up at the toes because of their size. He looked more closely at the shoes; they were spiked baseball ones. He told Nate they'd never let him play in those, because he might cut somebody to ribbons. Tubby said that Klein was wearing them to show that he had the Fifty-eighth Street fighting spirit.

"This ain't tiddledy-winks; the guy I cut up will be a Monitor, and that's his tough tiddy," Nate said, hard-boiled.

He and Tubby disregarded Studs' advice to save themselves, and went on fooling around with the ball. Studs turned his back to them, and let his hands fall on his hips; his helmet was over his right elbow, and his blond hair was a trifle curly. His broad face revealed absorption. A middle-aged guy with a paunch doped along; Studs hoped that the guy had noticed him, wished he was young like he was, and able to go out and play a game of football, still full of the vim and vitality of youth. A quick feeling of contrition came over him. Suppose he should get hurt? Suppose he should never come back alive? His mother would always remember how he had slammed the door in her face. But damn it, couldn't they be reasonable?

"Hell, Flannel Mouth! How's the brother?" asked Studs, as Young Fat Malloy showed up.

"He'll be there, and he was saying that if you guys lose your first game of the season, he was going to kick your tails around the block to hell and gone. And don't think he can't! He may be a little runt, but let me tell you, Hugo was one of the toughest sergeants they ever had in the army."

"I know it," Studs said, thinking that it was another case of a good little man.

"Look at Klein, that crazy hebe! He's liable to break his neck trying to catch that football!" Fat said.

"Yeah, he's that way because he got gassed in the war."

"But he has guts. You know, Studs, you guys ought to have a crack team this year. And with a good coach like Hugo, you oughtn't to lose a game."

Studs nodded. He thought that maybe, this year, they would all get to working together like a well-oiled machine, and then, next season they could join the Mid-West League. He saw himself flashing through the semi-pro circuit like a comet, and getting himself signed up to play in the backfield with Paddy Driscoll on the Chicago Cardinals.

There was excitement; a wild fling of Nate's nearly hit a baby being wheeled along. The father crabbed like hell, but finally pushed his buggy on. Nate told Studs that wise guys like that bird needed to be punched full of holes.

More players came around, and a gang of them started over to the football field in Washington Park.

II

Wearing a large white sweater, and his old army breeches, bow-legged Coach Hugo Zip Malloy stood with arms folded, his tough mug intent, as he watched the Fifty-eighth Street Cardinals clown through signal practice.

"Come on over here, you birds, and sit on your cans a minute. That's what they're for," he yelled, regally waving his short right arm.

The players dragged over and planked themselves down, facing him. Strangers collected to gape at them. He glared at the strangers.

"Everybody not associated with the team, please fade!" he commanded; some obeyed; others dropped backwards a few feet, and then commenced to inch forwards again. Courageous gawkers stood in their tracks.

Kenny Kilarney suddenly appeared, and did a take-off on a college cheer leader:

> *We ain't rough!*
> *We ain't tough!*
> *But oh! . . . are we determined?*

"Say, Monkey Face!" Coach Hugo said to Kenny.

"No hope for him," Bill Donoghue said.

"Now I want you birds to listen to what I tell you!"

"But say, Hugo?" Bill Donoghue called.

"That's my name."

"Would you mind taking the cigar out of your mouth so we can see you?"

"Sonnyboy, the playground is on the other side of the drive, in back of me," Coach Hugo replied.

"Another thing, coach? Don't you think we ought to give Klein a rising vote? He hasn't been hurt yet this season?"

"Jesus, wouldn't the squirrels make mince-pie out of you?" Coach Hugo said, darting a no-hope look at Bill.

"Now, when the clowns get finished pulling the whiskers off their jokes, I'll talk. . . . And by the way, can't you guys leave the cigarettes alone for a minute. It takes wind to win a football game, and you don't get wind eating them coffin nails!"

"You tell 'em coach, I stutter," said Shrimp Haggerty, lurching drunkenly into their midst; he was thin and sallow, and dogged out in classy clothes. He wore a black band on his top-coat sleeve.

"Haggerty! The other team needs a couple of mudguards. Go on over there," Coach Hugo said.

"Now that the children have finished throwing spitballs around, teacher will talk. . . . Haggerty, get the hell out of here before I have to throw your pieces away! . . ."

Haggerty saw that Coach Hugo was really sore. He staggered away, singing.

"All right, you birds, keep your dirty ears open! I ain't gonna repeat myself! You're goin' out there now for your first crack of the season, and you're gonna play a man's game. There's only one way to play it. Play hard! Hard! Get the other guy, before he gets you! Knock him down! Let them drag him out! If you don't, you might be the unlucky chump that's dragged out. And if any of you birds are carried off that gridiron, cold, don't expect me to break down and weep for you like I was your old lady! Because you won't get knocked cuckoo if you keep your heads up, and play hard! It's the soft guy that gets knocked silly in this game. And if there's any soft babies on this team, the sooner they get it in the neck, the better off they will be, and we too! You guys got to go in there and hit hard, hit often, and every time you hit, make the guy you hit think he's collided with a battleship. Don't worry about giving the ambulance drivers work; they got wives and kiddies to support, and need it. . . . ."

"Hey, Hugo, what undertaker's giving you a rakeoff?" interrupted Arnold Sheehan.

"Sheehan, step into the second grade. You're too bright a boy for first. . . . And now, you birds, you're goin' in that football game in about a minute. If you want to win it, you got to do it yourself! I can't win it for you. That's your job, and if you want this game, you'll have to get it by fighting (he slammed his right fist demonstratively into his left palm). I watched you guys go through signal practice. You stunk! If you go into this game like that, it'll be like the Fort Dearborn massacre. And get me, if you guys don't fight, you can get an old lady to coach you. I won't. All right, snap into it. And, oh, yes, a final word. If any bird on this other team starts dirty work . . . give him the works!"

The team arose. Nate tore forwards. The others walked slowly towards the football field, Coach Hugo making up the rear.

"Say, coach, that's a ripe husky bunch of boys you got there. Tell 'em to try center rushes, and they'll win as easy as taking candy from a baby. Now, when I was a kid. . . ."

"Say, fellow, will you do me a favor?"

"Sure, glad to coach!"

"All right. See that automobile drive? Well, walk across it, and keep on going until you lose yourself in the lagoon."

Coach Hugo roughly yelled gangway, as he went through a crowd, and stepped over the ropes. He clapped his hands together, and yelled to his team:

"All right, you guys, show me if you got any guts in your veins."

III

C
Nate Klein

L G				R G
Harold Dowson				*Carroll Dowson*
L T				R T
Red Kelly				*Dan Donoghue*

F B
Hink Weber

L E	L H B	R H B	R E
Weary Reilley	*Arnold Sheehan*	*Art Hahn*	*Jim Nolan*

Q B
Studs Lonigan

waited, while the ball was put into position for the kick. It fell off the little mound on the forty-yard line four times, so a Monitor stretched himself out and held it in position.

Referee Charley Bathcellar, wearing an astrakhan coat and a new derby, importantly signalled the two captains. Studs felt a thrill of pride as he signalled the readiness of his team; hundreds of people were watching, saw that he was captain. The whistle blew. A thin fellow in street pants and and old red jersey booted the ball on a line. Studs muffed it. The Fifty-eighth Street Cardinals formed disorganized interference. Studs scooped the ball up on the go, and thundered forwards, head down as if he were bucking the line, knees pumping. One Monitor clutched at his left sleeve. Another pulled at his pants from behind. A third dragged at his jersey from the right side. A fourth leaped to make a flying tackle around his ears. The whistle declared the ball dead. Nate Klein and a Monitor player were in the center of the field, bucking each other with arms folded together chest high.

The Cardinals lackadaisically took position in a balanced line formation. The defensive Monitor line crowded together, both tackles kneeling down inside of Dan Donoghue and Red Kelly. Hink Weber told Kelly not to play standing up. Red knelt down. Hink told him to crouch low so that he could charge. Red gave Hink a soreheaded look, but squatted in a weak position.

"Signals," Studs yelled huskily, leaning with hands on knees, eyes on the ground.

Studs tossed a lateral pass to Arnold Sheehan, who went through a mile-wide hole at right tackle. The fellow in the red jersey, Jewboy Schwartz, plugged up the hole. Arnold started to pivot, and Jewboy Schwartz got him while off balance. Three Monitors piled on, and Arnold groaned.

"Watch that piling on!" Weary yelled, rushing up.

"We ain't piling on!" Jake Schaeffer, the big Monitor captain, retorted.

"Well, he was down, wasn't he?"

"He might have crawled."

Hink Weber drew Weary back to avoid a fight.

Arnold limped, his face twisted with pain. Nate angrily asked if they had played dirty, because if they did—the works. Taking short, ziggedy steps, Coach Hugo appeared. Arnold was helped to the sidelines, and as he sat down, Fat Malloy told him that he'd played a swell game.

Weary Reilley switched to left halfback, and Tubby Connell took Weary's end. On the next play, Studs slapped the ball into Hink's guts as Hink thundered at center, hitting like a ton of bricks. He fell over Nate Klein. Getting up, he just looked at Nate and shook his head. Nate said he had been holding out his man, hadn't he? Weary Reilley was tackled by Jewboy Schwartz after a three-yard gain. When the players picked themselves up, Nate Klein was stretched out, ostensibly hurt. Coach Hugo strode importantly onto the field, followed by Fat Malloy, who lugged a water bucket. Fat rushed to Nate, and doused him.

"For Jesus sake!" Nate protested.

"Well, you were out, weren't you?"

Nate groaned weakly, rose to tottering feet, and moved dazedly, with his head hanging as if his neck were broken. But he told Coach Hugo he would stick in the game and get those bastards. Coach Hugo called it the old ginger. Nate floundered into position over the ball, and his face became a mirror of jungle ferocity.

Hink Weber punted down the field, and it was the Monitors' ball.

Studs took a defensive position, twenty yards behind the scrimmage line, and placed his hands on his hips. People in the crowd might notice how collected he seemed to be. He might get his chance to be spectacular. A fellow might break through, and Studs would stave off a touchdown with a flying tackle. Jewboy Schwartz started around the end, outran Tubby, who was boxed in, dodged Weary's lunge with a side leap, graceful as an antelope, and tore towards Studs. Studs dashed forwards a few paces, arms encircled outwards and tensed himself. Schwartz came, fast. Five yards from Studs, Jewboy Schwartz performed a feint with his right foot. Studs lunged. Schwartz would have been free had he not slipped, and Studs, in his lunge, caught Schwartz's foot. Jewboy dragged Studs along, and slipped free, but Dan Donoghue was up to make the tackle.

They patted Studs' back for such nice work. Studs' glow of pride quickly faded. He had been out-smarted, and the fellow would have been free to make a touchdown if he hadn't slipped. He was only wearing street shoes. With cleats, he wouldn't have slipped. Studs waited in back of the scrimmage line. Next time, the guy might make a monkey of him. If he was playing the other half, he might not break through as easily because Jim Nolan and Dan were better than Red and Tubby. Studs' confidence seemed gone. The Jew was too speedy and clever for him. No, goddamn it, he'd leave his feet next time before that feint! Nail him! Studs moved forwards a few feet with the pass from center. Dan smeared the play for a loss. The teams lined up and Nate staggered into his place as defensive center.

The game see-sawed through the first quarter, slow, argumentative, marred by fumbles. On the last play of the period, Studs took a punt, ran forwards, swinging the ball from side to side for effect, running forwards, thinking he was making a long run, hearing cheering from the side, and ... Jewboy Schwartz dove into him, his shoulder smashing Studs in the solar plexus. Studs went down with a thud, and lost the ball. His guts pained; he gasped. He slowly picked himself up, a sick expression on his face. The whistle saved him from having to call time out.

IV

Early in the second quarter, Jewboy Schwartz broke loose, and fleeted down the side line. Studs ran over, left his feet, smashed through the air as Schwartz sidestepped, and picked up speed again, rolled over offside four times in a histrionic effort to show the crowd that his try had been fearless and desperate, sat up and yelled to get him. Schwartz was over for a touchdown.

Studs' shame and disappointment was lessened a little when he heard Tommy Doyle call that it was a good try. The kick for extra point was missed. Hink and Weary walked by Studs, into position. Hink said that they would have to slow the Jew up with some rough tackling. Weary declared that if he got his guts slapped a couple of times, he'd slow down because all Jews were yellow. Nate ran awkwardly to Studs and started bawling him out. Studs told Nate to freeze it. Nate megaphoned to all of them that they had to fight now. Studs waited, hands on knees, worrying himself, forgetting the crowd, thinking that they had to win, had to stop that fast Jew.

The Cardinals pepped up and shouted after taking the ball to the Monitor thirty-yard line on four plays. They were going over now, but on the next play Art Hahn went through tackle, and he was stopped by Red Kelly who stood in his way. Nate yelled to Red that it wasn't a sanitarium, and Red told him to shut up while he was all together. Weary yelled to can the beefing and play football. Studs flung a pass. Jewboy Schwartz picked it neatly out of the air, and ran in the clear. Studs, playing safety, went for him without confidence, left his feet in a blind dive, opened his eyes as he encircled the Jew's slippery, powerful thighs, clenched them, tumbled him down. Hearing a cheer, he realized it had been neat work. He jumped up, forgetting that it had been lucky in the glory of being cheered. He walked casually way. The thrill of leaving his feet, rushing through the air, hitting him, dragging him down no nicely, lingered. He wanted to do it again. Weary patted his back, and called it a sweet tackle in the most genuine words he'd uttered to Studs since their fight. Studs felt good again. But, boy, that Jew was built like steel. Light and fast, and hard as nails. They'd need a club, or a tank to put him out. Still, the memory of that tackle, a split second of keen release and thrill, hung with him.

Jim Nolan recovered on a bad pass from the Monitor center. Hink Weber took the ball on the first play, and ran forty yards down the left side of the field for a touchdown. He kicked the point after touchdown. The Fifty-eighth Street Cardinals talked to each other like happy children.

Jewboy Schwartz took the kickoff. His own men got in his way, and Weary tackled him. There was a pile on, and Weary jammed his knee into Schwartz's groin. They got off, and Schwartz lay there, moaning and rolling, with both hands gripping his crotch. Schaeffer rushed to Reilley and told him to cut it out. Weary snarled back that he didn't like people to talk with their tongues; fists spoke a harder language. Hink pulled Weary aside, and again avoided a fight.

Jewboy Schwartz tried to play. When he had to punt, his kick went weakly to Art Hahn. He limped off the field, and at the half, the Fifty-eighth Street Cardinals led 7 to 6.

V

Between halves, Coach Hugo Zip Malloy told his team they weren't hitting hard enough. He promised to buy a drink for every one who laid out a Monitor so that the guy stayed out. He told Austin McAuliffe to go in at quarter and unleash their trick plays, because Austin, a thin, weak-faced, red-haired chap, was a scientific player. Studs took Art Hahn's half, Arnold was to go back in, and Weary was to play end in place of Tubby. Bill Donoghue was to take Kelly's tackle.

Jewboy Schwartz was back and returned the kickoff twenty yards. Weary grouped the team together after the play, and said this time, they had to put that Jew out for keeps. Studs took his position at defensive half, keen to be more in the game, tackling, running the ends, bucking the line, smearing passes. Only they couldn't let the Jew get loose. Austin was a poor safety man. But they'd stop him dead now. He waited for the play, suddenly wishing he'd gone to high school and been a star like Dan had. Studs smashed in with the play, but Dan nabbed Schwartz behind the line. Schaeffer carried the ball on the next play. Arnold Sheehan was clipped from behind, and Schaeffer got twenty yards before Hink sliced into him from the side. Arnold went out with a wrenched knee, and Art Hahn came on the field. Nolan recovered a fumble. Austin called a trick play. The ball was passed from Austin to Studs to Hahn to Nolan, and eighteen yards were lost. Austin called another trick play, a quarterback sneak, and he circled backwards, running wide. Tacklers closed in on him. He outran them to the sidelines for a twenty-five yard loss. Hink punted.

Schwartz took the ball on first down and came flying through tackle without interference. Dodging to break into the open, he was hit simultaneously by Studs, Weary, and Hink. He arose groggy.

"They'll be picking up the kike's pieces now," Weary said, walking off with Studs.

Schwartz started a wide end run. Nolan smashed in, and made a flying tackle, catching Jewboy by the heels to dump him on his head. The crowd could hear the thud. He lay unconscious. He was revived and insisted on playing. Jewboy dropped back to punt. Weary and Nate Klein broke through, and piled into him blocking the kick. He got up with a bloody nose, and a hand slightly scratched from Nate's spikes. There was a row, but Hink Weber sent Nate to the sidelines to borrow another pair of shoes.

Hink took the ball through the line. Schwartz dove for him, and was stiff-armed on the chin, his head jerking back as he flopped. Hink scored another touchdown.

Hink kicked off to Schwartz. Five Cardinals hit him. He was out again, bleeding from the mouth, his upper lip crusted with congealed blood from his nose. A Monitor yelled that he was dead. Jake Schaeffer helped carry him off and walked back onto the field in tears, vowing he'd get the sonsofbitches. Weary recovered a Monitor fumble, and Schaeffer piled on him.

"What's the idea?" Weary challenged, arising.

"Play football, and quit squawking. You half killed my buddy!"

"And I'll kill you too, kike!" Weary said, clipping Schaeffer on the jaw. Before he knew what hit him, Schaeffer got two more clouts, and went down.

"Get up and fight, louse!" Weary sneered, hovering over him.

Both teams started swinging. Spectators and substitutes rushed onto the field. The three cops, at the game, struggled in vain. One of them whistled loudly. Another fled to call for reenforcements. Hugo Malloy parted through the crowd with a billy. Three Monitors went for Weary. He laid two of them cold with punches, and picked the third up and tossed him four yards away. Studs caught him as he stumbled, and he went down. A fellow stepped on his face. Nate Klein kicked him, and was smacked in the eye from behind. He slunk towards the edge of the crowd. Weary shoved about, swinging when he had to, trying to find Schaeffer. He caught him, and let him have both guns. A billy came down on his shoulder. He wheeled around, getting force, and belted the guy with the billy, flush in the mouth, closed in, and gave him the knee. He kicked the guy for good measure.

A park cop grabbed Weary. He wriggled loose, slipped behind him, and gave him a rabbit punch. A bruiser, guard on the Monitors, slugged wildly at Studs. Studs ducked, in desperation at the guy's size, and swung blindly, landing in the guts. The ham's guard dropped, and he whittled down to Studs' size. Studs let an uppercut go from his heels and caught the fellow under the chin. The bruiser fled. Slug Mason came into action, pumping with both fists. He caught two guys, and crashed their heads together.

"The cops!" somebody yelled.

The cry was taken up. The mob separated in all directions. Police reenforcements came across the park, and clubs were swung, as everybody ran. Studs, running, passed a group carrying Schwartz.

"You bastards, come down to Forty-seventh Street!"

Studs turned and thumbed his nose. An opened pocket-knife zizzed by his ears. He ran.

"Swell work, Studs!" said Fat Malloy ranging alongside of him. Shots in the distance were heard.

Studs came out of the park at Fifty-sixth Street, out of breath, his side paining.

VI

The poolroom was crowded. Rumors spread quickly. Talk went of arrests, broken heads, people dead. Studs passed along from one excited group to another, liking it all, the praise, the talk, the excitement. He came upon Arnold Sheehan, who had a sprained ankle, a twisted knee, and a shiner. He had been sitting down, and when the fighting came close, he had arisen and hobbled along the ropes. It had been just his luck to get sloughed in the eye. Weary tried to stir Studs up to go down to Forty-seventh. Nobody was interested.

Fifty-eighth Street had won the game and the fight anyway, they all said. Nate came to tell Studs how he'd gloriously gotten his shiner. Young Rocky Kansas interrupted to tell how he had mashed in a big baboon. Studs knew they were liars. Guys always lied like that about how they fought, how they drank, how they jazzed. He told of hitting the big guy, and lied, too, saying he had knocked the guy cold with a punch. It was like being on a glorious jag, a little bit like it had been on Armistice Day.

He heard Dan Donoghue near him ask Danny O'Neill what he thought of the game.

"Most of them don't know how to play. They tackle high, can't block, don't even know how to play their positions."

"Well, they are uncoached, but don't you think it was a fair bunch for an uncoached team?" asked Dan Donoghue.

Studs frowned when O'Neill superciliously answered yes. Remembered the punk when he ran around with his stockings falling and snot running out of his nose. Uncoached! Ought to slap his teeth! Seemed to think he was god, droopy punk!

"That Schwartz is a player. I never tackled anybody as hard to get in my high school career with Loyola and I played against some tough men," Dan said.

"He was good. But some of the guys, Kelly, McAuliffe, and Klein, for instance, were jokes."

"What do you think of Studs?" asked Donoghue.

Studs tensed. Waited. Oughtn't care what the punk thought. Waited.

"A bit slow, but he knows what to do, leaves his feet when he tackles, and handles himself well."

"Studs is a natural-born football player," Donoghue said.

O'Neill wasn't so bad. Heard too that he was a high school star. Studs sidled to them.

"Now that you're a star on the team at the Saint Stanislaus high school, what did you think of our . . . amateur game?" Studs asked, fatuously.

Before O'Neill could answer, the rumor spread that Schwartz had died on the way to the hospital. Everybody gabbed and shouted at the same time.

"Will anything be done about it?" Studs asked Kelly.

"They might hold us for manslaughter."

"Why? We played a fair game. The fight was afterwards."

"Well, they might, only, of course, we'll get out of it, and anyway, besides, we were in the right. We can get drag through my old man, who's sergeant down at Fiftieth now, and your old man knowing politicians, and some other guys the same way," Red said.

"We can get enough witnesses," said Studs.

The rumor was still being discussed when Studs left for home. If they did throw them all in the jug! He saw himself in the pen for a manslaughter charge. But they couldn't get him. He'd played a clean game.

He realized how tired he was, and his shoulders drooped. But it had been a great game, and a great fight, and he could feel proud of his part in both. He'd showed them all. He remembered that first clean tackle he had made, leaving his feet, the way he smashed into the runner, that sudden rush of his body through the air for a split second, and bang, the guy was down. Hundreds of people, too, had seen it. He was nostalgic to be still playing, making tackles like that.

Dumb, too, not to have gone to high school. If punks like O'Neill could make the grade, what couldn't he have done? He cursed, though, realizing that they would lose their permits to play in Washington Park, and that they couldn't get up a good team to travel, particularly after a fight like this; because if they traveled and didn't have a big enough mob along, they'd get the clouts plenty somewhere. Damn Reilley! And just when the scrap had started, he had been getting into top form, he felt. But the fight, too, had been a wow. The way he had hit that big yellow bastard. Only, gee, he might have been a bigger star in the game than even Schwartz, if it hadn't started.

He stuck his shoulders back, and forced himself to walk briskly. Proud of himself and his body. In his prime right now.

He became aware that it was dark, and an autumn mist was settling over Fifty-eighth Street. Street lights were on at the alley between Indiana and Michigan. There were lights in windows. He heard the scrape of shoes in back of him, and the rumble of an elevated train. Down at State Street, a street car was going, the bell donging. An automobile passed. The lonesome part of the day.

If Lucy had seen it, him! Well, what if he did admit to himself; he had played and acted like a hero!

That poor bastard Schwartz, game, had to grant that, lying dead in a hospital or morgue. It could have been him, perhaps. No, he knew he wouldn't die that way; he knew that he had some kind of a destiny to live for, and that he would live until that destiny was fulfilled. Maybe he would be a damn important guy later on, politician or something. That poor Jew bastard in a morgue. On the impulse, he mumbled a prayer for the guy!

The street around him seemed gloomy, and he was gloomy too. He couldn't get the thought of that dead Jew out of his mind. He didn't feel so cocky. He felt now like he wanted something in life, and didn't know what. That game and fight now, it had been swell. But there was something more he wanted than the glory of it, and he didn't even know what it was. Funny that he kept coming back to thoughts like this.

JACK KEROUAC

HIGH SCHOOL FOOTBALL DAYS

from *Vanity of Duluoz*

All footballers know that the best football players started on sandlots. Take Johnny Unitas for instance, who never even went to high school, and take Babe Ruth too in baseball. From those early sandlot games we went on to some awful blood-flying games in North Common against the Greeks: the North Common Panthers. Naturally when a Canuck like Leo Boisleau (now on my team) and a Greek like Socrates Tsoulias come head on, blood will fly. The blood my dear flew like in a Homeric battle those Saturday mornings. Imagine Putsy Keriakalopoulos trying to dance his way on that dusty crazy field around Iddyboy or a crazy charging bull like Al Didier. It was the Canucks against the Greeks. The beauty of it all, these two teams later formed the nucleus of the Lowell High School football team. Imagine me trying to dive off tackle through Orestes Gringas or his brother Telemachus Gringas. Imagine Christy Kelakis trying to lay a pass over the fingers of tall Al Roberts. These later sandlot games were so awful I was afraid to get up on Saturday mornings and show up. Other such games were played in Bartlett Junior High field, where we'd all gone as kids, some in Dracut Tigers field, some in the cowfield near St. Rita's Church. There were other, wilder Canuck teams from around Salem Street who never contacted us because they didnt know how to ask for a game via the sports page of the newspaper; otherwise I think the combination of their team with ours, and the combination of other Greek or even Polish or Irish teams around town . . . O me, in other words, Homeric wouldnt have been the word for it.

But as an example of where I learned football. Because I wanted to go to college and somehow I knew my father would never be able to afford the tuition, as it turned out to be true. I, of all things, wanted to end up on a campus somewhere smoking a pipe, with a buttondown sweater, like Bing Crosby serenading a coed in the moonlight down the old Ox Road as the strains of alma mater song come from the frat house. This was our dream, gleaned from going to the Rialto Theater and seeing movies. The further dream was to graduate from college and become a big insurance salesman wearing a gray felt hat getting off the train in Chicago with a briefcase and being embraced by a blond wife on the platform, in the smoke and soot of the bigcity hum and excitement. Can you picture what this would be like today? What with air pollution and all, and the ulcers of the executive, and the ads in *Time* Magazine, and our nowadays highways with cars zipping along by the millions in all directions in and around rotaries from one ulceration of the joy of the spirit of the other? And then I pictured myself, college grad, insurance success, growing old with my wife in a paneled house where hang my moose heads from successful Labradorian hunting expeditions and as I'm sipping bourbon from my liquor cabinet with white hair I bless my son to the next mess of sheer heart attack (as I see it now).

As we binged and banged in dusty bloody fields, we didnt even dream we'd all end up in World War II, some of us killed, some of us wounded, the rest of us eviscerated of 1930's innocent ambition.

I wont go into my junior year in Lowell High School, it was the usual thing about the boy too young, or with not enough seniority, to get to play regularly, though because coach Tam Keating thought I was a sophomore because I was fifteen he didnt let me play but was "saving me up" for junior and senior years. Also there was something fishy in the state of Merrimack because in practice scrimmage he ran me pretty hard and I made perfectly good hard gains and could have done the same in any official games, or there are politics involved, none of which my father countenanced as he was so honest that when a committee of men of Lowell came to him in about 1930 to ask him if he'd run for mayor he answered "Sure, I'll run for mayor, but if I win, I'll have to throw every crook out of Lowell and there'll be nobody left in town."

All I know is how my senior year season went and judge for yourself, or if you dont understand, let a coach judge: I started the first game of the year only because Pie Menelakos had an injured ankle. Granted he was a nice tricky runner but he was so small that when somebody hit him he flew 10 feet. Granted again, he was slippery. But because, somehow, the coach figured he needed a blocker, a "fullback" like Rick Pietryka, and that neat little passer Christy Kelakis, there was no room for me the runner, in the starting backfield. Yet as for being fullback I, in scrimmage, could put my head down and ball right through for 10 yards without even looking. As for being halfback, I could catch a badly thrown pass that was zipping behind me by simply pivoting, gathering it in, and whirling back to my run and go all the way. I admit I couldnt block like Bill Demmons the quarterback or pass like Kelakis. Somehow they had to have Pietryka and Menelakos in there and my father claimed somebody was being paid. "Typical of stinktown on the Merrimack," he said. Besides he wasn't very popular in Lowell because whenever somebody gave him some guff he let em have it. He punched a wrestler in the mouth in the showers at Laurier Park after a wrestling match had been thrown, or fixed. He took a Greek patriarch by the black robes at the bottom and shoved him out of his printing shop for arguing about the price of circulars. He did the same thing to the owner of the Rialto Theater, Buck-a-Thousand Grossman he called him. He had been cheated out of his business by a group of Canuck "friends," and he said the Merrimack River wouldnt be cleaned up before 1984. He'd already told the mayoral committee what the hell he thought about honesty. He ran a little weekly newspaper called the Lowell *Spotlight* that exposed graft in City Hall. We know all cities are the same but he was an exceptionally honest and frank man. He was only Mister Five-by-Five, 5 foot 7 tall and 235 pounds, yet he wasnt afraid of anybody. He admitted I was a lousy hitter in baseball but when it came to football he said they hardly came better as runner. This opinion of his was later corroborated by Francis Fahey, then coach of Boston College and later of Notre Dame, who actually came to the house and talked with my father in the parlor.

But he had good reason to be sore as the record will show. As I say, I started the first game. Let me say, though, first, we had a magnificent line: Big Al Swoboda was right end, a 6 foot 4 Lithuanian or Pole strong as an ox and as mild. Telemachus Gringas (aforementioned) at right tackle, nicknamed Duke and brother to great Orestes Gringas, both of them the toughest, boniest and most honest Greeks to meet. Duke himself actually a boyhood buddy of mine in the short month's duration at age twelve or so we'd decided to be friends, Saturday nights walking a mile and a half leaning on each other's arm over shoulders from the glittering lights of Kearney Square, Duke now grown into a quiet fellow but a 210-pound blockbuster with merry black eyes. Hughie Wain right guard, a big 225-pound quiet fellow from Andover Street where the rich folks lived, with the power and demeanor of a bull. Joe Melis center, a Pole of dynamic booming dramatic crewcutted tackles, later elected captain to next year's team and destined to play fullback and a good 300-yard runner in track. Chet Rave left guard, a strange talkative rock of a man of seventeen destined to be the only other member of this Lowell team besides myself to be seriously sought after by bigtime college teams (in his case, Georgia University). Jim Downing left tackle, a 6 foot 4 lackadaisical Irishman and beware of them. And Harry Kiner left end, speedy and good on defense and made of rocky bones.

So I started the first game of the year against Greenfield Hi (and here's the record I spoke of, the whole year) (game by game) and made two touchdowns that were called back, actually made five of the seven first downs in the whole game, averaged about 10 yards a try, and made a 20-yard run to within inches of a touchdown and Kelakis assigned himself the honor of carrying it over (he was the signal caller).

In the second game of the season, despite this performance of mine,

Menelakos' ankle (Menny's) had healed and he started in my place. I was allowed to play only the last two minutes, at Gardner High in western Massachusetts, carried the ball but twice, hit for first down both tries, for 12 and 13 yards respectively, got a bloody nose and ate some Chair City ice cream after the game (it's made in Gardner).

(Both those first two games won easily by Lowell.)

In the third game I wasnt even assigned to start but was sent in for the last half only, against Worcester Classical, and ran back a punt 64 yards through the whole team for a touchdown, then knocked off two more touchdowns of about 25 yards apiece, carrying the ball only seven times for 20.6 yards per crack. This is in the newspaper records. (Lowell won that, too.)

Nevertheless, when the "big test" came for Lowell against Manchester even then I was not a big heroic "starter" but sat on the bench as now the kids of school in the stands took up a chant "We want Duluoz, we want Duluoz." Can you beat or figure that? I had to sit there and watch some of those bums prance and dance, one little leg sprain and there's heroic Pietryka making sure to remove his helmet when he was helped limping off the field so everybody could see his tragic hair waving in the autumn breeze. Supposed to be a piledriving fullback he really plowed and plumped like an old cow, and without the grim silent blocking of Bill Demmons in front of him he wouldnt have reached the line of scrimmage in time for an opening. Vaunted Manchester was overrated however, Lowell High won 20-0 and I was allowed to carry the ball just once in the last moment, the quarterback's call being for a line dive when what I wanted to do was sweep the end, so I got buried in tackle and the cry "We want Duluoz" died and the game ended a minute or less than a minute later.

I admit they didnt need me anyway in that game (20–0), but when the fifth game came, I didnt start that either, but was allowed to play one quarter of it during which I scored 3 touchdowns, one called back, against Keith Academy, which we won 43–0. But quite understandably, if you understand football, either by now or before, quietly in the background I was now being scouted by Francis Fahey's men at Boston College who were already preparing to move to Notre Dame, in other words, I was getting interested attention from the highest echelons of American football, and on top of that the Boston *Herald* ran a headline on the sports pages that week, right across the top, saying DULUOZ IS THE 12TH MAN ON THE LOWELL HIGH SCHOOL ELEVEN, which was strange no matter how you slice it. Even in my own sixteen-year-old dewy brain there lurked the suspicion that something was wrong though I couldnt altogether (or wouldnt) believe my father's claim of favoritism. The coach, Tam Keating, seemed to glance at me sometimes with a kind of distant rugged regret, I thought, as though this misattention of my palpable straight powers was out of his hands. My father by now was enraged. A sportswriter, Joe Callahan, who was later to become publicity director at Notre Dame in the Francis Fahey regime and then president of the Boston Patriots in the American Football League, began to hint in his sports column about me that "figures don't lie." An enemy sportswriter who hated my Pa wrote of me as "looking" like a football player. Wasnt that sweet?

The next game against Malden was a meeting of the titans of Massachusetts high school football that year, tho I'd say Lynn Classical was tougher than both of us. Malden's huge beefy guards and tackles with grease under their eyes like war-painted Iroquois held us to a 0–0 tie over the whole afternoon (I still say Iddyboy Bissonnette should have been there but the coach told me his marks were not good enough, they'd sent Iddyboy home after a few practice sessions where he clobbered everyboy and coulda clobbered Everyman too). Nobody was hardly in possession of the ball all that Malden afternoon. But our magnificent line of Swoboda, Wain, Rave, Downing, Melis, Gringas, etc. brooked no boloney from them either. This afternoon made no difference whether I carried the ball, or started, or played just a quarter or not; it was a defensive pingpoing B L O N G of a game: dull enough but watched by interested observers.

My only real goof of the season was in the Lynn Classical game: they beat us 6-0 in Lynn, but had I not dropped that damned pass with my slippery idiot fingers at the goal line, a pass from Kelakis straight and true into my hands, we might have won, or tied, one. I've never gotten over the guilt of dropping that pass. If there had been no pigskin in football but just a good old floppy sock like you play with at ten. In fact I used to carry the pigskin with one hand while running and fumbled often. This was one thing the coach may not have liked. But it was the only way for me to run hard and dodge hard with full trackman's range and I didnt fumble any more than anybody else, anyhow.

Malden game was followed by a ridiculous game to be played at New Britain Connecticut, big team, with all our whole squad screaming in hotel suites the night before the game, not drinking beer or anything like the kids must do nowadays but just no chance to sleep like at home on Friday nights, and so we lost that one cold. (Some had sneaked out to a dance.)

So now, being all discouraged, the great starters of the team, the heroes, had to rest after the fiasco in Connecticut, so I was left with a bunch of second-string kids to face Nashua (hometown of both my parents) in the raining mud, and as I say, it was an example of how they were treating me. After the game, mind you ... well wait a minute. It was the toughest best game of football I ever played and it was the game that decided Fahey and also caught the attention of Lu Libble of Columbia and other sources like Duke University. Naturally, the heroes resting in Turkish baths at the Rex, I started this one, in mud that smells so sickly sweet, facing a lot of big tough Greeks, Polocks, Canucks and Yankee boys and collided with them till we were caked beyond recognition of face or numerals on the jersey. The newspaper account concentrated on a report of the scoring plays, 19–13 favor of Nashua, but didnt keep tabs on the yardage by rushing because with my head down I averaged 130 out of 149 total yards for Lowell including one 60-yard run where I was caught from behind by a longlegged end but did make a 15-yard touchdown run with a pass in my arm. There were slippery fumbles on all sides, blocked kicks, sliding into the waiting arms of sideline spectators, yet this game remains in my mind the most beautiful I ever played and the most significant because I was being used (along with Bill Demmons) as a workhorse without glory and played the kind of game only a professional watcher could have applauded, a lonely secret backbone game piledriving through the murk with mud-blooded lips, the dream that goes back to old Gipper and Albie Booth games on old rainy newsreels.

With the regular team of course we could have won this one, nobody's a one-man team, but no, the heroes didnt like rainy mud.

That night at home I woke up in the middle of sleep with bunched cramp muscles called Charlie Horses that made me scream: yet no one had offered me a Turkish bath at the Rex after all that insane pile-driving slippery plowing and bashing with mostly children on my side.

(But was somebody trying to raise the odds on the big Thanksgiving football game coming up next in ten days?)

Okay, but comes the big Thanksgiving Day football game, the hallowed enemies are to meet, Lowell vs. Lawrence, in a zero weather field so hard it was like ice. Now the "heroes" were ready and started without me. The heroes had to have their day on radio with eighteen thousand watching. I'm sitting in the straw at the foot of the bench, with, as they say in French, *mon derrière dans paille* ("my arse in the straw"). Comes the end of the first half, no score whatever. Second half they figure they might need me and put me in. (Maybe they figure I looked awful bad in that Nashua game and nobody'll care.) At one point I am almost loose, but some kid from Lawrence just barely trips me with a meaty Italian hand. But a few plays later Kelakis flips me a 3-yard lob over the outside end's hands and I take this ball and turn down the sidelines and bash and drive head down, head up, pause, move on. Downing throws a beautiful block, somebody else too, bumping I go, 18 yards, and just make it to the goal line where a Lawrence guy hits me and hangs on but I just jump out of his arms and over on my face with the game's only touchdown. The score is 8–0 because Harry Kiner has already blocked a Lawrence punt and jumped on it in the end zone for a 2-point safety. We could have won 2–0 anyway. Some line we had. But as the game ends, pandemonium and et cetera, I run immediately into the locker rooms in front of everybody else on the field so I can change fast for Thanksgiving Dinner at home and who's in the locker room of Lowell High cursing and kicking his helmet around, but Pie Menelakos, as though we'd lost, and cursing because it was I and not himself who scored the only touchdown of the game?

So there you have it.

He gets an offer from Norwich in Vermont while Francis Fahey comes to my house followed by Lu Libble's men a few days later.

So in this case, wifey, I could be bitter, I am bitter, but God gave my chance to help myself.

Poor Pa meanwhile, at home, turkey, cherry pies, free bowling in the alleys, hooray, my dream of going to college was in like Flynn.

Still I say, what means it? You may say I'm a braggart about football, although all these records are available in the newspaper files called morgue, I admit I'm a braggart, but I'm not calling it thus because what was the use of it all anyway, for as the Preacher sayeth: "Vanity of vanities . . . all is vanity." You kill yourself to get to the grave. Especially you kill yourself to get to grave before you even die, and the name of that grave is "success," the name of that grave is hullaballoo boomboom horseshit.

IRWIN SHAW

THE EIGHTY-YARD RUN

The pass was high and wide and he jumped for it, feeling it slap flatly against his hands, as he shook his hips to throw off the halfback who was diving at him. The center floated by, his hands desperately brushing Darling's knee as Darling picked his feet up high and delicately ran over a blocker and an opposing linesman in a jumble on the ground near the scrimmage line. He had ten yards in the clear and picked up speed, breathing easily, feeling his thigh pads rising and falling against his legs, listening to the sound of cleats behind him, pulling away from them, watching the other backs heading him off toward the sideline, the whole picture, the men closing in on him, the blockers fighting for position, the ground he had to cross, all suddenly clear in his head, for the first time in his life not a meaningless confusion of men, sounds, speed. He smiled a little to himself as he ran, holding the ball lightly in front of him with his two hands, his knees pumping high, his hips twisting in the almost girlish run of a back in a broken field. The first halfback came at him and he fed him his leg, then swung at the last moment, took the shock of the man's shoulder without breaking stride, ran right through him, his cleats biting securely into the turf. There was only the safety man now, coming warily at him, his arms crooked, hands spread. Darling tucked the ball in, spurted at him, driving hard, hurling himself along, all two hundred pounds bunched into controlled attack. He was sure he was going to get past the safety man. Without thought, his arms and legs working beautifully together, he headed right for the safety man, stiff-armed him, feeling blood spurt instantaneously from the man's nose onto his hand, seeing his face go awry, head turned, mouth pulled to one side. He pivoted away, keeping the arm locked, dropping the safety man as he ran easily toward the goal line, with the drumming of cleats diminishing behind him.

How long ago? It was autumn then, and the ground was getting hard because the nights were cold and leaves from the maples around the stadium blew across the practice fields in gusts of wind, and the girls were beginning to put polo coats over their sweaters when they came to watch practice in the afternoons. . . . Fifteen years. Darling walked slowly over the same ground in the spring twilight, in his neat shoes, a man of thirty-five dressed in a double-breasted suit, ten pounds heavier in the fifteen years, but not fat, with the years between 1925 and 1940 showing in his face.

The coach was smiling quietly to himself and the assistant coaches were looking at each other with pleasure the way they always did when one of the second stringers suddenly did something fine, bringing credit to them, making their $2,000 a year a tiny bit more secure.

Darling, trotted back, smiling, breathing deeply but easily, feeling wonderful, not tired, though this was the tail end of practice and he'd run eighty yards. The sweat poured off his face and soaked his jersey and he liked the feeling, the warm moistness lubricating his skin like oil. Off in a corner of the field some players were punting and the smack of leather against the ball came pleasantly through the afternoon air. The freshmen were running signals on the next field and the quarterback's sharp voice, the pound of the eleven pairs of cleats, the "Dig, now *dig!*" of the coaches, the laughter of the players all somehow made him feel happy as he trotted back to midfield listening to the applause and shouts of the students along the sidelines, knowing that after that run the coach would have to start him Saturday against Illinois.

Fifteen years, Darling thought, remembering the shower after the workout, the hot water steaming off his skin and the deep soapsuds and all the young voices singing with the water streaming down and towels going and managers running in and out and the sharp sweet smell of oil of wintergreen and everybody clapping him on the back as he dressed and Packard, the captain, who took being captain very seriously, coming over to him and shaking his hand and saying, "Darling, you're going to go places in the next two years."

The assistant manager fussed over him, wiping a cut on his leg with alcohol and iodine, the little sting making him realize suddenly how fresh and whole and solid his body felt. The manager slapped a piece of adhesive tape over the cut, and Darling noticed the sharp clean white of the tape against the ruddiness of the skin, fresh from the shower.

He dressed slowly, the softness of his shirt and the soft warmth of his wool socks and his flannel trousers a reward against his skin after the harsh pressure of the shoulder harness and thigh and hip pads. He drank three glasses of cold water, the liquid reaching down coldly inside of him, soothing the harsh dry places in his throat and belly left by the sweat and running and shouting of practice.

Fifteen years.

The sun had gone down and the sky was green behind the stadium and he laughed quietly to himself as he looked at the stadium, rearing above the trees, and knew that on Saturday when the 70,000 voices roared as the team came running out onto the field, part of that enormous salute would be for him. He walked slowly, listening to the gravel crunch satisfactorily under his shoes in the still twilight, feeling his clothes swing lightly against his skin, breathing the thin evening air, feeling the wind more softly in his damp hair, wonderfully cool behind his ears and at the nape of his neck.

Louise was waiting for him at the road, in her car. The top was down and he noticed all over again, as he always did when he saw her, how pretty she was, the rough blond hair and the large, inquiring eyes and the bright mouth, smiling now.

She threw the door open. "Were you good today?" she asked.

"Pretty good," he said. He climbed in, sank luxuriously into the soft leather, stretched his legs far out. He smiled, thinking of the eighty yards. "Pretty damn good."

She looked at him seriously for a moment, then scrambled around, like a little girl, kneeling on the seat next to him, grabbed him, her hands along his ears, and kissed him as he sprawled, head back, on the seat cushion. She let go of him, but kept her head close to his, over his. Darling reached up slowly and rubbed the back of his hand against her cheek, lit softly by a street lamp a hundred feet away. They looked at each other, smiling.

Louise drove down to the lake and they sat there silently, watching the moon rise behind the hills on the other side. Finally he reached over, pulled her gently to him, kissed her. Her lips grew soft, her body sank into his, tears formed slowly in her eyes. He knew, for the first time, that he could do whatever he wanted with her.

"Tonight," he said. "I'll call for you at seven-thirty. Can you get out?"

She looked at him. She was smiling, but the tears were still full in her eyes. "All right," she said. "I'll get out. How about you? Won't the coach raise hell?"

Darling grinned. "I got the coach in the palm of my hand," he said. "Can you wait till seven-thirty?"

She grinned back at him. "No," she said.

They kissed and she started the car and they went back to town for dinner. He sang on the way home.

Christian Darling, thirty-five years old, sat on the frail spring grass, greener now than it ever would be again on the practice field, looked thoughtfully up at the stadium, a deserted ruin in the twilight. He had started on the first team that Saturday and every Saturday after that for the next two years, but it had never been as satisfactory as it should have been. He never had broken away, the longest run he'd ever made was thirty-five yards, and that in a game that was already won, and then that kid had come up from the third team, Diederich, a blank-faced German kid from Wisconsin, who ran like a bull, ripping lines to pieces Saturday after Saturday, plowing through, never getting hurt, never changing his expression, scoring more points, gaining more ground than all the rest of the team put together, making everybody's All-American, carrying the ball three times out of four, keeping everybody else out of the headlines. Darling was a good blocker and he spent his Saturday afternoons working on the big Swedes and Polacks who played tackle and end for Michigan, Illinois, Purdue, hurling into huge pile-ups, bobbing his head wildly to elude the great raw hands swinging like meat-cleavers at him as he went charging in to open up holes for Diederich coming through like a locomotive behind him. Still, it wasn't so bad. Everybody liked him and he did his job and he was pointed out on the campus and boys always felt important when they introduced their girls to him at their proms, and Louise loved him and watched him faithfully in the games, even in the mud, when your own mother wouldn't know you, and drove him around in her car keeping the top down because she was proud of him and wanted to show everybody that she was Christian Darling's girl. She bought him crazy presents because her father was rich, watches, pipes, humidors, an icebox for beer for his room, curtains, wallets, a fifty-dollar dictionary.

"You'll spend every cent your old man owns," Darling protested once when she showed up at his rooms with seven different packages in her arms and tossed them onto the couch.

"Kiss me," Louise said, "and shut up."

"Do you want to break your poor old man?"

"I don't mind. I want to buy you presents."

"Why?"

"It makes me feel good. Kiss me. I don't know why. Did you know that you're an important figure?"

"Yes," Darling said gravely.

"When I was waiting for you at the library yesterday two girls saw you coming and one of them said to the other, 'That's Christian Darling. He's an important figure.' "

"You're a liar."

"I'm in love with an important figure."

"Still, why the hell did you give me a forty-five pound dictionary?"

"I wanted to make sure," Louise said, "that you had a token of my esteem. I want to smother you in tokens of my esteem."

Fifteen years ago.

They'd married when they got out of college. There'd been other women for him, but all casual and secret, more for curiosity's sake, and vanity, women who'd thrown themselves at him and flattered him, a pretty mother at a summer camp for boys, an old girl from his home town who'd suddenly blossomed into a coquette, a friend of Louise's who had dogged him grimly for six months and had taken advantage of the two weeks that Louise went home when her mother died. Perhaps Louise had known, but she'd kept quiet, loving him completely, filling his rooms with presents, religiously watching him battling with the big Swedes and Polacks on the line of scrimmage on Saturday afternoons, making plans for marrying him and living with him in New York and going with him there to the night clubs, the theaters, the good restaurants, being proud of him in advance, tall, white-teethed, smiling, large, yet moving lightly, with an athlete's grace, dressed in evening clothes, approvingly eyed by magnificently dressed and famous women in theater lobbies, with Louise adoringly at his side.

Her father, who manufactured inks, set up a New York office for Darling to manage and presented him with three hundred accounts, and they lived on Beekman Place with a view of the river with fifteen thousand dollars a year between them, because everybody was buying everything in those days, including ink. They saw all the shows and went to all the speakeasies and spent their fifteen thousand dollars a year and in the afternoons Louise went to the art galleries and the matinees of the more serious plays that Darling didn't like to sit through and Darling slept with a girl who danced in the chorus of *Rosalie* and with the wife of a man who owned three copper mines. Darling played squash three times a week and remained as solid as a stone barn and Louise never took her eyes off him when they were in the same room together, watching him with a secret, miser's smile, with a trick of coming over to him in the middle of a crowded room and saying gravely, in a low voice, "You're the handsomest man I've ever seen in my whole life. Want a drink?"

Nineteen twenty-nine came to Darling and to his wife and father-in-law, the maker of inks, just as it came to everyone else. The father-in-law waited until 1933 and then blew his brains out and when Darling went to Chicago to see what the books of the firm looked like he found out all that was left were debts and three or four gallons of unbought ink.

"Please, Christian," Louise said, sitting in their neat Beekman Place apartment, with a view of the river and prints of paintings by Dufy and Braque and Picasso on the wall, "please, why do you want to start drinking at two o'clock in the afternoon?"

"I have nothing else to do," Darling said, putting down his glass, emptied of its fourth drink. "Please pass the whisky."

Louise filled his glass. "Come take a walk with me," she said. "We'll walk along the river."

"I don't want to walk along the river," Darling said, squinting intensely at the prints of paintings by Dufy, Braque and Picasso.

"We'll walk along Fifth Avenue."

"I don't want to walk along Fifth Avenue."

"Maybe," Louise said gently, "you'd like to come with me to some art galleries. There's an exhibition by a man named Klee. . . ."

"I don't want to go to any art galleries. I want to sit here and drink Scotch whisky," Darling said. "Who the hell hung these goddamn pictures up on the wall?"

"I did," Louise said.

"I hate them."

"I'll take them down," Louise said.

"Leave them there. It gives me something to do in the afternoon. I can hate them." Darling took a long swallow. "Is that the way people paint these days?"

"Yes, Christian. Please don't drink any more."

"Do you like painting like that?"

"Yes, dear."

"Really?"

"Really."

Darling looked carefully at the prints once more. "Little Louise Tucker. The middle-western beauty. I like pictures with horses in them. Why should you like pictures like that?"

"I just happen to have gone to a lot of galleries in the last few years. . . ."

"Is that what you do in the afternoon?"

"That's what I do in the afternoon," Louise said.

"I drink in the afternoon."

Louise kissed him lightly on the top of his head as he sat there squinting at the pictures on the wall, the glass of whisky held firmly in his hand. She put on her coat and went out without saying another word. When she came back in the early evening, she had a job on a woman's fashion magazine.

They moved downtown and Louise went to work every morning and Darling sat home and drank and Louise paid the bills as they came up. She made believe she was going to quit work as soon as Darling found a job, even though she was taking over more responsibility day by day at the magazine, interviewing authors, picking painters for the illustrations and covers, getting actresses to pose for pictures, going out for drinks with the right people, making a thousand new friends whom she loyally introduced to Darling.

"I don't like your hat," Darling said, once, when she came in in the evening and kissed him, her breath rich with Martinis.

"What's the matter with my hat, Baby?" she asked, running her fingers through her hair. "Everybody says it's very smart."

"It's too damned smart," he said. "It's not for you. It's for a rich, sophisticated woman of thirty-five with admirers."

Louise laughed. "I'm practicing to be a rich, sophisticated woman of thirty-five with admirers," she said. He stared soberly at her. "Now, don't look so grim, Baby. It's still the same simple little wife under the hat." She took the hat off, threw it into a corner, sat on his lap. "See? Homebody Number One."

"Your breath could run a train," Darling said, not wanting to be mean, but talking out of boredom, and sudden shock at seeing his wife curiously a stranger in a new hat, with a new expression in her eyes under the little brim, secret, confident, knowing.

Louise tucked her head under his chin so he couldn't smell her breath. "I had to take an author out for cocktails," she said. "He's a boy from the Ozark Mountains and he drinks like a fish. He's a Communist."

"What the hell is a Communist from the Ozarks doing writing for a woman's fashion magazine?"

Louise chuckled. "The magazine business is getting all mixed up these days. The publishers want to have a foot in every camp. And anyway, you can't find an author under seventy these days who isn't a Communist."

"I don't think I like you to associate with all those people, Louise," Darling said. "Drinking with them."

"He's a very nice, gentle boy," Louise said. "He reads Ernest Dowson."

"Who's Ernest Dowson?"

Louise patted his arm, stood up, fixed her hair. "He's an English poet."

Darling felt that somehow he had disapppointed her. "Am I supposed to know who Ernest Dowson is?"

"No, dear. I'd better go in and take a bath."

After she had gone, Darling went over to the corner where the hat was lying and picked it up. It was nothing, a scrap of straw, a red flower, a veil, meaningless on his big hand, but on his wife's head a signal of something . . . big city, smart and knowing women drinking and dining with men other than their husbands, conversation about things a normal man wouldn't know much about. Frenchmen who painted as though they used their elbows instead of brushes, composers who wrote whole symphonies without a single melody in them, writers who knew all about politics and women who knew all about writers, the movement of the proletariat, Marx, somehow mixed up with five-dollar dinners and the best-looking women in America and fairies who made them laugh and half-sentences immediately understood and secretly hilarious and wives who called their husbands "Baby." He put the hat down, a scrap of straw and a red flower, and a little veil. He drank some whisky straight and went into the bathroom where his wife was lying deep in her bath, singing to herself and smiling from time to time like a little girl, paddling the water gently with her hands, sending up a slight spicy fragrance from the bath salts she used.

He stood over her, looking down at her. She smiled up at him, her eyes half closed, her body pink and shimmering in the water, scented water. All over again, with all the old suddenness, he was hit deep inside him with the knowledge of how beautiful she was, how much he needed her.

"I came in here," he said, "to tell you I wish you wouldn't call me 'Baby.' "

She looked up at him from the bath, her eyes quickly full of sorrow, half-understanding what he meant. He knelt and put his arms around her, his sleeves plunged heedlessly in the water, his shirt and jacket soaking wet as he clutched her wordlessly, holding her crazily tight, crushing her breath from her, kissing her desperately, searchingly, regretfully.

He got jobs after that, selling real estate and automobiles, but somehow, although he had a desk with his name on a wooden wedge on it, and he went to the office religiously at nine each morning, he never managed to sell anything and he never made any money.

Louise was made assistant editor, and the house was always full of strange men and women who talked fast and got angry on abstract subjects like mural painting, novelists, labor unions. Negro short-story writers drank Louise's liquor, and a lot of Jews, and big solemn men with scarred faces and knotted hands who talked slowly but clearly about picket lines and battles with guns and leadpipe at mine-shaft-heads and in front of factory gates. And Louise moved among them all, confidently, knowing what they were talking about just as though she were a man. She knew everybody, condescended to no one, devoured books that Darling had never heard of, walked along the streets of the city, excited, at home, soaking in all the million tides of New York without fear, with constant wonder.

Her friends liked Darling and sometimes he found a man who wanted to get off in the corner and talk about the new boy who played fullback for Princeton, and the decline of the double wing-back, or even the state of the stock market, but for the most part he sat on the edge of things, solid and quiet in the high storm of words. "The dialectics of the situation . . . The theater has been given over to expert jugglers . . . Picasso? What man has a right to paint old bones and collect ten thousand dollars for them? . . . I stand firmly behind Trotsky . . . Poe was the last American critic. When he died they put lilies on the grave of American criticism. I don't say this because they panned my last book, but . . ."

Once in a while he caught Louise looking soberly and consideringly at him through the cigarette smoke and the noise and he avoided her eyes and found an excuse to get up and go into the kitchen for more ice or to open another bottle.

"Come on," Cathal Flaherty was saying, standing at the door with a girl, "you've got to come down and see this. It's down on Fourteenth Street, in the old Civic Repertory, and you can only see it on Sunday nights and I guarantee you'll come out of the theater singing." Flaherty was a big young Irishman with a broken nose who was the lawyer for a longshoreman's union, and he had been hanging around the house for six months on and off, roaring and shutting everybody else up when he got in an argument. "It's a new play, *Waiting for Lefty;* it's about taxi-drivers."

"Odets," the girl with Flaherty said. "It's by a guy named Odets."

"I never heard of him," Darling said.

"He's a new one," the girl said.

"It's like watching a bombardment," Flaherty said. "I saw it last Saturday night. You've got to see it."

"Come on, Baby," Louise said to Darling, excitement in her eyes already. "We've been sitting in the Sunday *Times* all day, this'll be a great change."

"I see enough taxi-drivers every day," Darling said, not because he meant that, but because he didn't like to be around Flaherty, who said things that made Louise laugh a lot and whose judgment she accepted on almost every subject. "Let's go to the movies."

"You've never seen anything like this before," Flaherty said. "He wrote this play with a baseball bat."

"Come on," Louise coaxed, "I bet it's wonderful."

"He has long hair," the girl with Flaherty said. "Odets. I met him at a party. He's an actor. He didn't say a goddam thing all night."

"I don't feel like going down to Fourteenth Street," Darling said, wishing Flaherty and his girl would get out. "It's gloomy."

"Oh, hell!" Louise said loudly. She looked coolly at Darling, as though she'd just been introduced to him and was making up her mind about him, and not very favorably. He saw her looking at him, knowing there was something new and dangerous in her face and he wanted to say something, but Flaherty was there and his damned girl, and anyway, he didn't know what to say.

"I'm going," Louise said, getting her coat. "I don't think Fourteenth Street is gloomy."

"I'm telling you," Flaherty was saying, helping her on with her coat, "it's the Battle of Gettysburg, in Brooklynese."

"Nobody could get a word out of him," Flaherty's girl was saying as they went through the door. "He just sat there all night."

The door closed. Louise hadn't said good night to him. Darling walked around the room four times, then sprawled out on the sofa, on top of the Sunday *Times*. He lay there for five minutes looking at the ceiling, thinking of Flaherty walking down the street talking in that booming voice between the girls, holding their arms.

Louise had looked wonderful. She'd washed her hair in the afternoon and it had been very soft and light and clung close to her head as she stood there angrily putting her coat on. Louise was getting prettier every year, partly because she knew by now how pretty she was, and made the most of it.

"Nuts," Darling said, standing up. "Oh, nuts."

He put on his coat and went down to the nearest bar and had five drinks off by himself in a corner before his money ran out.

The years since then had been foggy and downhill. Louise had been nice to him, and in a way, loving and kind, and they'd fought only once, when he said he was going to vote for Landon. ("Oh, Christ," she'd said, "doesn't *anything* happen inside your head? Don't you read the papers? The penniless Republican!") She'd been sorry later and apologized for hurting him, but apologized as she might to a child. He'd tried hard, had gone grimly to the art galleries, the concert halls, the bookshops, trying to gain on the trail of his wife, but it was no use. He was bored, and none of what he saw or heard or dutifully read made much sense to him and finally he gave it up. He had thought, many nights as he ate dinner alone, knowing that Louise would come home late and drop silently into bed without explanation, of getting a divorce, but he knew the loneliness, the hopelessness, of not seeing her again would be too much to take. So he was good, completely devoted, ready at all times to go any place with her, do anything she wanted. He even got a small job, in a broker's office and paid his own way, bought his own liquor.

Then he'd been offered a job of going from college to college as a tailor's representative. "We want a man," Mr. Rosenberg had said, "who as soon as you look at him, you say, 'There's a university man.' " Rosenberg had looked approvingly at Darling's broad shoulders and well-kept waist, at his carefully brushed hair and his honest, wrinkle-less face. "Frankly, Mr. Darling, I am willing to make you a proposition. I have inquired about you, you are favorably known on your old campus, I understand you were in the backfield with Alfred Diederich."

Darling nodded. "Whatever happened to him?"

"He is walking around in a cast for seven years now. An iron brace. He played professional football and they broke his neck for him."

Darling smiled. That, at least, had turned out well.

"Our suits are an easy product to sell, Mr. Darling," Rosenberg said. "We have a handsome, custom-made garment. What has Brooks Brothers got that we haven't got? A name. No more."

"I can make fifty-sixty dollars a week," Darling said to Louise that night. "And expenses. I can save some money and then come back to New York and really get started here."

"Yes, Baby," Louise said.

"As it is," Darling said carefully, "I can make it back here once a month, and holidays and the summer. We can see each other often."

"Yes, Baby." He looked at her face, lovelier now at thirty-five than it had ever been before, but fogged over now as it had been for five years with a kind of patient, kindly, remote boredom.

"What do you say?" he asked. "Should I take it?" Deep within him he hoped fiercely, longingly, for her to say "No, Baby, you stay right here," but she said, as he knew she'd say, "I think you'd better take it."

He nodded. He had to get up and stand with his back to her, looking out the window, because there were things plain on his face that she had never seen in the fifteen years she'd known him. "Fifty dollars is a lot of money," he said. "I never thought I'd ever see fifty dollars again." He laughed. Louise laughed, too.

Christian Darling sat on the frail green grass of the practice field. The shadow of the stadium had reached out and covered him. In the distance the lights of the university shone a little mistily in the light haze of evening. Fifteen years. Flaherty even now was calling for his wife, buying her a drink, filling whatever bar they were in with that voice of his and that easy laugh. Darling half-closed his eyes, almost saw the boy fifteen years ago reach for the pass, slip the halfback, go skittering lightly down the field, his knees high and fast and graceful, smiling to himself because he knew he was going to get past the safety man. That was the high point, Darling thought, fifteen years ago, on an autumn afternoon, twenty years old and far from death, with the air coming easily into his lungs, and a deep feeling inside him that he could do anything, knock over anybody, outrun whatever had to be outrun. And the shower after and the three glasses of water and the cool night air on his damp head and Louise sitting hatless in the open car with a smile and the first kiss she ever really meant. The high point, an eighty-yard run in the practice, and a girl's kiss and everything after that a decline. Darling laughed. He had practiced the wrong thing, perhaps. He hadn't practiced for 1929 and New York City and a girl who would turn into a woman. Somewhere, he thought, there must have been a point where she moved up to me, was even with me for a moment, when I could have held her hand, if I'd known, held tight, gone with her. Well, he'd never known. Here he was on a playing field that was fifteen years away and his wife was in another city having dinner with another and better man, speaking with him a different, new language, a language nobody had ever taught him.

Darling stood up, smiled a little, because if he didn't smile he knew the tears would come. He looked around him. This was the spot. O'Connor's pass had come sliding out just to here . . . the high point. Darling put up his hands, felt all over again the flat slap of the ball. He shook his hips to throw off the halfback, cut back inside the center, picked his knees high as he ran gracefully over two men jumbled on the ground at the line of scrimmage, ran easily, gaining speed, for ten yards, holding the ball lightly in his two hands, swung away from the halfback diving at him, ran, swinging his hips in the almost girlish manner of a back in a broken field, tore into the safety man, his shoes drumming heavily on the turf, stiff-armed, elbow locked, pivoted, raced lightly and exultantly for the goal line.

It was only after he had sped over the goal line and slowed to a trot that he saw the boy and girl sitting together on the turf, looking at him wonderingly.

He stopped short, dropping his arms. "I . . ." he said, gasping a little, though his condition was fine and the run hadn't winded him. "I—once played here."

The boy and the girl said nothing. Darling laughed embarrassedly, looked hard at them sitting there, close to each other, shrugged, turned and went toward his hotel, the sweat breaking out on his face and running down into his collar.

JANET FRAME

THE FOOTBALLER IN THE SMALL ROOM

Now he roars through an unlit stadium of silence.
A curve of pain in his head
corresponds to this teamless loneliest game
where his blood has less worth than orange juice,
but the spectator walls do not know his name.

LILLIAN MORRISON

IN THE BEGINNING WAS THE

In the beginning was the

Kickoff.
The ball flew
spiralling true
into the end zone
where it was snagged,
neatly hugged
by a swivel-hipped back
who ran up the field
and was smeared.

The game has begun.
The game has been won.
The game goes on.
Long live the game.
Gather and lock
tackle and block
move, move,
around the arena
and always the beautiful
trajectories.

JAMES WRIGHT

AUTUMN BEGINS IN MARTINS FERRY, OHIO

In the Shreve High football stadium,
I think of Polacks nursing long beers in Tiltonsville,
And gray faces of Negroes in the blast furnace at
    Benwood,
And the ruptured night watchman of Wheeling Steel,
Dreaming of heroes.

All the proud fathers are ashamed to go home.
Their women cluck like starved pullets,
Dying for love.

Therefore,
Their sons grow suicidally beautiful
At the beginning of October,
And gallop terribly against each other's bodies.

A MAD FIGHT SONG FOR WILLIAM S. CARPENTER, 1966 [1]

Varus, varus, gib mir meine Legionen wieder[2]

Quick on my feet in those Novembers of my loneliness,
I tossed a short pass,
Almost the instant I got the ball, right over the head
Of Barrel Terry before he knocked me cold.

1. Carpenter, a West Pointer, called for his own troops to be napalmed rather than
have them surrender. General Westmoreland called him "hero" and made him his aide,
and President Johnson awarded him a Silver Star for courage.
2. "Varus, Varus, give me back my legions." Octavius Augustus, Emperor of Rome,
said this to Varus, his general, after the Roman legions were badly defeated by the
Germanic tribes at the Battle of Teutoburger Wald in 9 A.D. Note also that Carpenter
was the famous "lonely end" for Red Blaik's West Point football team.—ED.

When I woke, I found myself crying out
Latin conjugations, and the new snow falling
At the edge of a green field.

Lemoyne Crone had caught the pass, while I lay
Unconscious and raging
Alone with the fire ghost of Catullus, the contemptuous
    graces tossing
Garlands and hendecasyllabics over the head
Of Cornelius Nepos the mastodon,
The huge volume.

At the edges of southeast Asia this afternoon
The quarterbacks and the lines are beginning to fall,
A spring snow,

And terrified young men
Quick on their feet
Lob one another's skulls across
Wings of strange birds that are burning
Themselves alive.

JAMES   DICKEY

THE BEE

To the football coaches of Clemson College, 1942

One dot
Grainily shifting   we at roadside and
The smallest wings coming   along the rail fence out
Of the woods   one dot   of all that green. It now
Becomes flesh-crawling   then the quite still
Of stinging. I must live faster for my terrified
Small son   it is on him. Has come. Clings.

Old wingback, come
To life. If your knee action is high
Enough, the fat may fall in time   God damn
You, Dickey, *dig*   this is your last time to cut
And run   but you must give it everything you have
Left, for screaming near your screaming child is the sheer
Murder of California traffic: some bee hangs driving

Your child
Blindly onto the highway. Get there however
Is still possible. Long live what I badly did
At Clemson   and all of my clumsiest drives
For the ball   all of my trying to turn
The corner downfield   and my spindling explosions
Through the five-hole over tackle. O backfield

Coach Shag Norton,
Tell me as you never yet have told me
To get the lead out   scream whatever will get
The slow-motion of middle age off me   I cannot
Make it this way   I will have to leave
My feet   they are gone   I have him where
He lives   and down we go singing with screams into

The dirt,
Son-screams of fathers   screams of dead coaches turning
To approval   and from between us the bee rises
        screaming
With flight   grainily shifting   riding the rail fence
Back into the woods   traffic blaring past us
Unchanged, nothing heard through the air-
conditioning glass   we lying at roadside full

Of the forearm prints
Of roadrocks   strawberries on our elbows as from
Scrimmage with the varsity   now we can get
Up   stand   turn away from the highway   look straight

Into trees. See, there is nothing coming out   no
Smallest wing   no shift of a flight-grain   nothing
Nothing. Let us go in, son and listen

For some tobacco-
mumbling voice in the branches   to say "That's
a little better,"   to our lives still hanging
By a hair. There is nothing to stop us   we can go
Deep   deeper   into elms, and listen to traffic die
Roaring, like a football crowd from which we have
Vanished. Dead coaches live in the air, son   live

In the ear
Like fathers, and *urge*   and *urge*. They want you better
Than you are. When needed, they rise and curse you
          they scream
When something must be saved. Here, under this tree,
We can sit down. You can sleep, and I can try
To give back what I have earned by keeping us
Alive, and safe from bees: the smile of some kind

Of savior—
Of touchdowns, of fumbles, battles,
Lives. Let me sit here with you, son
As on the bench, while the first string takes back
Over, far away   and say with my silentest tongue, with
          the man-
creating bruises on my arms   with a live leaf a quick
Dead hand on my shoulder, "Coach Norton, I am your
          boy."

DON DeLILLO

THE FIRST BLACK STUDENT

from *End Zone*

1

Taft Robinson was the first black student to be enrolled at Logos College in west Texas. They got him for his speed.

By the end of that first season he was easily one of the best running backs in the history of the Southwest. In time he might have turned up on television screens across the land, endorsing eight-thousand-dollar automobiles or avocado-flavored instant shave. His name on a chain of fast-food outlets. His life story on the back of cereal boxes. A drowsy monograph might be written on just that subject, the modern athlete as commercial myth, with footnotes. But this doesn't happen to be it. There were other intonations to that year, for me at least, the phenomenon of anti-applause—words broken into brute sound, a consequent silence of metallic texture. And so Taft Robinson, rightly or wrongly, no more than haunts this book. I think it's fitting in a way. The mansion has long been haunted (double metaphor coming up) by the invisible man.

But let's keep things simple. Football players are simple folk. Whatever complexities, whatever dark politics of the human mind, the heart—these are noted only within the chalked borders of the playing field. At times strange visions ripple across that turf; madness leaks out. But wherever else he goes, the football player travels the straightest of lines. His thoughts are wholesomely commonplace, his actions uncomplicated by history, enigma, holocaust or dream.

A passion for simplicity, for the true old things, as of boys on bicycles delivering newspapers, filled our days and nights that fierce summer. We practiced in the undulating heat with nothing to sustain us but the conviction that things here were simple. Hit and get hit; key the pulling guard; run over people; suck some ice and reassume the three-point stance. We were a lean and dedicated squad run by a hungry coach and his seven oppressive assistants. Some of us were more simple than others; a few might be called outcasts or exiles; three or four, as on every football team, were crazy. But we were all—even myself—we were all dedicated.

We did grass drills at a hundred and six in the sun. We attacked the blocking sleds and strutted through the intersecting ropes. We stood in what was called the chute (a narrow strip of ground bordered on two sides by blocking dummies) and we went one on one, blocker and pass-rusher, and hand-fought each other to the earth. We butted, clawed and kicked. There were any number of fistfights. There was one sprawling free-for-all, which the coaches allowed to continue for about five minutes, standing on the sidelines looking pleasantly bored as we kicked each other in the shins and threw dumb rights and lefts at caged faces, the more impulsive taking off their helmets and swinging them at anything that moved. In the evenings we prayed.

I was one of the exiles. There were many times, believe it, when I wondered what I was doing in that remote and unfed place, that summer tundra, being hit high and low by a foaming pair of 240-pound Texans. Being so tired and sore at night that I could not raise an arm to brush my teeth. Being made to obey the savage commands of unreasonable men. Being set apart from all styles of civilization as I had known or studied them. Being led in prayer every evening, with the rest of the squad, by our coach, warlock and avenging patriarch. Being made to lead a simple life.

Then they told us that Taft Robinson was coming to school. I looked forward to his arrival—an event, finally, in a time of incidents and small despairs. But my teammates seemed sullen at the news. It was a break with simplicity, the haunted corner of a dream, some piece of forest magic to scare them in the night.

Taft was a transfer student from Columbia. The word on him was good all the way. (1) He ran the hundred in 9.3 seconds. (2) He had good moves and good hands. (3) He was strong and rarely fumbled. (4) He broke tackles like a man pushing through a turnstile. (5) He could pass-block—when in the mood.

But mostly he could fly—a 9.3 clocking for the hundred. Speed. He had sprinter's speed. Speed is the last excitement left, the one thing we haven't used up, still naked in its potential, the mysterious black gift that thrills the millions.

2

(Exile or outcast: distinctions tend to vanish when the temperature exceeds one hundred.)

Taft Robinson showed up at the beginning of September, about two weeks before regular classes were to start. The squad, originally one hundred bodies, soon down to sixty, soon less, had reported in the middle of August. Taft had missed spring practice and twenty days of the current session. I didn't think he'd be able to catch up. I was in the president's office the day he arrived. The president was Mrs. Tom Wade, the founder's widow. Everybody called her Mrs. Tom. She was the only woman I had ever seen who might accurately be described as Lincolnesque. Beyond appearance I had no firm idea of her reality; she was tall, black-browed, stark as a railroad spike.

I was there because I was a northerner. Apparently they thought my presence would help make Taft feel at home, an idea I tended to regard as laughable. (He was from Brooklyn, having gone on to Columbia from Boys High, a school known for the athletes it turns out.) Mrs. Tom and I sat waiting.

"My husband loved this place," she said. "He built it out of nothing. He had an idea and he followed it through to the end. He believed in reason. He was a man of reason. He cherished the very word. Unfortunately he was mute."

"I didn't know that."

"All he could do was grunt. He made disgusting sounds. Spit used to collect at both corners of his mouth. It wasn't a real pretty sight."

Taft walked in flanked by our head coach, Emmett Creed, and backfield coach, Oscar Veech. Right away I estimated height and weight, about six-two, about 210. Good shoulders, narrow waist, acceptable neck. Prize beef at the county fair. He wore a dark gray suit that may have been as old as he was.

Mrs. Tom made her speech.

"Young man, I have always admired the endurance of your people. You've a tough row to hoe. Frankly I was against this from the start.

When they told me their plan, I said it was bushwah. Complete bushwah. But Emmett Creed is a mighty persuasive man. This won't be easy for any of us. But what's reason for if not to get us through the hard times? There now. I've had my say. Now you go on ahead with Coach Creed and when you're all thoo talking football you be sure to come on back here and see Mrs. Berry Trout next door. She'll get you all settled on courses and accommodations and things. History will be our ultimate judge."

Then it was my turn.

"Gary Harkness," I said. "We're more or less neighbors. I'm from upstate New York."

"How far up?" he said.

"Pretty far. Very far in fact. Small town in the Adirondacks."

We went over to the players' dorm, an isolated unit just about completed but with no landscaping out front and WET PAINT signs everywhere. I left the three of them in Taft's room and went downstairs to get suited up for afternoon practice. Moody Kimbrough, our right tackle and captain on offense, stopped me as I was going through the isometrics area.

"Is he here?"

"He is here," I said.

"That's nice. That's real nice."

In the training room Jerry Fallon had his leg in the whirlpool. He was doing a crossword puzzle in the local newspaper.

"Is he here?"

"He is everywhere," I said.

"Who?"

"Supreme being of heaven and earth. Three letters."

"You know who I mean."

"He's here all right. He's all here. Two hundred and fifty-five pounds of solid mahogany."

"How much?" Fallon said.

"They're thinking of playing him at guard. He came in a little heavier than they expected. About two fifty-five. Left guard, I think Coach said."

"You kidding me, Gary?"

"Left guard's your spot, isn't it? I just realized."

"How much is he weigh again?"

"He came in at two fifty-five, two sixty. Solid bronze right from the foundry. Coach calls him the fastest two-five-five in the country."

"He's supposed to be a running back," Fallon said.

"That was before he added the weight."

"I think you're kidding me, Gary."

"That's right," I said.

"You son of a bitch," Fallon said.

We ran through some new plays for about an hour. Creed's assistants moved among us yelling at our mistakes. Creed himself was up in the tower studying overall patterns. I saw Taft on the sidelines with Oscar Veech. The players kept glancing that way. When the second unit took over on offense, I went over to the far end of the field and grubbed around for a spot of shade in which to sit. Finally I just sank into the canvas fence and remained more or less upright, contemplating the distant fury. These canvas blinds surrounded the entire practice field in order to discourage spying by future opponents. The blinds were one of the many innovations Creed had come up with —innovations as far as this particular college was concerned. He had also had the tower built as well as the separate living quarters for the football team. (To instill a sense of unity.) This was Creed's first year here. He had been born in Texas, in either a log cabin or a manger, depending on who was telling the story, on the banks of the Rio Grande in what is now Big Bend National Park. The sporting press liked to call him Big Bend. He made a few all-American teams as a tailback in the old single-wing days at SMU and then flew a B-27 during the war and later played halfback for three years with the Chicago Bears. He went into coaching then, first as an assistant to George Halas in Chicago and then as head coach in the Missouri Valley Conference, the Big Eight and the Southeast Conference. He became famous for creating order out of chaos, building good teams at schools known for their perennial losers. He had four unbeaten seasons, five conference champions and two national champions. Then a second-string quarterback said or did something he didn't like and Creed broke his jaw. It became something of a national scandal and he went into obscurity for three years until Mrs. Tom beckoned him to west Texas. It was a long drop down from the Big Eight but Creed managed to convince the widow that a good football team could put her lonely little school on the map. So priorities were changed, new assistants were hired, alumni were courted, a certain amount of oil money began to flow, a certain number of private planes were made available for recruiting purposes, the team name was changed from the Cactus Wrens to the Screaming Eagles—and Emmett Creed was on the comeback trail. The only thing that didn't make sense was the ton of canvas that hid our practice sessions. There was nothing out there but insects.

The first unit was called back in and I headed slowly toward the dust and noise. Creed up in the tower spoke through his bullhorn.

"Defense, I'd appreciate some pursuit. They don't give points for apathy in this sport. Pursue those people. Come out of the ground at them. Hit somebody. Hit somebody. Hit somebody."

On the first play Garland Hobbs, our quarterback, faked to me going straight into the line and then pitched to the other setback, Jim Deering. He got hit first by a linebacker, Dennis Smee, who drove him into the ground, getting some belated and very nasty help from a tackle and another linebacker. Deering didn't move. Two assistant coaches started shouting at him, telling him he was defacing the landscape. He tried to get up but couldn't make it. The rest of us walked over to the far hashmark and ran the next play.

It all ended with two laps around the goal posts. Lloyd Philpot Jr., a defensive end, fell down in the middle of the second lap. We left him there in the end zone, on his stomach, one leg twitching slightly. His father had won all-conference honors at Baylor for three straight years.

That evening Emmett Creed addressed the squad.

"Write home on a regular basis. Dress neatly. Be courteous. Articulate your problems. Do not drag-ass. Anything I have no use for, it's a football player who consistently drag-asses. Move swiftly from place to place, both on the field and in the corridors of buildings. Don't ever get too proud to pray."

3

Rolf Hauptfuhrer coached the defensive line and attended to problems of morale and grooming. He approached me one morning after practice.

"We want you to room with Bloomberg," he said.

"Why me?"

"John Billy Small was in there with him. Couldn't take the tension. We figure you won't mind. You're more the complicated type."

"Of course I'll mind."

"John Billy said he wets the bed. Aside from that there's no problem. He gets nervous. No doubt about that. A lot of tension in that frame. But we figure you can cope with it."

"I object. I really do. I've got my own tensions."

"Harkness, everybody knows what kind of reputation you brought down here. Coach is willing to take a chance on you only as long as you follow orders. So keep in line. Just keep in line—hear?"

"Who's rooming with Taft Robinson?" I said.

"Robinson rooms alone."

"Why's that?"

"You'll have to ask the powers that be. In the meantime move your stuff in with Bloomberg."

"I don't like tension," I said. "And I don't see why I have to be the one who gets put in with controversial people."

"It's for the good of the team," Hauptfuhrer said.

Five of us sneaked into the nearest town that night, a place called Rooster, to see what was happening. We ended up at Bing Jackmin's house, right outside town, where we drank beer for five hours. Bing's father joined us, falling off the porch when he came out to say good night. We drove back to campus and held a drunken Olympiad in the moonlight at the edge of the football field—slow-motion races, grass swimming, spitting for distance. Then we walked slowly back to the dorm and listened to Norgene Azamanian tell the story of his name.

"A lot of people take it for a girl's name. But it's no such thing. It comes from Norge refrigerators and from my uncle, Captain Gene Kinney. How it all came about, my being called Norgene, makes for a real interesting story. You see, everybody in my mother's family going back for generations, man or woman, always had a Christian name of just one syllable. Nobody knows how it started but at some point along the line they decided they'd keep it going. So I go and get born and it comes time to name me. Now it just so happens there was an old Norge refrigerator out on the back porch waiting to get thrown away. It also happens that my daddy wasn't too happy about the syllable thing, it being his belief that the bible carries a warning against one-syllable names, Cain being his brother's slayer. And finally there was the amazing coincidence that my uncle Gene Kinney was on leave and coming over to visit so he could see the new baby, which was me, and so he could get in on the naming of it to be sure the family tradition would be carried out. How all these different factors resulted in the name Norgene is the whole crux of the story."

"Very good," Bing said. "But first tell us how you got Azamanian."

I went up to my room. Bloomberg was asleep, on his belly, snoring softly into the pillow. He was absolutely enormous. It was easy to imagine him attached to the bed by guy-wires, to be floated aloft once a year like a Macy's balloon. His full name was Anatole Bloomberg and he played left tackle on offense. That was all I knew about him, that plus the fact that he wasn't a Texan. One of the outcasts, I thought. Or a voluntary exile of the philosophic type. I decided to wake him up.

"Anatole," I said. "It's Gary Harkness, your new roommate. Let's shake hands and be friends."

"We're roommates," he said. "Why do we have to be friends?"

"It's just an expression. I didn't mean undying comrades. Just friends as opposed to enemies. I'm sorry I woke you up."

"I wasn't asleep."

"You were snoring," I said.

"That's the way I breathe when I'm on my stomach. What happened to my original roommate?"

"John Billy? John Billy's been moved."

"Was that his name?"

"He's been moved. I hope you're not tense about my showing up. All I want to do is get off to a good start and avoid all possible tension."

"Who in your opinion was the greater man?" Bloomberg said. "Edward Gibbon or Archimedes?"

"Archimedes."

"Correct," he said.

In the morning Creed sent us into an all-out scrimmage with a brief inspirational message that summed up everything we knew or had to know.

"It's only a game," he said, "but it's the only game."

Taft Robinson and I were the setbacks. Taft caught a flare pass, evaded two men and went racing down the sideline. Bobby Iselin, a cornerback, gave up the chase at the 25. Bobby used to be the team's fastest man.

4

Through all our days together my father returned time and again to a favorite saying.

"Suck in that gut and go harder."

He never suggested that this saying of his ranked with the maxims of Teddy Roosevelt. Still, he was dedicated to it. He believed in the idea that a simple but lasting reward, something just short of a presidential handshake, awaited the extra effort, the persevering act of a tired man. Backbone, will, mental toughness, desire—these were his themes, the qualities that insured success. He was a pharmaceutical salesman with a lazy son.

It seems that wherever I went I was hounded by people urging me to suck in my gut and go harder. They would never give up on me—my father, my teachers, my coaches, even a girl friend or two. I was a challenge, I guess: a piece of string that does not wish to be knotted. My father was by far the most tireless of those who tried to give me direction, to sharpen my initiative, to piece together some collective memory of hard-won land or dusty struggles in the sun. He put a sign in my room.

WHEN THE GOING GETS TOUGH
THE TOUGH GET GOING

I looked at this sign for three years (roughly from ages fourteen to seventeen) before I began to perceive a certain beauty in it. The sentiment of course had small appeal but it seemed that beauty flew from the words themselves, the letters, consonants swallowing vowels, aggression and tenderness, a semi-self-re-creation from line to line, word to word, letter to letter. All meaning faded. The words became pictures. It was a sinister thing to discover at such an age, that words can escape their meanings. A strange beauty that sign began to express.

My father had a territory and a company car. He sold vitamins, nutritional supplements, mineral preparations and antibiotics. His customers included about fifty doctors and dentists, about a dozen pharmacies, a few hospitals, some drug wholesalers. He had specific goals, both geographic and economic, each linked with the other, and perhaps because of this he hated waste of any kind, of shoe leather, talent, irretrievable time. (Get cracking. Straighten out. Hang in.) It paid, in his view, to follow the simplest, most pioneer of rhythms—the eternal work cycle, the blood-hunt for bear and deer, the mellow rocking of chairs as screen doors swing open and bang shut in the gathering fragments of summer's sulky dusk. Beyond these honest latitudes lay nothing but chaos.

He had played football at Michigan State. He had ambitions on my behalf and more or less at my expense. This is the custom among men who have failed to be heroes; their sons must prove that the seed was not impoverished. He had spent his autumn Saturdays on the sidelines, watching others fall in battle and rise then to the thunder of the drums and the crowd's demanding chants. He put me in a football uniform very early. Then, as a high school junior, I won all-state honors at halfback. (This was the first of his ambitions and as it turned out the only one to be fulfilled.) Eventually I received twenty-eight offers of athletic scholarships—tuition, books, room and board, fifteen dollars a month. There were several broad hints of further almsgiving. Visions were painted of lovely young ladies with charitable instincts of their own. It seemed that every section of the country had much to offer in the way of scenery, outdoor activities, entertainment, companionship, and even, if necessary, education. On the application blanks, I had to fill in my height, my weight, my academic average and my time for the 40-yard dash.

I handed over a letter of acceptance to Syracuse University. I was eager to enrich their tradition of great running backs. They threw me out when I barricaded myself in my room with two packages of Oreo cookies and a girl named Lippy Margolis. She wanted to hide from the world and I volunteered to help her. For a day and a night we read to each other from a textbook on economics. She seemed calmed by the incoherent doctrines set forth on those pages. When I was sure I had changed the course of her life for the better, I opened the door.

At Penn State, the next stop, I studied hard and played well. But each day that autumn was exactly like the day before and the one to follow. I had not yet learned to appreciate the slowly gliding drift of identical things; chunks of time spun past me like meteorites in a universe predicated on repetition. For weeks the cool clear weather was unvarying; the girls wore white knee-high stockings; a small red plane passed over the practice field every afternoon at the same time. There was something hugely Asian about those days in Pennsylvania. I tripped on the same step on the same staircase on three successive days. After this I stopped going to practice. The freshman coach wanted to know what was up. I told him I knew all the plays; there was no reason to practice them over and over; the endless repetition might be spiritually disastrous; we were becoming a nation devoted to human xerography. He and I had a long earnest discussion. Much was made of my talent and my potential value to the varsity squad. Oneness was stressed—the oneness necessary for a winning team. It was a good concept, oneness, but I suggested that, to me at least, it could not be truly attractive unless it meant oneness with God or the universe or some equally redoubtable super-phenomenon. What he meant by oneness was in fact elevenness or twenty-twoness. He told me that my attitude was all wrong. People don't go to football games to see patterns run by theologians. He told me, in effect, that I would have to suck in my gut and go harder. (1) A team sport. (2) The need to sacrifice. (3) Preparation for the future. (4) Microcosm of life.

"You're saying that what I learn on the gridiron about sacrifice and oneness will be of inestimable value later on in life. In other words if I give up now I'll almost surely give up in the more important contests of the future."

"That's it exactly, Gary."

"I'm giving up," I said.

It was a perverse thing to do—go home and sit through a blinding white winter in the Adirondacks. I was passing through one of those odd periods of youth in which significance is seen only on the blankest of walls, found only in dull places, and so I thought I'd turn my back to the world and to my father's sign and try to achieve, indeed establish, some lowly form of American sainthood. The repetition of Penn State was small stuff compared to that deep winter. For five months I did nothing and then repeated it. I had breakfast in the kitchen, lunch in my room, dinner at the dinner table with the others, meaning my parents. They concluded that I was dying of something slow and incurable and that I did not wish to tell them in order to spare their feelings. This was an excellent thing to infer for all concerned. My father took down the sign and hung in its place a framed photo of his favorite pro team, the Detroit Lions—their official team picture. In late spring, a word appeared all over town. MILITARIZE. The word was printed on cardboard placards that stood in shop windows. It was scrawled on fences. It was handwritten on loose-leaf paper taped to the windshields of cars. It appeared on bumper stickers and signboards.

I had accomplished nothing all those months and so I decided to enroll at the University of Miami. It wasn't a bad place. Repetition gave way to the beginnings of simplicity. (A preparation thus for Texas.) I wanted badly to stay. I liked playing football and I knew that by this time I'd have trouble finding another school that would take me. But I had to leave. It started with a book, an immense volume about the possibilities of nuclear war—assigned reading for a course I was taking in modes of disaster technology. The problem was simple and terrible: I enjoyed the book. I liked reading about the deaths of tens of millions of people. I liked dwelling on the destruction of great cities. Five to twenty million dead. Fifty to a hundred million dead. Ninety percent population loss. Seattle wiped out by mistake. Moscow demolished. Airbursts over every SAC base in Europe. I liked to think of huge buildings toppling, of firestorms, of bridges collapsing, survivors roaming the charred countryside. Carbon 14 and strontium 90. Escalation ladder and subcrisis situation. Titan, Spartan, Poseidon. People burned and unable to breathe. People being evacuated from doomed cities. People diseased and starving. Two hundred thousand bodies decomposing on the roads outside Chicago. I read several chapters twice. Pleasure in the contemplation of millions dying and dead. I became fascinated by words and phrases like thermal hurricane, overkill, circular error probability, post-attack environment, stark deterrence, dose-rate contours, kill-ratio, spasm war. Pleasure in these words. They were extremely effective, I thought, whispering shyly of cycles of destruction so great that the language of past world wars became laughable, the wars themselves somewhat naive. A thrill almost sensual accompanied the reading of this book. What was wrong with me? Had I gone mad? Did others feel as I did? I became seriously depressed. Yet I went to the library and got more books on the subject. Some of these had been published well after the original volume and things were much more up-to-date. Old weapons vanished. Megatonnage soared. New concepts appeared—the rationality of irrationality, hostage cities, orbital attacks. I became more fascinated, more depressed, and finally I left Coral Gables and went back home to my room and to the official team photo of the Detroit Lions. It seemed the only thing to do. My mother brought lunch upstairs. I took the dog for walks.

In time the draft board began to get interested. I allowed my father to get in touch with a former classmate of his, an influential alumnus of Michigan State. Negotiations were held and I was granted an interview with two subalterns of the athletic department, types familiar to football and other paramilitary complexes, the square-jawed bedrock of the corporation. They knew what I could do on the football field, having followed my high school career, but they wouldn't accept me unless I could convince them that I was ready to take orders, to pursue a mature course, to submit my will to the common good. I managed to convince them. I went to East Lansing the following autumn, an aging recruit, and was leading the freshman squad in touchdowns, yards gained rushing, and platitudes. Then, in a game against the Indiana freshmen, I was one of three players converging on a safetyman who had just intercepted a pass. We seemed to hit him simultaneously. He died the next day and I went home that evening.

I stayed in my room for seven weeks this time, shuffling a deck of cards. I got to the point where I could cut to the six of spades about three out of five times, as long as I didn't try it too often, abuse the gift, as long as I tried only when I truly felt an emanation from the six, when I knew in my fingers that I could cut to that particular card.

Then I got a phone call from Emmett Creed. Two days later he flew up to see me. I liked the idea of losing myself in an obscure part of the world. And I had discovered a very simple truth. My life meant nothing without football.

BASKETBALL

When competition is fierce, sport can be deadly serious. But there are also many occasions of comic relief. The following selection from Larry McMurtry's novel, *The Last Picture Show,* portrays the lighter side of athletics. The satirical portrait of the coach is pointed though exaggerated, and the theme of masculinity is amusingly handled.

It is curious but true that hardly any literature, in the sense of poems and stories, is available about basketball. For reasons that might be profitably discussed, baseball and boxing seem to be the most common subjects of American sports literature.

"Ex-Basketball Player" by John Updike is another of the very few examples of basketball literature. The poem deals poignantly with the theme of what happens to the youthful athletic hero once he is past his prime. Thus the poem might be discussed in the context of works like Irwin Shaw's "Eighty-Yard Run" and A. E. Housman's "To an Athlete Dying Young." Updike has also written two novels, *Rabbit Run* and *Rabbit Redux,* that have an ex-basketball player as their main character.

LARRY McMURTRY

THE BASKETBALL GAME

from *The Last Picture Show*

The first basketball game of the season was with Paducah, a town well over a hundred miles from Thalia. It was the longest trip of the year and usually the wildest: in Paducah they played basketball as if it were indoor football, and they had everything in their favor, including a gym so small that the out-of-bounds lines were painted on the walls. The Paducah boys were used to the gym and could run up the walls like lizards, but visiting teams, accustomed to normal-sized courts, had a hard time. Every year two or three Thalia players smashed into the walls and knocked themselves out.

This time it happened to Sonny, and in the very first minutes of play. Leroy Malone managed to trip the gangly Paducah center and while the center was sprawled on the floor Sonny ran right along his back, in pursuit of the ball. Just as he was about to grab it somebody tripped *him* and he hit the wall head first. The next thing he knew he was stretched out beside the bench and one of the freshmen players was squeezing a wet washrag on his forehead. Sonny tried to keep his eyes closed as long as he could—he knew Coach Popper would send him back into the game as soon as he regained consciousness. He feigned deep coma for about five minutes, but unfortunately the coach was experienced in such matters. He came over and lifted one of Sonny's eyelids and saw that he was awake.

"Possuming," he said. "I thought so. Get up and get your butt back in there. We're forty points behind and it ain't but the second quarter."

"I think I got a concussion," Sonny said, trying to look dangerously ill. "Maybe I ought to stay out a little while."

"Get up," the coach insisted. "We just quit football practice ten days ago, you ain't had time to get that out shape. If you want to rest, by God go in there and foul out first. Knock the shit out of that forward two or three times—he's the one doin' all the scorin'. Hell, we come all this way, let's make a showing."

Sonny reluctantly got up and went back in. He managed three fouls before the half, but he was too weak to hit anybody very hard and none of the fouls was really satisfactory. The half-time score was Paducah 62 and Thalia 9. During the half the coach called them over for one of his little pep talks, this one very brief.

"You ten boys have got the shortest little peckers of any bunch of kids I've ever coached," he said sincerely. "By God, if you don't stomp some asses this next half I'll stomp a few tomorrow afternoon when we start practicing."

He scowled fiercely and strolled off to the concession stand to have some coffee.

In the second half things began to look really ominous. Sonny felt strangely light headed and went out on the floor not much caring what he did. Paducah defense had become virtually impenetrable: for one thing, they had started openly tackling whichever Thalia player had the ball. It seemed to Sonny that at last the time had come to shoot peg shots—there was not much chance of moving the ball down the court any other way. Whenever they tried, Paducah tackled them, tripped them, threw body blocks into them, or had the referee call fouls on them.

Actually, the refereeing was another very bad aspect of basketball in Paducah. Unusual as it was, Paducah had a male home economics teacher, a frail little man named Mr. Wean. The school board felt that teaching home ec was really too light a job for a man so they made Mr. Wean basketball referee. He had never managed to learn much about the game, but he was quite docile and called whatever the Paducah team told him to call. Also, he was in bad shape and couldn't possibly run up and down the court for forty-eight minutes. Instead of following the ball, he just stood on the center line and made all his calls from there.

After considering the matter for half a quarter or so Sonny concluded that peg shots were the only feasible tactic. He was simply too weak to dodge the blocks the Paducah boys were throwing. From then on, every time he got the ball he threw it at the backboard he was attacking. At the very worst it slowed down Paducah's scoring. The other Thalia players were quick to see the wisdom of such an offense and in five minutes they were all doing it. Whoever caught the throw-in after a Paducah score would immediately whirl and throw a full-court peg shot. The only one it didn't work for was Leroy Malone: the big Paducah center anticipated him, caught the ball, and threw a ten-yard peg shot right at Leroy's groin. It hurt so bad he later told Sonny he was unable to jack off for two weeks.

The groin shot drew such sustained applause from the Paducah bleachers that Sonny was angered. Mr. Wean had failed to see that it was a deliberate foul: indeed, Mr. Wean was seeing less and less all the time. Thalia's pegshot offense confused him—he had to keep turning around and around to keep up with the ball. After a while this made him so dizzy that he simply stopped and stood facing the Thalia goal—most of the Paducah team was down there anyway, catching the peg shots and throwing them back. Mr. Wean felt that he had somehow got involved in a game of ante over, and he didn't like it. He had a fat wife and all he really wanted to do was stay in the home ec classroom and teach young, small-breasted girls how to make pies. Instead he was standing on the center line, sweating and wishing the quarter would end. Suddenly, Sonny had an irresistible urge to chunk somebody. He unleashed a flat, low peg shot that caught Mr. Wean squarely in the back of the head and sent him sprawling.

The Thalia bench, boys and girls alike, arose with shrieks and cheers, their jubilation all the more noticeable because of the moment of total silence in the Paducah bleachers. The shot instantly made Sonny a celebrity, but it also scared hell out of him and his teammates who were on the floor at the time. They rushed over and tried to help Mr. Wean up, but his legs were like rubber. He had to be dragged off the floor. Paducah's assistant football coach was called in to referee the rest of the game—by the time he got his tennis shoes on, the hometown bleachers had recovered from their shock and were clamoring for Sonny's blood. He knew his only hope was to foul out immediately and get to the bench. While he was trying to decide on the safest way to foul, Coach Popper came to his rescue and took him out.

"Good lick," the coach said. "Nobody but a queer would teach home ec anyway."

From there on things were dismal for the Thalia five. Duane fouled out before the quarter ended, leaving no one but Joe Bob and the freshmen to play the fourth quarter. Paducah was ahead 88 to 14. Coach Popper got so mad at the freshmen that he couldn't see; he almost strangled himself tugging at the towel around his neck. He sent Sonny in again but Sonny quickly threw a couple of light body blocks and fouled out. That left Joe Bob and the freshmen to do the best they could. For the remainder of the game they never once managed to get the ball into their end of the court. As soon as they threw it in the Paducah players took it away from them and made another goal. In five minutes the score was 110 to 14 and Coach Popper called time out. A huddle was in order.

"I tell you," the coach said philosophically, "let's just forget about winning and try to hold the score down. We're gonna get beat over a hundred points if we ain't careful. Oaks, you throw the ball into Joe Bob and Joe Bob as soon as you get it lay down with it. That way they'll have to tie it up and jump for it every time. That'll slow 'em down a little."

The tactic worked fine the first time it was tried. Joe Bob swallowed the ball and Paducah had to tie it up to get possession. It took them about forty seconds to score. Thalia tried it again and three Paducah players gang-piled Joe Bob as he went down. He had to be carried off. The freshman who shot his free throw for him was so scared he barely got the ball half-way to the basket.

Joe Bob's injury left the four freshmen alone on the field for the last few minutes of the game. None of them wanted to swallow the ball and get gang-piled so they did what they could to cooperate with Paducah. The final score was 121 to 14.

"Well, hell, at least my B team got some experience," Coach Popper said. "Might as well look on the bright side. Let's go to the bus."

Basketball defeats weighed very lightly on the coach: football was the only sport that really counted. Ten minutes later he was flopped down in his bus seat, sound asleep.

The boys sat in a stupor for the first twenty miles or so, trying to get used to feeling safe again. Besides, Old Lady Fowler, the girl's coach, was still awake and they could not start to work on the girls until she dropped off. She went to sleep as they were pulling out of Vernon, and from there on it was dog-eat-dog.

The four little freshmen had no chance with the girls and had to get what amusement they could out of tormenting Joe Bob. They crowded him in a seat, took his underpants off, and threw them out the window. Joe Bob was too weak from the gang-piling to fight back, and he might not have bothered anyway. He lost so many pair of underwear that his mother bought them wholesale. He was the only boy on the team who wore his regulars, rather than a jockey strap: Brother Blanton wouldn't hear of him wearing anything so immodest.

"What if you got hurt and were taken to a hospital wearing a thing like that?" Brother Blanton said. "Our good name would be ruined."

Most of the kids had seen Joe Bob's underwear often enough to be thoroughly bored with it. The freshmen attracted no notice at all, and soon went to sleep.

Sonny started the return trip sitting by Leroy Malone, whose balls were so sore that the mere thought of girls made him writhe. After a little bargaining Sonny managed to switch with the kid in front of him, which put him next to the pretty but prudish sophomore he had had his eye on. Knocking Mr. Wean down gave him so much status that he was able to hold the girl's hand almost immediately. Martha Lou was her name. By the time they reached Electra she was willing to let him kiss her, but the results were pretty discouraging. Her teeth were clenched as tightly as if she had lockjaw, and even Sonny's status couldn't unlock them. His only reward was a taste of lipstick, in a flavor he didn't much care for.

The only real excitement on the bus ride home involved Jacy and Duane, the star couple. That was usually the case. None of the other kids excited one another much. There was a fat blond named Vida May who would feel penises, but the teachers knew about her and made her sit so close to the front that it was dangerous to fool with her even when the teachers were asleep.

Jacy and Duane, as a matter of course, were sitting in the very back seat. Duane didn't like the back seat much because there was a little overhead light above it that the bus driver refused to turn off. The bus driver's name was Wilbur Tim and he wasn't about to trust any kids in a totally dark bus. One time years earlier his wife Jessie had found two prophylactics when she was sweeping out the bus, and it just about sent her into hysterics. She was the apprehensive type and went around for months worried sick that some nice girl had got pregnant on her husband's bus. After that Wilbur installed the light.

It was a small bulb that didn't really give any light, just a nice orange glow. Jacy loved it and wouldn't sit anywhere else, despite Duane's protests. She thought the light was very romantic and suggestive: everyone in the bus could tell when the couple in the back seat were kissing or doing something sexy, but the light wasn't strong enough for them to see too clearly. Courting with Duane when all the kids on the school bus could watch gave Jacy a real thrill, and made her feel a little like a movie star: she could bring beauty and passion into the poor kids' lives.

Because Jacy enjoyed them so much, the kissing sessions in the back seat had become a sort of regular feature on basketball road trips. All the kids watched, even though it made them itchy and envious. Jacy, after all, was the prettiest girl in school and watching her get kissed and played with was something to do on the long drives home. The element that made it really exciting to everyone was the question of how far Jacy would go. Once Duane got started kissing he was completely indifferent to whether he had an audience or not: all he wanted was more. The dim light made it impossible to tell precisely how much more Jacy allowed: everyone caught shadowy glimpses, and occasionally a gasp or a little moan from Jacy indicated that Duane was making some headway at least, but no one ever knew how much or what kind.

Only Jacy and Duane knew that he was making a great deal of headway indeed. Jacy would kiss and play around any time, but she seldom got excited past the point of control unless she was on the school bus, where people were watching. Being in the public eye seemed to heighten the quality of every touch. On the bus seat she never had to feign passion—she was burning with it. It was easy for Duane to get his hands inside her loose uniform and touch her breasts, and she loved it. Also, since she was in shorts, it was easy for him to do even more abandoned things to her. She loved to have him slide his hands up the underside of her legs, and sometimes she would even get to the point where she wanted him to touch her crotch. It was a matter that took very delicate managing, but if Duane's hand were cupped against her at the right time so she could squeeze it with her legs, something nice would happen. That was not for the audience, however: she didn't want the kids to see that. When the moment came near she would try to get Duane to crowd her back in the corner, so they couldn't be seen so well. Sometimes it worked beautifully. The younger and more naïve kids were sure Duane went all the way; the juniors and seniors knew better, but felt he must be going a pretty significant distance, anyhow. Every trip added to Jacy's legend. The following day at school she would be on every tongue. Some of the girls said bitter things about her, but the boys took notice when she walked by. The only one seriously discommoded by bus-seat sessions was Duane, who frequently ached painfully by the time the bus reached home. He didn't like it, but he supposed such frustration was something he would simply have to bear until they were married.

Just before the bus got back to Thalia Coach Popper woke up and looked around. Most of the kids were asleep by that time, Jacy and Duane among them, but Jacy had gone to sleep with her legs across Duane's and when the coach saw that he was infuriated. It would put him in an awful spot if Lois Farrow somehow found out he had let her daughter go to sleep with her legs across Duane's. Gene Farrow was on the school board, and an incident like that could cost a coach his job. He stormed back and shook Jacy until she was awake enough to stumble down the aisle to the front seat, where she stayed the rest of the way home.

When all the kids had been delivered to their houses the coach got to thinking about it and began to cuss. There was no end to the trouble a couple of silly-ass kids might cause, particularly if one of them was Lois Farrow's daughter. Lois Farrow was the one person in Thalia who didn't give a damn for the fact that he was football coach.

Wilbur Tim dropped him off at his home, and he stomped inside, still angry. When he turned on the light in his bedroom closet it woke Ruth up. She had just had her breast operation a few days before and was still taking pain medicine. As he was taking off his shoes she sat up in bed.

"Herman, could you bring me a pain pill?" she asked. "It's hurting a little and I'm too groggy to get up."

"You sound goddamn wide awake to me," the coach said, fed up with women. "I bet if I let you you could lay there and talk for two hours. Get up and get your own pills, I ain't no pharmacist."

After a moment, Ruth did. She was dizzy and had to guide herself along the wall, holding her sore breast with one hand. She had washed that day and her white cotton nightgown smelled faintly of detergent. The coach ignored her and flopped on the bed. So far as he could tell, it had not been enough of an operation to make a fuss about. The scar on her breast was barely three inches long. He had cut himself worse than that many times, usually when he was hurrying through a barbed-wire fence to get a covey of quail. The only thing that worried him about Ruth was the chance that they hadn't removed all the tumor and might have to operate again, in which case there would be no end to the expense. The cheapest and most sensible thing would have been for them to take the whole breast off while they were at it. The breast wasn't doing Ruth any good anyway, and if they had taken it all that would have been the end of the matter. He had told them so, too, but the doctor had ignored him and Ruth had gone off in another room and bawled. A woman like her would try the patience of a saint.

The next day at basketball practice the coach gave Duane a dressing down in front of the whole squad. He told him if he ever again so much as sat with Jacy on a basketball trip he would give him fifteen licks with a basketball shoe. A basketball shoe was the only thing the coach ever whipped boys with, but since he wore a size thirteen that was enough. He also told Duane to run fifty laps around the outside of the gym, and at that point Duane rebelled.

"I ain't runnin' no fifty laps all at one time," he said. "I'll do ten a day."

"You'll do fifty right now or check your suit in, by God," the coach said. "If you check it in you don't need to come out for track or baseball, neither. We can get along without you."

Duane went to the locker room, took his suit off, and left. It was just what the coach had hoped for. Any mess the boy got into with Jacy Farrow could no longer be laid at his door. It put him in such good spirits that he worked the boys until seven o'clock that night. The next day he commandeered a sophomore, and the team had ten players again.

JOHN UPDIKE

EX-BASKETBALL PLAYER

Pearl Avenue runs past the high-school lot,
Bends with the trolley tracks, and stops, cut off
Before it has a chance to go two blocks,

At Colonel McComsky Plaza. Berth's Garage
Is on the corner facing west, and there,
Most days, you'll find Flick Webb, who helps Berth out.

Flick stands tall among the idiot pumps—
Five on a side, the old bubble-head style,
Their rubber elbows hanging loose and low.
One's nostrils are two S's, and his eyes
An E and O. And one is squat, without
A head at all—more of a football type.

Once Flick played for the high-school team, the Wizards.
He was good: In fact, the best. In '46,
He bucketed three hundred ninety points,
A county record still. The ball loved Flick.
I saw him rack up thirty-eight of forty
In one home game. His hands were like wild birds.

He never learned a trade, he just sells gas,
Checks oil, and changes flats. Once in a while,
As a gag, he dribbles an inner tube,
But most of us remember anyway.
His hands are fine and nervous on the lug wrench.
It makes no difference to the lug wrench, though.

Off work, he hangs around Mae's Luncheonette.
Grease-grey and kind of coiled, he plays pinball,
Sips lemon cokes, and smokes those thin cigars;
Flick seldom speaks to Mae, just sits and nods
Beyond her face towards bright applauding tiers
Of Necco Wafers, Nibs, and Juju Beads.

BASEBALL

Baseball is *the* most poetic sport, if the frequency of its occurrence as a subject for poets is to be a criterion. Why this is so would be a good subject for discussion. Perhaps a clue to the answer lies in these lines from Marianne Moore's poem "Baseball and Writing":

> Fanaticism? No. Writing is exciting
> and baseball is like writing.

Robert Wallace's poem makes the connection between sport and art even stronger in his precise evocation of the fluid beauty of the well-executed double-play.

Marianne Moore, legendary fan of the old Brooklyn Dodgers, expressed the appreciation of one whose life has been enriched by a strong feeling for the players as individuals. The use of the players' names also connotes an atmosphere of a particular place and time, thus suggesting the importance of history and the past to the overall impact of the game of baseball.

Rolfe Humphries uses a similar method in "Polo Grounds," except that his players recede into the dim, almost mythological origins of the sport, until a link is made by the poet with his own ancestor, one of the old-time ballplayers. In this manner, the abstract idea that "time is of the essence" is made surprisingly concrete.

John Updike's "Tao in the Yankee Stadium Bleachers" is another poem that deals with difficult abstractions through the concrete means of the game of baseball, which may be viewed as a game tending toward contemplative pleasure because of its measured, bucolic pace.

Both Robert Fitzgerald and Robert Francis excellently express more aspects of baseball. The amazing last line of Francis' "The Base Stealer" expresses particularly well the poised action that is so much a part of baseball.

Gregory Corso's "Dream of a Baseball Star" touches upon several ideas already raised—the enthusiasm of the fan, the athlete as artist, and large, abstract concepts which, in this case, are handled whimsically.

Diane Wakoski's "Indian Giver" nicely implies the battle between the sexes and the social pressure on girls not to excel in competition with boys. How many times has a girl deliberately lost after coming perilously close to beating her boy friend in some game?

Deena Metzger's caustic portrait of Little League mothers may be unfair, but it does deal with a real problem—the usurping of children's games by vicariously involved parents.

May Swenson's "Analysis of Baseball" reduces the game to its basic components, as analysis should. Yet, as a poem, it also conveys a sense of enjoyment.

Sonia Sanchez' "on watching a world series game" angrily raises the question of racism in our society. With the emergence of the black athlete as a powerful postwar force, racism is an issue that should inevitably be raised in any consideration of the meaning of sport in American society.

Over the years, since Jackie Robinson broke the color barrier in baseball, racism has been transformed from overt bigotry to more subtle discrimination. In our time, overt bigotry has somewhat diminished (though it certainly revived during Hank Aaron's assault on Babe Ruth's home-run record). However, in the selection from Eliot Asinof's novel, *Man on Spikes*, we see discrimination in its early postwar stages when black baseball players were rare and open baiting was common.

ROBERT WALLACE

THE DOUBLE PLAY

In his sea lit
distance, the pitcher winding
like a clock about to chime comes down with

the ball, hit
sharply, under the artificial
banks of arc-lights, bounds like a vanishing string

over the green
to the shortstop magically
scoops to his right whirling above his invisible

shadows
in the dust redirects
its flight to the running poised second baseman

pirouettes
leaping, above the slide, to throw
from mid-air, across the colored tightened interval,

to the leaning-
out first baseman ends the dance
drawing it disappearing into his long brown glove

stretches. What
is too swift for deception
is final, lost, among the loosened figures

jogging off the field
(the pitcher walks), casual
in the space where the poem has happened.

MARIANNE MOORE

HOMETOWN PIECE FOR MESSRS. ALSTON AND REESE

To the tune:
"Li'l baby, don't say a word: Mama goin' to buy you a
                                        mockingbird.
Bird don't sing: Mama goin' to sell it and buy a brass ring."

"Millennium," yes; "pandemonium"!
Roy Campanella leaps high. Dodgerdom

crowned, had Johnny Podres on the mound.
Buzzie Bavasi and the Press gave ground;

the team slapped, mauled, and asked the Yankees' match,
"How did you feel when Sandy Amoros made the catch?"

"I said to myself"—pitcher for all innings—
"as I walked back to the mound I said, 'Everything's

getting better and better.' " (Zest: they've zest.
" 'Hope springs eternal in the Brooklyn breast.' "

And would the Dodger Band in 8, row 1, relax
if they saw the collector of income tax?

Ready with a tune if that should occur:
"Why Not Take All of Me—All of Me, Sir?")

Another series. Round-tripper Duke at bat,
"Four hundred feet from home-plate"; more like that.

A neat bunt, please; a cloud-breaker, a drive
like Jim Gilliam's great big one. Hope's alive.

Homered, flied out, fouled? Our "stylish stout"
so nimble Campanella will have him out.

A-squat in double-headers four hundred times a day,
he says that in a measure the pleasure is the pay:

catcher to pitcher, a nice easy throw
almost as if he'd just told it to go.

Willie Mays should be a Dodger. He should—
a lad for Roger Craig and Clem Labine to elude;

but you have an omen, pennant-winning Peewee,
on which we are looking superstitiously.

Ralph Branca has Preacher Roe's number; recall?
and there's Don Bessent; he can really fire the ball.

As for Gil Hodges, in custody of first—
"He'll do it by himself." Now a specialist—versed

in an extension reach far into the box seats—
he lengthens up, leans and gloves the ball. He defeats

expectation by a whisker. The modest star,
irked by one misplay, is no hero by a hair;

in a strikeout slaughter when what could matter more,
he lines a homer to the signboard and has changed the
      score.

Then for his nineteenth season, a home run—
with four of six runs batted in—Carl Furillo's the big gun;

almost dehorned the foe—has fans dancing in delight.
Jake Pitler and his Playground "get a Night"—

Jake, that hearty man, made heartier by a harrier
who can bat as well as field—Don Demeter.

Shutting them out for nine innings—hitter too—
Carl Erskine leaves Cimoli nothing to do.

Take off the goat-horns, Dodgers, that egret
which two very fine base-stealers can offset.

You've got plenty: Jackie Robinson
and Campy and big Newk, and Dodgerdom again
watching everything you do. You won last year. Come on.

ROLFE HUMPHRIES

POLO GROUNDS

Time is of the essence. This is a highly skilled
And beautiful mystery. Three or four seconds only
From the time that Riggs connects till he reaches first,
And in those seconds Jurges goes to his right,
Comes up with the ball, tosses to Witek at second
For the force on Reese, Witek to Mize at first,
In time for the out—a double play.

(Red Barber crescendo. Crowd noises, obbligato;
Scattered staccatos from the peanut boys,
Loud in the lull, as the teams are changing sides) . . .

Hubbell takes the sign, nods, pumps, delivers—
A foul into the stands. Dunn takes a new ball out,
Hands it to Danning, who throws it down to Werber;
Werber takes off his glove, rubs the ball briefly,
Tosses it over to Hub, who goes to the rosin bag,
Takes the sign from Danning, pumps, delivers—

Low, outside, ball three. Danning goes to the mound,
Says something to Hub. Dunn brushes off the plate,
Adams starts throwing in the Giant bull pen,
Hub takes the sign from Danning, pumps, delivers,
Camilli gets hold of it, a *long* fly to the outfield,
Ott goes back, back, back, against the wall, gets under it,
Pounds his glove, and takes it for the out.
That's all for the Dodgers. . . .

Time is of the essence. The rhythms break,
More varied and subtle than any kind of dance;
Movement speeds up or lags. The ball goes out
In sharp and angular drives, or long, slow arcs,
Comes in again controlled and under aim;
The players wheel or spurt, race, stoop, slide, halt,
Shift imperceptibly to new positions,
Watching the signs, according to the batter,
The score, the inning. Time is of the essence.
Time is of the essence. Remember Terry?
Remember Stonewall Jackson, Lindstrom, Frisch,
When they were good? Remember Long George Kelly?
Remember John McGraw and Benny Kauff?
Remember Bridwell, Tenney, Merkle, Youngs,
Chief Myers, Big Jeff Tesreau, Shufflin' Phil?
Remember Matthewson, and Ames, and Donlin,
Buck Ewing, Rusie, Smiling Mickey Welch?
Remember a left-handed catcher named Jack Humphries,
Who sometimes played the outfield, in '83?

Time is of the essence. The shadow moves
From the plate to the box, from the box to second base,
From second to the outfield, to the bleachers.

Time is of the essence. The crowd and players
Are the same age always, but the man in the crowd
Is older every season. Come on, play ball!

JOHN UPDIKE

TAO IN THE YANKEE STADIUM BLEACHERS[1]

Distance brings proportion. From here
the populated tiers
as much as players seem part of the show:
a constructed stage beast, three folds of Dante's rose,
or a Chinese military hat
cunningly chased with bodies.
"Falling from his chariot, a drunk man is unhurt
because his soul is intact. Not knowing his fall,
he is unastonished, he is invulnerable."
So, too, the "pure man"—"pure"
in the sense of undisturbed water.

"It is not necessary to seek out
a wasteland, swamp, or thicket."
The old men who saw Hans Wagner
scoop them up in lobster hands,
the opposing pitcher's pertinent hesitations,
the sky, this meadow, Mantle's thick baked neck,
the old men who in the changing rosters see
a personal mutability,
green slats, wet stone are all to me
as when an emperor commands
a performance with a gesture of his eyes.

1. *Tao* is a Chinese word meaning the way of all life. Chuang-tzu was a Taoist philosopher who speaks with a skull in one of his parables. Taoism is intended to create poise, serenity, and complete assurance, qualities that may be associated with the invincible Yankees of old.—ED.

"No king on his throne has the joy of the dead,"
the skull told Chuang-tzu.
The thought of death is peppermint to you
when games begin with patriotic song
and a democratic sun beats broadly down.
The Inner Journey seems unjudgeably long
when small boys purchase cups of ice
and, distant as a paradise,
experts, passionate and deft,
wait while Berra flies to left.

ROBERT FITZGERALD

COBB WOULD HAVE CAUGHT IT

In sunburnt parks where Sundays lie,
Or the wide wastes beyond the cities,
Teams in grey deploy through sunlight.

Talk it up, boys, a little practice.

Coming in stubby and fast, the baseman
Gathers a grounder in fat green grass,
Picks it stinging and clipped as wit
Into the leather: a swinging step
Wings it deadeye down to first.
Smack. Oh, attaboy, attyoldboy.

Catcher reverses his cap, pulls down
Sweaty casque, and squats in the dust:
Pitcher rubs a new ball on his pants,
Chewing, puts a jet behind him;
Nods past batter, taking his time.
Batter settles, tugs at his cap:
A spinning ball: step and swing to it,

Caught like a cheek before it ducks
By shivery hickory: socko, baby:
Cleats dig into the dust. Outfielder,
On his way, looking over shoulder,
Makes it a triple. A long peg home.

Innings and afternoons. Fly lost in sunset.
Throwing arm gone bad. There's your old ball game.
Cool reek of the field. Reek of companions.

ROBERT FRANCIS

THE BASE STEALER

Poised between going on and back, pulled
Both ways taut like a tightrope-walker,
Fingertips pointing the opposites,
Now bouncing tiptoe like a dropped ball
Or a kid skipping rope, come on, come on,
Running a scattering of steps sidewise,
How he teeters, skitters, tingles, teases,
Taunts them, hovers like an ecstatic bird,
He's only flirting, crowd him, crowd him,
Delicate, delicate, delicate, delicate—now!

PITCHER

His art is eccentricity, his aim
How not to hit the mark he seems to aim at,

His passion how to avoid the obvious,
His technique how to vary the avoidance.

The others throw to be comprehended. He
Throws to be a moment misunderstood.

Yet not too much. Not errant, arrant, wild,
But every seeming aberration willed.

Not to, yet still, still to communicate
Making the batter understand too late.

GREGORY CORSO

DREAM OF A BASEBALL STAR

I dreamed Ted Williams
leaning at night
against the Eiffel Tower, weeping.

He was in uniform
and his bat lay at his feet
—knotted and twiggy.

"Randall Jarrell say's you're a poet!" I cried.
"So do I! I say you're a poet!"

He picked up his bat with blown hands;
stood there astraddle as he would in the batter's box,
and laughed! flinging his schoolboy wrath
toward some invisible pitcher's mound
—waiting the pitch all the way from heaven.

It came; hundreds came! all afire!
He swung and swung and swung and connected not one
sinker curve hook or right-down-the-middle.
A hundred strikes!

The umpire dressed in strange attire
thundered his judgment: YOU'RE OUT!
And the phantom crowd's horrific boo
dispersed the gargoyles from Notre Dame.

And I screamed in my dream:
God! throw thy merciful pitch!
Herald the crack of bats!
Hooray the sharp liner to left!
Yea the double, the triple!
Hosannah the home run!

DIANE WAKOSKI

INDIAN GIVER

You gave me
this knife
yesterday

an act
of friendship
            because
I gave you
part of my lunch,
so you wouldn't have to eat
in the school cafeteria
and miss the ball game

Today you
take it
back.
      Indian giver,
I call you,
remembering I made a home run
yesterday at noon
and you
struck
out.

DEENA METZGER

LITTLE LEAGUE WOMEN °

The women are larger than I
fed on beefsteak and beer
guzzled from nippled bottles
like Jap cows
in a film I saw once.
Their flanks ripple with fat
above thin hoofs.
The women take it from the earth first.
The juices flow up and make milk
to dribble in one and another
goat red mouth.
Yet the kids are thin
as stalks and corn blond.
The women grow
beyond comfort,
nimble only when surprised.
There is nothing sympathetic about them
They sweat under their breasts
and swat flies.
Herding in dumb bulk,
the women are cows
eating grass and men.
What cud there is
once chewed
is spit.

° This poem was written in 1969 at a time when I was still afflicted with the self-hate
which is a product of the general devaluation of women in our society. At that time, it
was difficult to establish the self without dissociating oneself from other women and
women's roles. Rather than experiencing sympathy or empathy, I had absorbed the
anger, the stereotypes which are directed at women and mothers in order to maintain us
in the inferior female role. Since that time, I have come to see that the women whom I
portrayed so cruelly were victims, and that the poem is a lie. Now I honor their efforts,
my efforts, to survive by whatever means we found in a society which denied us almost
all meaningful participation.

I could pretend that the poem was not written, or could write another (I may,
someday) but I think it more honest and appropriate to let the poem stand as a sign of
my own ignorance and pain at that time. I am pleased that times have changed and the
daughters of these women are now playing ball in Little League and that, hopefully, the
fathers are selling hot dogs and standing by the sidelines. In time, I expect we will
advance sufficiently so that no one is on the sidelines and everyone plays.

MAY SWENSON

ANALYSIS OF BASEBALL

It's about
the ball,
the bat,
and the mitt.
Ball hits
bat, or it
hits mitt.
Bat doesn't
hit ball, bat
meets it.
Ball bounces
off bat, flies
air, or thuds
ground (dud)
or it
fits mitt.

Bat waits
for ball
to mate.
Ball hates
to take bat's
bait. Ball
flirts, bat's
late, don't
keep the date.
Ball goes in
(thwack) to mitt,
and goes out
(thwack) back
to mitt.

Ball fits
mitt, but
not all
the time.
Sometimes
ball gets hit
(pow) when bat
meets it,
and sails
to a place
where mitt
has to quit
in disgrace.
That's about
the bases
loaded,
about 40,000
fans exploded.

It's about
the ball,
the bat,
the mitt,
the bases
and the fans.
It's done
on a diamond,
and for fun.
It's about
home, and it's
about run.

SONIA SANCHEZ

on watching a world series game

O say can u see
on the baseball diamond
all the fans
            clappen for they nigger/players
yeah.
            there ain't nothing like a
            nigger playen in the noon/day
            sun for us fun/loving/spectators.
                                    sometimes
they seem even human.
                    (that is to say
                            every now and then.)
Hooray. hurrah. hooray.
                    my. that nigger's
tough on that mound.
                    can't git no
batters past him.
                wonder where he
was found
            makes u wonder if
it's still a wite man's game.
                    WHO that flexing
his wite muscles.
                oh god yes. another wite hero
to save us from total blk/ness.
                    Carl YASTRZEMSKi
yastruski.   YASTROOSKI.
    ya - fuck - it.   yeh.
                        it's america's
most famous past time
                    and the name
    of the game
                    ain't baseball.

ELIOT ASINOF

THE NEGRO

from *Man on Spikes*

On the players' bench, Ben Franks sat wedged in amongst the hot, tired bodies, listening to the sullen obscenities that reflected their mood. The dugout suddenly seemed like a small, overcrowded house with a huge picture-window looking out over the diamond. Quiet, he stewed in his own sweat, waiting for the turn at bat that would permit him to leave; and he thought that this was a helluva place to feel so damn alone.

He tried to concentrate on the ball game, nursing a weird feeling that he hadn't been in it. Everything was strange. Strange park. Strange city. Strange ballplayers. It made the day seem unreal, almost dreamlike. (What the hell, man! You slept last night in a crummy flea bag in Scranton, Pennsylvania, and here you are like a bird, suddenly, in Kansas City, hustling your ass with Minneapolis in a nifty triple A circuit. Man, that's something; so get with it!)

Up at the plate, the hitter was Kutner, waving his bat at the pitcher like he would knock the guy's head off. Ben leaned back and suppressed a routine desire to holler encouragement, for he sensed this was not wanted from him. Not now, especially not for Kutner. For today Ben had moved in cold and taken over center field as though he were the greatest prospect since Tris Speaker. The manager had announced it in the locker room, apologizing for something he had no control over.

"This is Franks, men. He'll play center field for us. Kutner moves to left."

Orders from Chicago, Ben knew. "Move the big nigger in there and see what he can do!" It seemed like a damn-fool way to run a ball club.

The silence that followed had crushed him. They had looked at him as if he had engineered the deal himself. He had sneaked a first glance at this Kutner and saw the man barely nod to the manager, the muscle on his jaw twitching nervously. Ben had swallowed heavily, and it sounded like thunder to him.

So he sat back on the bench now, quiet and alone, contemplating his coming time at bat for he followed the next hitter. The prospects of belting one excited him, as always. He knew he would have to talk with his bat and talk big. This was not his ball club just because he wore the uniform. He tried to forget everything else.

Even as he saw Kutner lift a simple pop foul, his stomach fluttered anticipating trouble. He waited until the catcher had settled under it before going to the bat rack. He grabbed three bats and started out of the dugout toward the batter's circle, suddenly hating the baseball tradition that required him to be there. He saw Kutner coming toward him, his eyes lowered to the ground, sputtering his anger and frustration between his teeth.

"Sonofabitch!"

Ben grumbled to himself as he heard. Listen to the man cussing himself. That ain't nothing to what they gonna be callin' me! He spat through his broken tooth and moved nervously into the batter's circle.

The voices greeted him again.

"Well, well. Look who's here!"

"Shine, boy?"

He tried to shut them out of his consciousness, to close his brain to their viciousness. But he was too vulnerable there, a kneeling duck, trapped by a white circle of lime and an old article in the rule book.

"Nigger! shine! boogie! coon! slave!"

They used all the words on him. There was a sudden harshness to their yelling, now more agitated and severe than before, as though they were building up to something. It seemed like more than a razzing job to get his goat. He'd played ball for four years in the Negro leagues and they could jockey with the best of them. But this was more, much more. This was the hoarse, rasping voice of hate, and it struck close to home.

He had guessed it would be something like this when he had signed. This was white men's baseball. Up in Chicago Jim Mellon had told him as much: "You'll have to swallow plenty, boy. This is still a new thing. You'll just have to learn how to control yourself!"

He was getting plenty of practice.

"Hey, porter, take my bags."

"Yeah, where's your red cap?"

"Ya big ape! Go on back to the zoo!"

He thought wryly that back in the dugout he was lonely and wanted out. Now he was worried and wanted back in. O.K., big Ben. Take it easy. Remember this is where you want to be. What did you expect, cookies and tea between innings?

"Watch out, nigger. The chucker's got a real hard one."

"He's gonna stick it in yer ear, black boy."

"Look here, nigger!"

"Hey, boy, here!"

In front of him, he saw the pitcher step off the mound, suddenly distracted by the spectators. Mechanically, Ben turned to see them, the faces behind the jeering voices.

Someone was dangling a handmade noose from a long pole.

Big joke. He heard their mocking calls and their savage laughter, and a slight chill ran through him. Then he saw them on his own bench, peering over the dugout like kids at a ten-cent peep show, and they were laughing too. Sure . . . great big gag. He wiped the sweat off his hands on the rosin bag and turned back to the game.

"Come on!" he roared at the hitter. "Ride one!"

He wanted them to know: Ben Franks was here to play ball.

He watched the feeble grounder and the simple play at first and he moved in to hit. It was his moment now, and he would make it good. He saw only the pitcher and a beautiful vision of a drive riding over the big fence in right. He knew this chucker was duck soup for him, that he could pick out the throw he liked and blast it. The thing to do was to be loose up there, to think only of hitting . . . only of hitting.

The pitcher had more respect for him than the jockeys, or, at least, a different kind, and he kept the ball away from him. Ben fouled off one, then another, and the count worked up to three and two. He got set for the big one, and watched the curve ball sweep down and away. He held his swing for the obviously bad pitch, but even as he did, he heard the umpire's call, the much-too-hasty grunt meant to cut him down.

"Stee-rike three!"

He turned like a cat at a sudden noise, his whole body alive with protest. This wasn't jockeying any more. A man can't hit a pitch like that, no matter what. In the stands they saw his contorted face, and they hooted with joy at this unexpected treat.

("You'll have to swallow plenty, boy. You'll just have to learn control!")

He bit his lip at the fury rushing through him. Control, Ben. Control. Don't throw your bat. Don't argue. Dont!"

He moved back from the umpire, and as he did, he saw the stupid smile through the fat mask.

It was time for him to get out of there.

He dropped his bat and jogged back to the outfield, fighting back his rage. He picked up his glove and pounded the pocket viciously.

The sonsofbitches.

His mind was knotted with his anger. He knew it was the goddamn jockeys who had called that pitch, not the umpire's eyesight. The ump was riding on their catcalls as he waited for the pitch, ready to holler "strike three" before he even saw it. The guy was playing it safe; he'd call them with the crowd whenever possible.

So he stood out there in the field, balancing his pride and hopes and ambitions against this monster of hate and pressure. He tried to believe he could live with this kind of thing and play ball despite it. He knew he was plenty good at bat, that he could hit with the best of them. But it was the other factors that tore at the roots of his confidence—the fans on him, the umps against him, his teammates cool toward him. He thought of Jackie Robinson up there breaking in with Brooklyn and he let his mind speculate over what it might be like in the big leagues. Pretty rough, he knew. People are people whatever the circuit. There's good folk and there's bad. The bad ones will put the spike in your leg and the hard knee in your groin, and the good ones will sit back while it happens and just be damn sorry that it does. Sure, a man would have to be pretty terrific to stick, not just good enough. Pretty damn terrific. He wondered whether he'd ever be that.

Then, as if out of nowhere, he heard the crack of the bat. His body tensed, waiting for his eye to focus on the drive soaring out toward him. He turned with a jerk to take off for it, terrified that he hadn't even seen it hit! At once his concentration returned to the game, and somehow, through his reverie, he had recorded that there was a man on. He panicked at his unreadiness. He drove his legs desperately over the turf, wondering how hard it was hit, and as he ran, he sensed suddenly he was misjudging it. He tried to shift his direction, but his big body seemed unwieldy. At the last moment, he twisted his arm behind him in a wild, clumsy maneuver. The best he could do was to get a piece of his glove on the ball.

He turned quickly to pick it up, and couldn't. It was as if the ball were alive, eluding him. Out of the corner of his eye, he saw Kutner, standing there a few feet away, and he almost laughed through his exasperation. He grabbed at it again, and whirled to throw.

"Home," he heard.

He threw desperately, with all his power, and before he let it go, he knew he would throw it away.

The savage roaring of the crowd blasted in his ears. Ben stood there for a moment, looking at the players around home plate.

"Shit!" he heard Kutner snarl with disgust.

"Shit . . ." he nodded.

He walked back to his position, torturing himself with a recount of his actions. In those few moments, he had been all wrong as a ball-player. In fact, he'd been no ballplayer at all. He had let his concentration drift from the game. A ballplayer should be thinking. A ball-player should always be thinking.

He set himself for the next hitter, who popped out to third, and the next, his teeth clenched with concentration on every pitch. He begged for the ball to be hit to him. He prayed for the chance to redeem himself with a great catch this time, or a great throw. To me, goddammit! To me! Hit that sonofabitchin' thing out here again. And he felt he would burn up at the terrible waiting that is baseball.

Then he saw the pitch, the swing, and the ball floating out into left center like an answer to his plea. He cut loose after it, thinking only that he was happy that there were two men on, that with two outs they'd be running, and that the game would be over if he failed to make the catch. He took off for it with everything he had. Then, near the end of his dash, he heard the hurried cry a few yards away:

"I got it! I got it!"

He had all but forgotten that Kutner was out there in left field.

Ben's big body was charging like a locomotive and he didn't want to stop. He saw the ball in its downward flight and he knew he could get there in time. This should be his catch. Somehow or other he felt that they owed it to him.

"No!" he cried "Mine! Mine!"

But at the same moment, Ben heard him again, repeating his call. It was too late; the decision would have to be made by instinct, without corroboration by the other. There was too much of Ben's will in his race for that ball; the commitment had been made even before the ball was hit, and he could not control it. His body drove for the catch, but as it did, Kutner's body crossed into his line of vision. Ben automatically swerved violently, throwing himself to the ground to avoid a crash. He rolled over twice with the momentum of his fall, and when he stopped, he turned to see Kutner standing over him, his face red with anger.

A few feet behind him, Ben saw the white ball, slowly trickling to a stop. He realized then how far he had moved into left field.

Slowly he got to his feet, listening to the hooting and laughter of the crowd. The game was over and the crowd had won it. He stuffed his glove into his hip pocket and began the terrible walk to the clubhouse.

In the locker room, the players sat on the benches taking too much time to undress. Ben fingered the laces on his shoes, wanting to take his shower and get out of there. He remembered he hadn't eaten since this morning, at a stopover in Chicago. Christ! What a day! But he felt the rest of them half-eyeing him, as if they were defying him to be first after what he had done. Furtively, he stopped unlacing, resigned to taking the scorn they were throwing at him without so much as opening their mouths. Somehow, he had hoped there would be quick respite for him, that they'd offer him some pollyannish word of encouragement to prop him up. And when the manager came in, Ben looked up toward him and winced as the man threw his little cap at the corner in a ludicrous, adolescent gesture that passed for rage. Like the others, he could say nothing but merely moped in the special chair reserved for him.

Goddamn you all! Ben was ready to explode. Say it! Go ahead and say it!

Then he wondered what he wanted them to say. There was too much against him to package into a few choice words of profanity. He had walked in there a few hours before, hated for as good a reason as any white man could have dreamed up to hate a Negro.

Ben Franks was labeled to go up *because* he was black.

He knew it. They all knew it. Up in Chicago, Jim Mellon had his eyes on Brooklyn, shifting from the gate receipts to Robinson's ability and back to the gate receipts. The black man was being accepted and the ball club was making a fat dollar for its "crusade." So Jim Mellon had to get himself a black man.

Ben looked down at the color of his arms. Coal black. Sure. Mellon's boy would have to be black. With kinky hair and big feet. He remembered Mellon suggesting slyly that Robinson seemed like the wrong kind of black boy to bring up. Too smart, too aggressive, too tricky. His feet were too small. The public might not like too much of that. But a big, lumbering, quiet boy who can blast that long ball. The crowds would really go for that.

Big and dumb, Ben grunted. But not too dumb. He hated Mellon for that, and he hated himself now because he hadn't proved the old bastard wrong. Ben was big, yes, and he lumbered on the base paths without grace or too much speed. Therefore, it followed that he must be dumb. Jesus, he thought now, they hadn't even told him the signals before the game, as though he wasn't expected to play that kind of baseball!

The whole deal had a peculiar flavor to it. It seemed too arbitrary, too simple. He felt he was being judged by a special set of standards that applied only to him. Back in Scranton, just a few weeks ago, a foolish young pitcher had grooved one with the bases crowded, and Ben had laid his power into it. The ball had soared over the lights in deep right center, out of the park and into the huge parking lot, some 560 feet from home plate. It created a big stir. No ball had ever been hit that far in Scranton. He was told that Jim Mellon had hopped a plane the next night and flown to Scranton to watch him play. Then he went out to the parking area after the game to see where the ball landed. They had even sought out the man whose windshield had been smashed by the blow, and they paid him ten bucks to drive to the spot where his car had been parked.

Apparently this had been enough to sell old man Mellon on him. It was crazy. He knew he was good enough. But he also knew he was no better than dozens of others, black or white. But he alone had belted one 560 feet. You're a freak, Ben, he told himself. A 560-foot publicity stunt. You're gonna be Chicago's symbol of tolerance and democracy, and you'll be paid for your pigment, your yardage, and your docility.

He sat there now, brooding, unable to undress until the last man had showered, as though this were a kind of self-inflicted punishment, a token of his guilt. There was something sickening about all this. He was being used to exploit the breaking color line in baseball by a man who was simply trying a new angle for an extra buck. Ben would be fed nickels and the familiar pot of sugar about how thrilled he should be to be playing white man's baseball, to be a hero to his people. And he'd go up the ladder to the top, hated most by the men he was told to walk on, like Kutner here.

He took off his shirt and hung it neatly on the hanger. MINNEAPOLIS it read, bridging across the zipper down the middle. He told himself to be proud. What the hell, he was doing fine. The world was a crazy place and it wasn't up to him to explain it. Things had moved fast for him since April, faster during these four months than for most people in a lifetime. He was going up and that's what counted. Forget today, Ben. Tomorrow will be better. Everything's gonna be O.K.

But it wasn't that simple. There was a tense pressure in AAA baseball that was strange to him. They played to win with a new kind of concentration, for these were the eager boys close to the top, knocking at the big doors. They looked for likely targets and knew a million ways to knock a man down. That he should become such a target did not stagger him. It was a way of winning he knew all about.

But a bad beginning can hound a man; the breaks can turn against him, developing a reputation that makes him out a complete bust. After a week, Ben found his confidence severely shaken, especially since he had done nothing to prove himself. Those first three days in Kansas City had been a nightmare. After that first game, they never gave him a chance to climb out of the hole he had dug for himself. The pitchers had given him nothing to hit at. At the risk of walking him once or twice a game, they dusted him off with their high hard ones, and he spent half his time at the plate thinking about protecting himself. He was not going to make the big leagues on a record number of bases on balls. If he belted a few, at least some of the fans would welcome him in Minneapolis. He wanted that. He needed the crowds behind him.

He also needed his teammates, but some of them made it rough on him. He came to feel a weird kind of pressure as though they were making him a slave to his new reputation. Quietly, he was needled in a hundred different ways with irritating pricks at his nerves that left him raw and edgy. His bats would disappear from the rack just before game time, and he would have to borrow someone's stick he didn't feel comfortable with. In batting practice, he'd occasionally be fed bad pitches so he couldn't get loose and swing away freely. At night, he'd get strange phone calls in his hotel room, interrupting his sleep. He even received a letter threatening him if he didn't go back "where he belonged."

Yet he knew who they were. He could tell by the way they looked at him. A couple of drawling punks so full of hatred they reeked of it. He tried not to care. He told himself it didn't matter; he wasn't here to win a popularity contest. He kept to himself.

One afternoon he arrived early at the ball park with a pair of new bats and a dried turkey bone to rub them down with. He was thankful for the quiet of the locker room, and sitting on the bench in front of his locker, he went to work on his bats lovingly. From across the room, he saw Kutner and Meade come in. They nodded and went to the table to play cards. Ben nodded back, relieved that they did not choose to talk to him.

For some time he rubbed, deriving pleasure from the work for it lent itself to the kind of daydreams he most enjoyed, the pictures of the fat barrel of the bat laid powerfully to the ball and that long, wonderful ride up and out before his eyes.

"Aren't those bats already treated, Franks?"

Ben looked up and saw Kutner.

"Yeah . . . I guess so. But not like this. Seal up the grain real hard and the wood won't chip on you."

Kutner was watching him.

"See the difference?" Ben said. "Rubbed this side, not this."

They examined the barrel, and nodded.

Ben smiled, encouraged. "Josh Gibson, he showed me. He had some sticks, they last for five, maybe six years. Bone-rubbed the hell out of them." Ben chuckled. "I think he went out and found his own tree."

"You play ball with Gibson?"

The question made him feel good.

"Yeah. Two years."

Kutner shook his head. "I never saw such a hitter. Played one lousy semipro game against him. That guy hit one by me so hard I could've been playing infield. I never had a chance to move for it."

Franks nodded and they were silent again. Ben heard the cards shuffling above him as he worked. He thought of Gibson, the greatest of all Negro catchers, and he wondered what Josh'd be thinking about him, going up like this. It seemed crazy, for Josh had been ten times the ballplayer Ben was. Ben let his mind picture Gibson in the majors, jogging his squat body around the bases while they scrambled for the ball deep in the bleachers. He knew how much Gibson wanted to play there. Too late. They were too late for Josh Gibson. And damn lucky for them white-boy catchers like Cochrane and Dickey. Old Josh would've showed 'em how.

That's a waste, ain't it, Ben thought. A lousy waste. He remembered Josh with that little picture he carried around which showed him shaking hands with Babe Ruth. That was as close as they let him come to the major leagues.

"Say, Franks. You ever hit against this guy Satchel Paige?"

It did not escape Ben that they must have been thinking along the same lines as he was. It made him smile.

"No hitting, just swinging," he said.

"Really rough, eh?"

Ben nodded.

"He threw 'em and they looked like peas hopping in the wind."

"They say he's mighty quick."

"He has several speeds. And the plate is all corners, no middle."

It was quiet again for a moment. Ben sat there containing his laughter. He felt he could see right into Kutner's mind and it amused him. The man was thinking that black men were coming up, wondering if there was a mess of them who might beat him out.

"I suppose they'll bring Paige up, if he's not too old," Kutner said.

"They have to pay him some, 'cause that boy don't pitch for peanuts any more." Meade and Kutner listened over their cards. "Why, Satch has a private plane. Did you know that? Flies to work, he does. I heard one day he pitched in three different states all in one damn day! He works the first three innings of a double-header in Charleston, South Carolina. He hops his plane and hustles down to work the last three in Savannah, Georgia. Then he takes his time and has a good feed. That night, he goes for nine in Jacksonville."

Kutner and Meade laughed.

"He must've been tired," Meade said.

"Maybe. But he left a trail of goose eggs across a good slice of the country. And he was ready to work again the next day, I'll bet."

"What's it like in the Negro leagues, Franks? Anything like this?"

Ben looked around at the pleasant locker room, at the half-dozen showers with hot water. He thought of the well-planned AAA schedule, the almost leisurely three-day stopovers, the high-class Pullman rides, the first-rate hotels, the five-bucks-a-day meal money, the beautiful well-trimmed diamonds; and he thought back to the all-night bus rides, the double-headers followed by night games in another town, the flea bags they ate and slept in, the sand-lot ball parks, some of them where they didn't have lockers and you rode all night in your sweaty suit. You got paid by the week, and not much either, and they'd keep you working as many exhibition games as they could book.

"Not much like this," he answered finally. "But they sure play a lot of ball."

Kutner persisted. "How would you rate it? What class?"

Ben thought for a moment. "I don't know. Some of them clubs were pretty damn good."

"As good as this?"

He didn't like the questioning now. He had a feeling that maybe he'd talked enough.

"I don't know," he repeated. "I guess I ain't been around long enough to say."

He looked up at them as he replied, wondering what they were thinking of him. He hadn't intended to talk at all, and here he'd been spinning out the story of his career. And especially, why in front of these two? His arrival had pushed them out of their regular spots and shuffled them around the outfield. Meade had been the left fielder; he was an older guy and apparently a buddy of Kutner's for Ben saw them together frequently. In some ways he would have found it easier if these two had hated him. Then he could hate them back. But it was clear that they didn't. For all the stolid expression, in Kutner's face, Ben saw no hatred. Resentment maybe, but no hatred.

For the most part, Kutner had kept away from him. Until this moment, there had been few words between them, even after his blunder in the outfield that first game. Ben had found it rough to shake it off; it was so much more than just another error in another ball game.

But in his way, Kutner exploited the situation. Ben saw it happening and shrugged it off. At first, it seemed almost ludicrous. He had been with the club less than a week when a crucial fly ball looped out to left center field, a short easy run for him. He moved in for the catch that would end the inning when suddenly he heard Kutner's yell: "I've got it!" He stopped quickly and watched the other tear in front of him, making the catch on a dead run.

On the way back to the dugout, neither of them said anything.

Then it happened again the following night, this time with a runner on third base, tagging up for a dash home after the catch. The fly ball was clearly Ben's, but Kutner claimed it, moving over toward center field as though his throwing arm was needed to make the play. Ben stood by, helplessly, and found no relief in the fact that the run scored.

He knew how plays like that looked to everyone. They put a stigma on a man. A ballplayer doesn't go up holding another guy's glove.

His ear became tuned to all kinds of talk, a word here and there, a line in the newspapers, a stranger's voice over a glass of beer. "This guy Franks ain't much; Kutner takes the show from him." Kutner was playing ball like a demon. He was all over the place. He'd back up Ben on a simple can of corn, scurrying across the outfield as if there was a chance that Ben might let the ball get away. Ben hated it. He'd hear him charging toward him, yelling advice when none was needed, always at his elbow on every play.

The treatment would have to stop.

One afternoon after the game, he waited for Kutner until the locker room had emptied.

"Let's have a talk, Kutner," he said. "Got something on my mind."

Kutner nodded.

"O.K. Let's have it."

"I want you to get off my back, little man. You're giving me too much trouble."

Kutner shrugged. "Your trouble ain't my fault."

"Some of it is, man. You can turn it off. I'm here to play ball, not to play games with you out there in the gardens. You can't stop me, Kutner. You'll be wasting your time trying. It may be a lousy deal for you and that's t.s., but it all adds up for me. They brought me up here, see, and I don't aim to step aside for you."

Kutner looked up at him.

"And what the hell am I supposed to do? Pick my goddamn nose? I been in pro ball for ten years and I don't like to get pushed around."

"I ain't pushin' nobody."

"That's not what's written in my book. I was due to go up next spring. Me. Mike Kutner. I was due to go up because I've fought for it and deserve it. Then you come along and I get shoved over. Sonofabitch. I never played anything but center field in my life and you shove my ass over."

"You blame me for that?"

"O.K., O.K. All I know is you're the bastard who's stealing my pie, Franks, and I'm the kid to protect it. That should be clear enough." He started to walk away.

Ben grabbed his arm. He didn't want to leave things like this. He didn't want a perpetual fight with this little man.

"Wait a minute!" he snapped. "You talk about what's fair! You got some idea this is a picnic for me?" Then he said aloud to a white man the words that had been going around in circles in his head for days. "Even without you bastards on my hump this is no picnic. Every goddamn chucker thinks he's throwing balls at my head like I'm a Little Black Sambo at a carnival. Yeah, that's it. Three balls for a dime. Win a kewpie doll if you can stick it in his ear! And they try to cut me down on the bases with them sharp spikes like I was hamburger; and the polite folk in the stands will look at the gashes and say, now ain't that too damn bad. And all the time the friggen holler-guys, on and off the field, night after night, calling me a black sonofabitch because they mean it. That ain't no way to become a ballplayer, Kutner. No way at all. It's like getting up to bat with two strikes on you; you ain't even when you start!"

He looked at Kutner, trying to find a measure of understanding. He saw the man's indecision. Then Kutner shook his head slowly and pulled off his glasses.

"See these stinking things?" he said quietly. "I got troubles of my own."

The bite had left his voice. He looked almost sadly at Ben for a moment, holding his glasses in his hand. Then he turned and left.

It had never occurred to Ben that Kutner's glasses made any difference. But he saw it now. There was more than one way for the odds to stack up against you. He'd heard about the trouble guys with specs had, though he never figured it himself. He remembered one kid going into the Negro leagues back home who wore them. Some man loaned him fifty bucks to get himself a pair of those lenses you wear right on your eyeballs so no one could tell he needed them.

Yeah, Kutner had troubles of his own. And he was the kind who would fight all the harder because of them.

And so it happened.

Kutner kept working on him, crowding him, backing him up, showing his greater knowledge of the hitters by conspicuously advising him to move as each one stepped up to bat. It seemed to Ben that Kutner was spending half his time in center field and the other half calling and beckoning to him from left.

But Ben ignored him. Things began to go better for him. Late one game, he homered with two on to put them ahead, and he jogged out to his position sensing the elation that rides with a turn in the tide. He'd be O.K. now, he felt. He'd blast another and they'd get off his back. When a man's producing, there ain't a thing they can do but love him.

But a tight ball game is a fickle thing, and a late rally snuffed out the lead from his hit. He stood out there waiting, feeling the power of his old confidence and wishing for the ball to be hit to him. And when it came, a savage drive through the infield, he legged it rapidly, prepared to scoop it up on the run and cut down the runner moving around third with the big tally. He knew the runner was fast—he was prepared, this time, he'd been thinking—and had the jump on him. Though a long shot, this was the tying run and a long throw home was the correct play. But as he stabbed for it, he heard the sharp call from behind him.

"Third!"

At once his mind reacted, automatically. He whirled to throw to third, figuring the runner had cut back or stumbled. It could happen. But this time it hadn't. He watched his throw hop beautifully into third base, and he choked on the truth he saw too late: The runner was crossing the plate standing up.

He looked back at Kutner and barked at him.

"What the hell did you do that for?" He fought back his rage.

Even as he said it he knew, and all he could do was stand there helplessly watching Kutner turn from him without bothering to answer. He stood there smoldering against a background of derisive yells from the bleachers. Control, boy . . . control! Sonofabitch. You'll control your ass right out of organized baseball.

He walked back to his position chewing on his anger, and he waited. He didn't know what he was waiting for, though he had to believe there was a way to prove himself once and for all.

He waited until the ninth. From center field, he watched a base hit and a walk with two outs threaten their one-run lead again. Then it came, the long fly ball to deep left center. Ben got a good start on it and pumped hard, determined to put it in his pocket for the final out. He saw Kutner sprinting over from left, still a long way from it.

At once, Ben called for it. "Mine! Mine!"

Kutner kept coming, moving rapidly toward the point where the ball would drop. Suddenly, Mike hollered:

"I got it! I got it!"

Ben drove his body harder.

"Mine, Kutner. Mine!"

Kutner waved his glove at him as he ran.

"Stay away! Stay away!"

They were converging rapidly now. Ben felt the fury rising in him.

"Get away, you bastard. Get away!" His voice boomed out across the thirty feet between them, and he wondered what was in Kutner's mind. Would the little man dare keep coming? Would he still try for it? Would he? *Would he?*

He measured his stride for the end flight of the ball and gritted his teeth for the catch and whatever else might follow. He saw the ball sinking rapidly toward his outstretched glove and then, with terrible suddenness, the body crashing into him. Ben fell heavily over him, and somersaulted awkwardly on the soft turf. He was conscious mainly of the ball securely wrapped in the webbing of his glove.

He got up to the screaming of the crowd and went to the body prostrate on the ground.

"You O.K., man?" Ben knelt beside him.

Kutner moaned and rolled slowly over on his back, gasping for breath.

"Yeah, I'll be O.K.," he said. "Just leave me be."

Ben saw the bruised face and the twisted metal frame of Mike's glasses. He pulled them off as gently as he could and turned aside to straighten them out. He twisted them carefully until they were properly fixed, and as he worked, he was proud of the steadiness of his hand, as though he almost did not expect this of himself.

The infielders came rushing out and stormed into him, shattering his mood with their hot faces spitting rage into his.

"You sonofabitch. What the hell you think you're doin'?"

"Goddammit, nigger, you trying to ruin this man?"

They pushed him violently, plucking at his uniform as if they wanted to strip him of it. He held one hand behind his back to protect the glasses and tried to ward them off with the other. There was nothing he could say.

There were more of them now. In the stands they probably think I'm being congratulated, Ben thought crazily. He stood there taking their shoving and their angry abuse. They could kill me, probably. Crowd around and kill me. Nobody'd know.

And then he saw the little man scrambling among them, pulling them off with a fury of his own.

"Stop it!" Kutner cried. "Pete! Lefty! Fer Chrissakes, lay off him!"

They saw who it was and they stopped, and suddenly Ben was free. The whole thing hadn't lasted thirty seconds; yet a sea of threatening faces had hemmed him in. They stood around him still, not yet ready to make peace, waiting for what Kutner would say. Kutner stood there breathing heavily.

"Leave him alone," he mumbled. "It was my goddamn fault."

They started to protest, and stopped. Kutner stared at them with his naked eyes. His whole face seemed naked.

"You heard me!" he said. "Come on, let's go in."

Then they broke up, quiet in their confusion and the baldness of their violence. Ben saw the hate drain from their faces and he stood there nodding his head as if in approval. He was shaking.

"Here, Mike." He handed Kutner his glasses. "It's lucky them things didn't smash, ain't it?"

Kutner looked up at him, red-eyed and pale.

"That's O.K.," he said quietly. "It's happened before. They bend, but they won't break."

He looked squarely at Ben, and smiled slightly. Then he put them back on and walked in with him.

BOXING

In boxing, competition is reduced to its very essence—man versus man. Boxing is one of the most ancient sports. For example, a bronze statue of a boxer exists which dates from the mid-first century B.C. It is not surprising to find that a nineteenth-century writer, William Hazlitt, has written about the fight game and that boxing has changed hardly at all since that time. Hazlitt puts the fighters in a mythological context when he compares them to Ajax and Diomed, and certainly the identification of athletes with mythological heroes is one of the most persistent characteristics of sport.

Conversely, Ring Lardner's "Champion" demythologizes the hero and shows that the reality behind the smooth public facade of sport may be quite ugly. Midge Kelly is a worse human being than even Lefty in J. F. Powers' "Jamesie." Although it is debatable whether sport will build character, sport will certainly *reveal* character, and at the end of this story we have a full revelation of the true Midge Kelly.

This brutality of boxing is put in an ancient context in Alan Dugan's poem "Hurricane Jackson," about a fighter who received a terrible beating in the ring. This brutality is an intrinsic part of boxing, but in the United States it has been specially colored by racial discrimination.

Thus the two selections by Richard Wright and Ralph Ellison show the worst side of boxing, when it becomes a surrogate lynching. In Richard Wright's selection from *Black Boy*, a powerful autobiography, there is a loose semblance to the rules of sport, but Ellison's "The Battle Royal" is simply anarchic brutality mixed with strong sexual overtones. In Ellison's piece, we have an ironic counterpoint with the use of Booker T. Washington's famous speech to indicate that at this point the victimized boy still has some stake in existing society, or at least a belief that he will, at bottom, not be repudiated.

In any case, boxing is used in all these selections as a way of writing about the worst in human nature. The will to destruction is a necessary part of the fight game as it is seen here. The rules of the Marquis of Queensbury are absent.

WILLIAM HAZLITT

THE FIGHT

Reader, have you ever seen a fight? If not, you have a pleasure to come, at least if it is a fight like that between the Gas-man and Bill Neate. The crowd was very great when we arrived on the spot; open carriages coming up, with streamers flying and music playing, and the country-people were pouring in over hedge and ditch in all directions, to see their hero beat or be beaten. The odds were still on Gas, but only about five to four. Gully had been down to try Neate, and had backed him considerably, which was a damper to the sanguine confidence of the adverse party. About two hundred thousand pounds were pending. The Gas says, he lost £3000, which were promised him by different gentlemen if he had won. He had presumed too much on himself, which had made others presume on him. This spirited and formidable young fellow seems to have taken for his motto the old maxim, that "there are three things necessary to success in life—*Impudence! Impudence! Impudence!*" It is so in matters of opinion, but not in the *Fancy*, which is the most practical of all things, though even here confidence is half the battle, but only half. Our friend had vapoured and swaggered too much, as if he wanted to grin and bully his adversary out of the fight. The difference of weight between the two combatants (14 stone to 12) was nothing to the sporting men. Great, heavy, clumsy, long-armed Bill Neate kicked the beam in the scale of the Gas-man's vanity. The amateurs were frightened at his big words, and thought that they would make up for the difference of six feet and five feet nine. Truly, the *Fancy* are not men of imagination. They judge of what has been, and cannot conceive of anything that is to be. The Gas-man had won hitherto; therefore he must beat a man half as big again as himself—that to a certainty. Besides, there are as many feuds, factions, prejudices, pedantic notions in the *Fancy* as in the state or in the schools. Mr. Cully is almost the only cool, sensible man among them, who exercises an unbiased discretion, and is not a slave to his passions in these matters. But enough of reflections, and to our tale.

The day, as I have said, was fine for a December morning. The grass was wet, and the ground miry, and ploughed up with multitudinous feet, except that, within the ring itself, there was a spot of virgin-green closed in and unprofaned by vulgar tread, that shone with dazzling brightness in the mid-day sun. For it was now noon, and we had an hour to wait. This is the trying time. It is then the heart sickens, as you think what the two champions are about, and how short a time will determine their fate. After the first blow is struck, there is no opportunity for nervous apprehensions; you are swallowed up in the immediate interest of the scene—but

> Between the acting of a dreadful thing
> And the first motion, all the interim is
> Like a phantasma, or a hideous dream.

I found it so as I felt the sun's rays clinging to my back, and saw the white wintry clouds sink below the verge of the horizon. "So," I thought, "my fairest hopes have faded from my sight!—so will the Gas-man's glory, or that of his adversary, vanish in an hour." The *swells* were parading in their white box-coats, the outer ring was cleared with some bruises on the heads and shins of the rustic assembly (for the *cockneys* had been distanced by the sixty-six miles); the time drew near, I had got a good stand; a bustle, a buzz ran through the crowd, and from the opposite side entered Neate, between his second and bottle-holder. He rolled along swathed in his loose great coat, his knock-knees bending under his huge bulk; and, with a modest cheerful air, threw his hat into the ring. He then just looked round, and began quietly to undress; when from the other side there was a similar rush and an opening made, and the Gas-man came forward with a conscious air of anticipated triumph, too much like the cock-of-the-walk. He strutted about more than became a hero, sucked oranges with a supercilious air, and threw away the skin with a toss of his head, and went up and looked at Neate, which was an act of supererogation. The only sensible thing he did was, as he strode away from the modern Ajax, to fling out his arms, as if he wanted to try whether they would do their work that day.

By this time they had stripped, and presented a strong contrast in appearance. If Neate was like Ajax, "with Atlantean shoulders, fit to bear" the pugilistic reputation of all Bristol, Hickman might be compared to Diomed, light, vigorous, elastic, and his back glistened in the sun, as he moved about, like a panther's hide. There was now a dead pause—attention was awe-struck. Who at that moment, big with a great event, did not draw his breath short—did not feel his heart throb? All was ready. They tossed up for the sun, and the Gas-man won. They were led up to the *scratch*—shook hands, and went at it.

In the first round everyone thought it was all over. After making play a short time, the Gas-man flew at his adversary like a tiger, struck five blows in as many seconds, three first, and then following him as he staggered back, two more, right and left, and down he fell, a mighty ruin. There was a shout, and I said, "There is no standing this." Neate seemed like a lifeless lump of flesh and bone, round which the Gas-man's blows played with the rapidity of electricity or lightning, and you imagined he would only be lifted up to be knocked down again. It was as if Hickman held a sword or a fire in that right hand of his, and directed it against an unarmed body. They met again, and Neate seemed, not cowed, but particularly cautious. I saw his teeth clenched together and his brows knit close against the sun. He held out both his arms at full length straight before him, like two sledgehammers, and raised his left an inch or two higher. The Gas-man could not get over this guard—they struck mutually and fell, but without advantage on either side.

It was the same in the next round; but the balance of power was thus restored—the fate of the battle was suspended. No one could tell how it would end. This was the only moment in which opinion was divided; for, in the next, the Gas-man aiming a mortal blow at his adversary's neck, with his right hand, and failing from the length he had to reach, the other returned it with his left at full swing, planted a tremendous blow on his cheek-bone and eyebrow, and made a red ruin of that side of his face. The Gas-man went down, and there was another shout—a roar of triumph as the waves of fortune rolled tumultuously from side to side. This was a settler. Hickman got up, and "grinned horrible a ghastly smile," yet he was evidently dashed in his opinion of himself; it was the first time he had ever been so punished; all one side of his face was perfect scarlet, and his right eye was closed in dingy blackness, as he advanced to the fight, less confident, but still determined.

After one or two more rounds, not receiving another such remembrancer, he rallied and went at it with his former impetuosity. But in vain. His strength had been weakened,—his blows could not tell at such a distance,—he was obliged to fling himself at his adversary, and could not strike from his feet; and almost as regularly as he flew at him with his right hand, Neate warded the blow, or drew back out of its reach, and felled with the return of his left. There was little cautious sparring—no half-hits—no tapping and trifling, none of the *petit-maîtreship* of the art—they were almost all knock-down blows:—the fight was a good stand-up fight. The wonder was the half-minute time. If there had been a minute or more allowed between each round, it would have been intelligible how they should by degrees recover strength and resolution; but to see two men smashed to the ground, smeared with gore, stunned, senseless, the breath beaten out of their bodies; and then, before you recover from the shock, to see them rise up with new strength and courage, stand ready to inflict or receive mortal offence, and rush upon each other "like two clouds over the Caspian"—this is the most astonishing thing of all:—this is the high and heroic state of man! From this time forward the event became more certain every round; and about the twelfth it seemed as if it must have been over.

Hickman generally stood with his back to me; but in the scuffle, he had changed positions, and Neate just then made a tremendous lunge at him, and hit him full in the face. It was doubtful whether he would fall backwards or forwards; he hung suspended for a second or two, and then fell back, throwing his hands in the air, and with his face lifted up to the sky. I never saw any thing more terrific than his aspect just before he fell. All traces of life, of natural expression, were gone from him. His face was like a human skull, a death's head, spouting blood. The eyes were filled with blood, the nose streamed with blood, the mouth gaped blood. He was not like an actual man, but like a preternatural, spectral appearance, or like one of the figures in Dante's *Inferno*.

Yet he fought on after this for several rounds, still striking the first desperate blow, and Neate standing on the defensive, and using the same cautious guard to the last, as if he had still all his work to do; and it was not till the Gas-man was so stunned in the seventeenth or eighteenth round, that his senses forsook him, and he could not come to time, that the battle was declared over.

Ye who despise the Fancy, do something to shew as much *pluck*, or as much self-possession as this, before you assume a superiority which you have never given a single proof of by any one action in the whole course of your lives!—When the Gas-man came to himself, the first words he uttered were, "Where am I? What is the matter, Tom—you have lost the battle, but you are the bravest man alive." And Jackson whispered to him, "I am collecting a purse for you, Tom."—Vain sounds, and unheard at that moment! Neate instantly went up and shook him cordially by the hand, and seeing some old acquaintance, began to flourish with his fists, calling out, "Ah, you always said I couldn't fight—What do you think now?" But all in good humour, and without any appearance of arrogance; only it was evident Bill Neate was pleased that he had won the fight.

When it was over, I asked Cribb if he did not think it was a good one? He said, *"Pretty well!"* The carrier-pigeons now mounted into the air, and one of them flew with the news of her husband's victory to the bosom of Mrs. Neate. Alas, for Mrs. Hickman!

RING   LARDNER

CHAMPION

Midge Kelly scored his first knockout when he was seventeen. The knockee was his brother Connie, three years his junior and a cripple. The purse was a half dollar given to the younger Kelly by a lady whose electric had just missed bumping his soul from his frail little body.

Connie did not know Midge was in the house, else he never would have risked laying the prize on the arm of the least comfortable chair in the room, the better to observe its shining beauty. As Midge entered from the kitchen, the crippled boy covered the coin with his hand, but the movement lacked the speed requisite to escape his brother's quick eye.

"Watcha got there?" demanded Midge.

"Nothin'," said Connie.

"You're a one legged liar!" said Midge.

He strode over to his brother's chair and grasped the hand that concealed the coin.

"Let loose!" he ordered.

Connie began to cry.

"Let loose and shut up your noise," said the elder, and jerked his brother's hand from the chair arm.

The coin fell onto the bare floor. Midge pounced on it. His weak mouth widened in a triumphant smile.

"Nothin', huh?" he said. "All right, if it's nothin' you don't want it."

"Give that back," sobbed the younger.

"I'll give you a red nose, you little sneak! Where'd you steal it?"

"I didn't steal it. It's mine. A lady give it to me after she pretty near hit me with a car."

"It's a crime she missed you," said Midge.

Midge started for the front door. The cripple picked up his crutch, rose from his chair with difficulty, and, still sobbing, came toward Midge. The latter heard him and stopped.

"You better stay where you're at," he said.

"I want my money," cried the boy.

"I know what you want," said Midge.

Doubling up the fist that held the half dollar, he landed with all his strength on his brother's mouth. Connie fell to the floor with a thud, the crutch tumbling on top of him. Midge stood beside the prostrate form.

"Is that enough?" he said. "Or do you want this, too?"

And he kicked him in the crippled leg.

"I guess that'll hold you," he said.

There was no response from the boy on the floor. Midge looked at him a moment, then at the coin in his hand, and then went out into the street, whistling.

An hour later, when Mrs. Kelly came home from her day's work at Faulkner's Steam Laundry, she found Connie on the floor, moaning. Dropping on her knees beside him, she called him by name a score of times. Then she got up and, pale as a ghost, dashed from the house. Dr. Ryan left the Kelly abode about dusk and walked toward Halsted Street. Mrs. Dorgan spied him as he passed her gate.

"Who's sick, Doctor?" she called.

"Poor little Connie," he replied. "He had a bad fall."

"How did it happen?"

"I can't say for sure, Margaret, but I'd almost bet he was knocked down."

"Knocked down!" exclaimed Mrs. Dorgan.

"Why, who—?"

"Have you seen the other one lately?"

"Michael? No, not since mornin'. You can't be thinkin'—"

"I wouldn't put it past him, Margaret," said the doctor gravely. "The lad's mouth is swollen and cut, and his poor, skinny little leg is bruised. He surely didn't do it to himself and I think Ellen suspects the other one."

"Lord save us!" said Mrs. Dorgan. "I'll run over and see if I can help."

"That's a good woman," said Doctor Ryan, and went on down the street.

Near midnight, when Midge came home, his mother was sitting at Connie's bedside. She did not look up.

"Well," said Midge, "what's the matter?"

She remained silent. Midge repeated his question.

"Michael, you know what's the matter," she said at length.

"I don't know nothin'," said Midge.

"Don't lie to me, Michael. What did you do to your brother?"

"Nothin'."

"You hit him."

"Well, then, I hit him. What of it? It ain't the first time."

Her lips pressed tightly together, her face like chalk, Ellen Kelly rose from her chair and made straight for him. Midge backed against the door.

"Lay off'n me, Ma. I don't want to fight no woman."

Still she came on breathing heavily.

"Stop where you're at, Ma," he warned.

There was a brief struggle and Midge's mother lay on the floor before him.

"You ain't hurt, Ma. You're lucky I didn't land good. And I told you to lay off'n me."

"God forgive you, Michael!"

Midge found Hap Collins in the showdown game at the Royal.

"Come on out a minute," he said.

Hap followed him out on the walk.

"I'm leavin' town for a w'ile," said Midge.

"What for?"

"Well, we had a little run-in up to the house. The kid stole a half buck off'n me, and when I went after it he cracked me with his crutch. So I nailed him. And the old lady came at me with a chair and I took it off'n her and she fell down."

"How is Connie hurt?"

"Not bad."

"What are you runnin' away for?"

"Who the hell said I was runnin' away? I'm sick and tired o' gettin' picked on; that's all. So I'm leavin' for a w'ile and I want a piece o' money."

"I ain't only got six bits," said Happy.

"You're in bad shape, ain't you? Well, come through with it."

Happy came through.

"You oughtn't to hit the kid," he said.

"I ain't astin' you who can I hit," snarled Midge. "You try to put somethin' over on me and you'll get the same dose. I'm goin' now."

"Go as far as you like," said Happy, but not until he was sure that Kelly was out of hearing.

Early the following morning, Midge boarded a train for Milwaukee. He had no ticket, but no one knew the difference. The conductor remained in the caboose.

On a night six months later, Midge hurried out of the "stage door" of the Star Boxing Club and made for Duane's saloon, two blocks away. In his pocket were twelve dollars, his reward for having battered up one Demon Dempsey through the six rounds of the first preliminary.

It was Midge's first professional engagement in the manly art. Also it was the first time in weeks that he had earned twelve dollars.

On the way to Duane's he had to pass Niemann's. He pulled his cap over his eyes and increased his pace until he had gone by. Inside Niemann's stood a trusting bartender, who for ten days had staked Midge to drinks and allowed him to ravage the lunch on a promise to come in and settle the moment he was paid for the "prelim."

Midge strode into Duane's and aroused the napping bartender by slapping a silver dollar on the festive board.

"Gimme a shot," said Midge.

The shooting continued until the wind-up at the Star was over and part of the fight crowd joined Midge in front of Duane's bar. A youth in the early twenties, standing next to young Kelly, finally summoned sufficient courage to address him.

"Wasn't you in the first bout?" he ventured.

"Yeh," Midge replied.

"My name's Hersch," said the other.

Midge received the startling information in silence.

"I don't want to butt in," continued Mr. Hersch, "but I'd like to buy you a drink."

All right," said Midge, "but don't overstrain yourself."

Mr. Hersch laughed uproariously and beckoned to the bartender.

"You certainly gave that wop a trimmin' tonight," said the buyer of the drink, when they had been served. "I thought you'd kill him."

"I would if I hadn't let up," Midge replied. "I'll kill 'em all."

"You got the wallop all right," the other said admiringly.

"Have I got the wallop?" said Midge. "Say, I can kick like a mule. Did you notice them muscles in my shoulders?"

"Notice 'em? I couldn't help from noticin' 'em," said Hersch. "I says to the fella settin' alongside o' me, I says: 'Look at them shoulders! No wonder he can hit,' I says to him."

"Just let me land and it's good-by, baby," said Midge. "I'll kill 'em all."

The oral manslaughter continued until Duane's closed for the night. At parting, Midge and his new friend shook hands and arranged for a meeting the following evening.

For nearly a week the two were together almost constantly. It was Hersch's pleasant rôle to listen to Midge's modest revelations concerning himself, and to buy every time Midge's glass was empty. But there came an evening when Hersch regretfully announced that he must go home to supper.

"I got a date for eight bells," he confided. "I could stick till then, only I must clean up and put on the Sunday clo'es, 'cause she's the prettiest little thing in Milwaukee."

"Can't you fix it for two?" asked Midge.

"I don't know who to get," Hersch replied. "Wait, though. I got a sister and if she ain't busy, it'll be O.K. She's no bum for looks herself."

So it came about that Midge and Emma Hersch and Emma's brother and the prettiest little thing in Milwaukee foregathered at Wall's, and danced half the night away. And Midge and Emma danced every dance together, for though every little onestep seemed to induce a new thirst of its own, Lou Hersch stayed too sober to dance with his own sister.

The next day, penniless at last in spite of his phenomenal ability to make someone else settle, Midge Kelly sought out Doc Hammond, matchmaker for the Star, and asked to be booked for the next show.

"I could put you on with Tracy for the next bout," said Doc.

"What's they in it?" asked Midge.

"Twenty if you cop," Doc told him.

"Have a heart," protested Midge. "Didn't I look good the other night?"

"You looked all right. But you aren't Freddie Welsh yet by a consid'able margin."

"I ain't scared of Freddie Welsh or none of 'em," said Midge.

"Well, we don't pay our boxers by the size of their chests," Doc said. "I'm offerin' you this Tracy bout. Take it or leave it."

"All right; I'm on," said Midge, and he passed a pleasant afternoon at Duane's on the strength of his booking.

Young Tracy's manager came to Midge the night before the show.

"How do you feel about this go?" he asked.

"Me?" said Midge, "I feel all right. What do you mean, how do I feel?"

"I mean," said Tracy's manager, "that we're mighty anxious to win, 'cause the boy's got a chanct in Philly if he cops this one."

"What's your proposition?" asked Midge.

"Fifty bucks," said Tracy's manager.

"What do you think I am, a crook? Me lay down for fifty bucks. Not me!"

"Seventy-five, then," said Tracy's manager.

The market closed on eighty and the details were agreed on in short order. And the next night Midge was stopped in the second round by a terrific slap on the forearm.

This time Midge passed up both Niemann's and Duane's, having a sizable account at each place, and sought his refreshment at Stein's farther down the street.

When the profits of his deal with Tracy were gone, he learned, by first-hand information from Doc Hammond and the matchmakers at other "clubs," that he was no longer desired for even the cheapest of preliminaries. There was no danger of his starving or dying of thirst while Emma and Lou Hersch lived. But he made up his mind, four months after his defeat by Young Tracy, that Milwaukee was not the ideal place for him to live.

"I can lick the best of 'em," he reasoned, "but there ain't no more chanct for me here. I can maybe go east and get on somewheres. And besides—"

But just after Midge had purchased a ticket to Chicago with the money he had "borrowed" from Emma Hersch "to buy shoes," a heavy hand was laid on his shoulders and he turned to face two strangers.

"Where are you goin', Kelly?" inquired the owner of the heavy hand.

"Nowheres," said Midge. "What the hell do you care?"

The other stranger spoke:

"Kelly, I'm employed by Emma Hersch's mother to see that you do right by her. And we want you to stay here till you've done it."

"You won't get nothin' but the worst of it, monkeying with me," said Midge.

Nevertheless he did not depart for Chicago that night. Two days later, Emma Hersch became Mrs. Kelly, and the gift of the groom, when once they were alone, was a crushing blow on the bride's pale cheek.

Next morning, Midge left Milwaukee as he had entered it—by fast freight.

"They's no use kiddin' ourself any more," said Tommy Haley. "He might get down to thirty-seven in a pinch, but if he done below that a mouse could stop him. He's a welter; that's what he is and he knows it as well as I do. He's growed like a weed in the last six mont's. I told him, I says, 'If you don't quit growin' they won't be nobody for you to box, only Willard and them.' He says, 'Well, I wouldn't run away from Willard if I weighed twenty pounds more.' "

"He must hate himself," said Tommy's brother.

"I never seen a good one that didn't," said Tommy. "And Midge is a good one; don't make no mistake about that. I wisht we could of got Welsh before the kid growed so big. But it's too late now. I won't make no holler, though, if we can match him up with the Dutchman."

"Who do you mean?"

"Young Goetz, the welter champ. We mightn't not get so much dough for the bout itself, but it'd roll in afterward. What a drawin' card we'd me, 'cause the people pays their money to see the fella with the wallop, and that's Midge. And we'd keep the title just as long as Midge could make the weight."

"Can't you land no match with Goetz?"

"Sure, 'cause he needs the money. But I've went careful with the kid so far and look at the results I got! So what's the use of takin' a chanct? The kid's comin' every minute and Goetz is goin' back fastern' big Johnson did. I think we could lick him now; I'd bet my life on it. But six mont's from now they won't be no risk. He'll of licked hisself before that time. Then all as we'll have to do is sign up with him and wait for the referee to stop it. But Midge is so crazy to get at him now that I can't hardly hold him back."

The brothers Haley were lunching in a Boston hotel. Dan had come down from Holyoke to visit with Tommy and to watch the latter's protégé go twelve rounds, or less, with Bud Cross. The bout promised little in the way of a contest, for Midge had twice stopped the Baltimore youth and Bud's reputation for gameness was all that had earned him the date. The fans were willing to pay the price to see Midge's hay-making left, but they wanted to see it used on an opponent who would not jump out of the ring the first time he felt its crushing force. Bud Cross was such an opponent, and his willingness to stop boxing-gloves with his eyes, ears, nose and throat had long enabled him to escape the horrors of honest labor. A game boy was Bud, and he showed it in his battered, swollen, discolored face.

"I should think," said Dan Haley, "that the kid'd do whatever you tell him after all you done for him."

"Well," said Tommy, "he's took my dope pretty straight so far, but he's so sure of hisself that he can't see no reason for waitin'. He'll do what I say, though; he'd be a sucker not to."

"You got a contrac' with him?"

"No, I don't need no contrac'. He knows it was me that drug him out o' the gutter and he ain't goin' to turn me down now, when he's got the dough and bound to get more. Where'd he of been at if I hadn't listened to him when he first come to me? That's pretty near two years ago now, but it seems like last week. I was settin' in the s'loon acrost from the Pleasant Club in Philly, waitin' for McCann to count the dough and come over, when this little bum blowed in and tried to stand the house off for a drink. They told him nothin' doin' and to beat it out o' there, and then he seen me and come over to where I was settin' and ast me wasn't I a boxin' man and I told him who I was. Then he ast me for money to buy a shot and I told him to set down and I'd buy it for him.

"Then we got talkin' things over and he told me his name and told me about fightin' a couple o' prelims out to Milwaukee. So I says, 'Well, boy, I don't know how good or how rotten you are, but you won't never get nowheres trainin' on that stuff.' So he says he'd cut it out if he could get on in a bout and I says I would give him a chanct if he played square with me and didn't touch no more to drink. So we shook hands and I took him up to the hotel with me and give him a bath and the next day I bought him some clo'es. And I staked him to eats and sleeps for over six weeks. He had a hard time breakin' away from the polish, but finally I thought he was fit and I give him his chanct. He went on with Smiley Sayer and stopped him so quick that Smiley thought sure he was poisoned.

"Well, you know what he'd did since. The only beatin' in his record was by Tracy in Milwaukee before I got hold of him, and he's licked Tracy three times in the last year.

"I've gave him all the best of it in a money way and he's got seven thousand bucks in cold storage. How's that for a kid that was in the gutter two years ago? And he'd have still more yet if he wasn't so nuts over clo'es and got to stop at the good hotels and so forth."

"Where's his home at?"

"Well, he ain't really got no home. He came from Chicago and his mother canned him out o' the house for bein' no good. She give him a raw deal, I guess, and he says he won't have nothin' to do with her unlest she comes to him first. She's got a pile o' money, he says, so he ain't worryin' about her."

The gentleman under discussion entered the café and swaggered to Tommy's table, while the whole room turned to look.

Midge was the picture of health despite a slightly colored eye and an ear that seemed to have no opening. But perhaps it was not his healthiness that drew all eyes. His diamond horse-shoe tie pin, his purple cross-striped shirt, his orange shoes and his light blue suit fairly screamed for attention.

"Where you been?" he asked Tommy. "I been lookin' all over for you."

"Set down," said his manager.

"No time," said Midge. "I'm goin' down to the w'arf and see 'em unload the fish."

"Shake hands with my brother Dan," said Tommy.

Midge shook hands with the Holyoke Haley.

"If you're Tommy's brother, you're O.K. with me," said Midge, and the brothers beamed with pleasure.

Dan moistened his lips and murmured an embarrassed reply, but it was lost on the young gladiator.

"Leave me take twenty," Midge was saying. "I prob'ly won't need it, but I don't like to be caught short."

Tommy parted with a twenty-dollar bill and recorded the transaction in a small black book the insurance company had given him for Christmas.

"But," he said, "It won't cost you no twenty to look at them fish. Want me to go along?"

"No," said Midge hastily. "You and your brother here prob'ly got a lot to say to each other."

"Well," said Tommy, "don't take no bad money and don't get lost. And you better be back at four o'clock and lay down a w'ile."

"I don't need no rest to beat this guy," said Midge. "He'll do enough layin' down for the both of us."

And laughing even more than the jest called for, he strode out through the fire of admiring and startled glances.

The corner of Boylston and Tremont was the nearest Midge got to the wharf, but the lady awaiting him was doubtless a more dazzling sight than the catch of the luckiest Massachusetts fisherman. She could talk, too—probably better than the fish.

"O you Kid!" she said, flashing a few silver teeth among the gold. "O you fighting man!"

Midge smiled up at her.

"We'll go somewheres and get a drink," he said. "One won't hurt."

In New Orleans, five months after he had rearranged the map of Bud Cross for the third time, Midge finished training for his championship bout with the Dutchman.

Back in his hotel after the final workout, Midge stopped to chat with some of the boys from up north, who had made the long trip to see a champion dethroned, for the result of this bout was so nearly a foregone conclusion that even the experts had guessed it.

Tommy Haley secured the key and the mail and ascended to the Kelly suite. He was bathing when Midge came in, half an hour later.

"Any mail?" asked Midge.

"There on the bed," replied Tommy from the tub.

Midge picked up the stack of letters and postcards and glanced them over. From the pile he sorted out three letters and laid them on the table. The rest he tossed into the waste-basket. Then he picked up the three and sat for a few moments holding them, while his eyes gazed off into space. At length he looked again at the three unopened letters in his hand; then he put one in his pocket and tossed the other two at the basket. They missed their target and fell on the floor.

"Hell!" said Midge, and stooping over picked them up.

He opened one postmarked Milwaukee and read:

> Dear Husband:
>
> I have wrote to you so manny times and got no anser and I dont know if you ever got them, so I am writeing again in the hopes you will get this letter and anser. I dont like to bother you with my trubles and I would not only for the baby and I am not asking you should write to me but only send a little money and I am not asking for myself but the baby has not been well a day sence last Aug. and the dr. told me she cant live much longer unless I give her better food and thats impossible the ways things are. Lou has not been working for a year and what I make dont hardley pay for the rent. I am not asking for you to give me any money, but only you should send what I loaned when convenient and I think it amts. to about $36.00. Please try and send that amt. and it will help me, but if you cant send the whole amt. try and send me something.
>
> Your wife,
> Emma.

Midge tore the letter into a hundred pieces and scattered them over the floor.

"Money, money, money!" he said. "They must think I'm made o' money. I s'pose the old woman's after it too."

He opened his mother's letter:

> dear Michael Connie wonted me to rite and say you must beet the dutchman and he is sur you will and wonted me to say we wont you to rite and tell us about it, but I gess you havent no time to rite or we herd from you long beffore this but I wish you would rite just a line or 2 boy becaus it wuld be better for Connie then a barl of medisin. It wuld help me to keep things going if you send me money now and then when you can spair it but if you cant send no

money try and fine time to rite a letter onley a few lines
and it will please Connie, jest think boy he hasent got out
of bed in over 3 yrs. Connie says good luck.

> Your Mother,
> ELLEN F. KELLY.

"I thought so," said Midge. "They're all alike."
The third letter was from New York. It read:

Hon:—This is the last letter you will get from me before
your champ, but I will send you a telegram Saturday, but I
can't say as much in a telegram as in a letter and I am
writeing this to let you know I am thinking of you and
praying for good luck.

Lick him good hon and don't wait no longer than you
have to and don't forget to wire me as soon as its over.
Give him that little old left of yours on the nose hon and
don't be afraid of spoiling his good looks because he
couldn't be no homlier than he is. But don't let him spoil
my baby's pretty face. You won't will you hon.

Well hon I would give anything to be there and see it,
but I guess you love Haley better than me or you wouldn't
let him keep me away. But when your champ hon we can
do as we please and tell Haley to go to the devil.

Well hon I will send you a telegram Saturday and I
almost forgot to tell you I will need some more money, a
couple hundred say and you will have to wire it to me as
soon as you get this. You will won't you hon.

I will send you a telegram Saturday and remember hon I
am pulling for you.

Well good-by sweetheart and good luck.'

> GRACE.

"They're all alike," said Midge. "Money, money, money."
Tommy Haley, shining from his ablutions, came in from the adjoining room.

"Thought you'd be layin' down," he said.

"I'm goin' to," said Midge, unbuttoning his orange shoes.

"I'll call you at six and you can eat up here without no bugs to pester you. I got to go down and give them birds their tickets."

"Did you hear from Goldberg?" asked Midge.

"Didn't I tell you? Sure; fifteen weeks at five hundred, if we win. And we can get a guarantee o' twelve thousand, with privileges either in New York or Milwaukee."

"Who with?"

"Anybody that'll stand up in front of you. You don't care who it is, do you?"

"Not me. I'll make 'em all look like a monkey."

"Well you better lay down aw'ile."

"Oh, say, wire two hundred to Grace for me, will you? Right away; the New York address."

"Two hundred! You just sent her three hundred last Sunday."

"Well, what the hell do you care?"

"All right, all right. Don't get sore about it. Anything else?"

"That's all," said Midge, and dropped onto the bed.

"And I want the deed done before I come back," said Grace as she rose from the table. "You won't fall down on me, will you, hon?"

"Leave it to me," said Midge. "And don't spend no more than you have to."

Grace smiled a farewell and left the café. Midge continued to sip his coffee and read his paper.

They were in Chicago and they were in the middle of Midge's first week in vaudeville. He had come straight north to reap the rewards of his glorious victory over the broken-down Dutchman. A fortnight had been spent in learning his act, which consisted of a gymnastic exhibition and a ten minutes' monologue on the various excellences of Midge Kelly. And now he was twice daily turning 'em away from the Madison Theater.

His breakfast over and his paper read, Midge sauntered into the lobby and asked for his key. He then beckoned to a bell-boy, who had been hoping for that very honor.

"Find Haley, Tommy Haley," said Midge. "Tell him to come up to my room."

"Yes, sir, Mr. Kelly," said the boy, and proceeded to break all his former records for diligence.

Midge was looking out of his seventh-story window when Tommy answered the summons.

"What'll it be?" inquired his manager.

There was a pause before Midge replied.

"Haley," he said, "twenty-five per cent's a whole lot o' money."

"I guess I got it comin', ain't I?" said Tommy.

"I don't see how you figger it. I don't see where you're worth it to me."

"Well," said Tommy, "I didn't expect nothin' like this. I thought you was satisfied with the bargain. I don't want to beat nobody out o' nothin', but I don't see where you could have got anybody else that would of did all I done for you."

"Sure, that's all right," said the champion. "You done a lot for me in Philly. And you got good money for it, didn't you?"

"I ain't makin' no holler. Still and all, the big money's still ahead of us yet. And if it hadn't of been for me, you wouldn't of never got within grabbin' distance."

"Oh, I guess I could of went along all right," said Midge. "Who was it that hung that left on the Dutchman's jaw, me or you?"

"Yes, but you wouldn't been in the ring with the Dutchman if it wasn't for how I handled you."

"Well, this won't get us nowheres. The idear is that you ain't worth no twenty-five per cent now and it don't make no diff'rence what come off a year or two ago."

"Don't it?" said Tommy. "I'd say it made a whole lot of difference."

"Well, I say it don't and I guess that settles it."

"Look here, Midge," Tommy said, "I thought I was fair with you, but if you don't think so, I'm willin' to hear what you think is fair. I don't want nobody callin' me a Sherlock. Let's go down to business and sign up a contrac'. What's your figger?"

"I ain't namin' no figger," Midge replied. "I'm sayin' that twenty-five's too much. Now what are you willin' to take?"

"How about twenty?"

"Twenty's too much," said Kelly.

"What ain't too much?" asked Tommy.

"Well, Haley, I might as well give it to you straight. They ain't nothin' that ain't too much."

"You mean you don't want me at no figger?"

"That's the idear."

There was a minute's silence. Then Tommy Haley walked toward the door.

"Midge," he said, in a choking voice, "you're makin' a big mistake, boy. You can't throw down your best friends and get away with it. That damn woman will ruin you."

Midge sprang from his seat.

"You shut your mouth!" he stormed. "Get out o' here before they have to carry you out. You been spongin' off o' me long enough. Say one more word about the girl or about anything else and you'll get what the Dutchman got. Now get out!"

And Tommy Haley, having a very vivid memory of the Dutchman's face as he fell, got out.

Grace came in later, dropped her numerous bundles on the lounge and perched herself on the arm of Midge's chair.

"Well?" she said.

"Well," said Midge, "I got rid of him."

"Good boy!" said Grace. "And now I think you might give me that twenty-five per cent."

"Besides the seventy-five you're already gettin'?" said Midge.

"Don't be no grouch, hon. You don't look pretty when you're grouchy."

"It ain't my business to look pretty," Midge replied.

"Wait till you see how I look with the stuff I bought this mornin'!"

Midge glanced at the bundles on the lounge.

"There's Haley's twenty-five per cent," he said, "and then some."

The champion did not remain long without a manager. Haley's successor was none other than Jerome Harris, who saw in Midge a better meal ticket than his popular-priced musical show had been.

The contract, giving Mr. Harris twenty-five per cent of Midge's earnings, was signed in Detroit the week after Tommy Haley had heard his dismissal read. It had taken Midge just six days to learn that a popular actor cannot get on without the ministrations of a man who thinks, talks and means business. At first Grace objected to the new member of the firm, but when Mr. Harris had demanded and secured from the vaudeville people a one-hundred dollar increase in Midge's weekly stipend, she was convinced that the champion had acted for the best.

"You and my missus will have some great old times," Harris told Grace. "I'd of wired her to join us here, only I seen the Kid's bookin' takes us to Milwaukee next week, and that's where she is."

But when they were introduced in the Milwaukee hotel, Grace admitted to herself that her feeling for Mrs. Harris could hardly be called love at first sight. Midge, on the contrary, gave his new manager's wife the many times over and seemed loath to end the feast of his eyes.

"Some doll," he said to Grace when they were alone.

"Doll is right," the lady replied, "and sawdust where her brains ought to be."

"I'm li'ble to steal that baby," said Midge, and he smiled as he noted the effect of his words on his audience's face.

On Tuesday of the Milwaukee week the champion successfully defended his title in a bout that the newspapers never reported. Midge was alone in his room that morning when a visitor entered without knocking. The visitor was Lou Hersch.

Midge turned white at sight of him.

"What do you want?" he demanded.

"I guess you know," said Lou Hersch. "Your wife's starvin' to death and your baby's starvin' to death and I'm starvin' to death. And you're dirty with money."

"Listen," said Midge, "if it wasn't for you, I wouldn't never saw your sister. And, if you ain't man enough to hold a job, what's that to me? The best thing you can do is keep away from me."

"You give me a piece o' money and I'll go."

Midge's reply to the ultimatum was a straight right to his brother-in-laws' narrow chest.

"Take that home to your sister."

And after Lou Hersch picked himself up and slunk away, Midge thought: "It's lucky I didn't give him my left or I'd of croaked him. And if I'd hit him in the stomach, I'd of broke his spine."

There was a party after each evening performance during the Milwaukee engagement. The wine flowed freely and Midge had more of it than Tommy Haley ever would have permitted him. Mr. Harris offered no objection, which was possibly just as well for his own physical comfort.

In the dancing between drinks, Midge had his new manager's wife for a partner as often as Grace. The latter's face as she floundered round in the arms of the portly Harris, belied her frequent protestations that she was having the time of her life.

Several times that week, Midge thought Grace was on the point of starting the quarrel he hoped to have. But it was not until Friday night that she accommodated. He and Mrs. Harris had disappeared after the matinee and when Grace saw him again at the close of the night show, she came to the point at once.

"What are you tryin' to pull off?" she demanded.

"It's none o' your business, is it?" said Midge.

"You bet it's my business; mine and Harris's. You cut it short or you'll find out."

"Listen," said Midge, "have you got a mortgage on me or somethin'? You talk like we was married."

"We're goin' to be, too. And tomorrow's as good a time as any."

"Just about," Midge said. "You got as much chanct o' marryin' me to-morrow as the next day or next year and that ain't no chanct at all."

"We'll find out," said Grace.

"You're the one's that got somethin' to find out."

"What do you mean?"

"I mean I'm married already."

"You lie!"

"You think so, don't you? Well, s'pose you go to this here address and get acquainted with my missus."

Midge scrawled a number on a piece of paper and handed it to her. She stared at it unseeingly.

"Well," said Midge, "I ain't kiddin' you. You go there and ask for Mrs. Michael Kelly, and if you don't find her, I'll marry you to-morrow before breakfast."

Still Grace stared at the scrap of paper. To Midge it seemed an age before she spoke again.

"You lied to me all this w'ile."

"You never ast me was I married. What's more, what the hell diff'rence did it make to you? You got a split, didn't you? Better'n fifty-fifty."

He started away.

"Where you goin'?"

"I'm goin' to meet Harris and his wife."

"I'm goin' with you. You're not goin' to shake me now."

"Yes, I am, too," said Midge quietly. "When I leave town to-morrow night, you're going to stay here. And if I see where you're goin' to make a fuss, I'll put you in a hospital where they'll keep you quiet. You can get your stuff to-morrow mornin' and I'll slip you a hundred bucks. And then I don't want to see no more o' you. And don't try and tag along now or I'll have to add another K.O. to the old record."

When Grace returned to the hotel that night, she discovered that Midge and the Harrises had moved to another. And when Midge left town the following night, he was again without a manager, and Mr. Harris was without a wife.

Three days prior to Midge Kelly's ten-round bout with Young Milton in New York City, the sporting editor of *The News* assigned Joe Morgan to write two or three thousand words about the champion to run with a picture lay-out for Sunday.

Joe Morgan dropped in at Midge's training quarters Friday afternoon. Midge, he learned, was doing road work, but Midge's manager, Wallie Adams, stood ready and willing to supply reams of dope about the greatest fighter of the age.

"Let's hear what you've got," said Joe, "and then I'll try to fix up something."

So Wallie stepped on the accelerator of his imagination and shot away.

"Just a kid; that's all he is; a regular boy. Get what I mean? Don't know the meanin' o' bad habits. Never tasted liquor in his life and would prob'bly get sick if he smelled it. Clean livin' put him up where he's at. Get what I mean? And modest and unassumin' as a school girl. He's so quiet you wouldn't never know he was round. And he'd go to jail before he'd talk about himself.

"No job at all to get him in shape, 'cause he's always that way. The only trouble we have with him is gettin' him to light into these poor bums they match him up with. He's scared he'll hurt somebody. Get what I mean? He's tickled to death over this match with Milton, 'cause everybody says Milton can stand the gaff. Midge'll maybe be able to cut loose a little this time. But the last two bouts he had, the guys hadn't no business in the ring with him, and he was holdin' back all the w'ile for the fear he'd kill somebody. Get what I mean?"

"Is he married?" inquired Joe.

"Say, you'd think he was married to hear him rave about them kiddies he's got. His fam'ly's up in Canada to their summer home and Midge is wild to get up there with 'em. He thinks more o' that wife and them kiddies than all the money in the world. Get what I mean?"

"How many children has he?"

"I don't know, four or five, I guess. All boys and every one of 'em a dead ringer for their dad."

"Is his father living?"

"No, the old man died when he was a kid. But he's got a grand old mother and a kid brother out in Chi. They're the first ones he thinks about after a match, them and his wife and kiddies. And he don't forget to send the old woman a thousand bucks after every bout. He's goin' to buy her a new home as soon as they pay him off for this match."

"How about his brother? Is he going to tackle the game?"

"Sure, and Midge says he'll be a champion before he's twenty years old. They're a fightin' fam'ly and all of 'em honest and straight as a die. Get what I mean? A fella that I can't tell you his name come to Midge in Milwaukee onct and wanted him to throw a fight and Midge give him such a trimmin' in the street that he couldn't go on that night. That's the kind he is. Get what I mean?"

Joe Morgan hung around the camp until Midge and his trainers returned.

"One o' the boys from *The News*," said Wallie by way of introduction. "I been givin' him your fam'ly hist'ry."

"Did he give you good dope?" he inquired.

"He's some historian," said Joe.

"Don't call me no names," said Wallie smiling. "Call us up if they's anything more you want. And keep your eyes on us Monday night. Get what I mean?"

The story in Sunday's *News* was read by thousands of lovers of the manly art. It was well written, and full of human interest. Its slight inaccuracies went unchallenged, though three readers, besides Wallie Adams and Midge Kelly, saw and recognized them. The three were

Grace, Tommy Haley and Jerome Harris and the comments they made were not for publication.

Neither the Mrs. Kelly in Chicago nor the Mrs. Kelly in Milwaukee knew that there was such a paper as the New York *News*. And even if they had known of it and that it contained two columns of reading matter about Midge, neither mother nor wife could have bought it. For *The News* on Sunday is a nickel a copy.

Joe Morgan could have written more accurately, no doubt, if instead of Wallie Adams, he had interviewed Ellen Kelly and Connie Kelly and Lou Hersch and Grace and Jerome Harris and Tommy Haley and Hap Collins and two or three Milwaukee bartenders.

But a story built on their evidence would never have passed the sporting editor.

"Suppose you can prove it," that gentleman would have said, "It wouldn't get us anything but abuse to print it. The people don't want to see him knocked. He's champion."

ALAN DUGAN

ON HURRICANE JACKSON

Now his nose's bridge is broken, one eye
will not focus and the other is astray;
trainers whisper in his mouth while one ear
listens to itself, clenched like a fist;
generally shadow-boxing in a smoky room,
his mind hides like the aching boys
who lost a contest in the Pan-Hellenic games
and had to take the back roads home,
but someone else, his perfect youth,
laureled in newsprint and dollar bills,
triumphs forever on the great white way
to the statistical Sparta of the champs.

RICHARD WRIGHT

FOUR ROUNDS FOR FIVE DOLLARS

from *Black Boy*

I had to make my round of errands to deliver eyeglasses and I stole a few minutes to run across the street to talk to Harrison. Harrison was sullen and bashful, wanting to trust me, but afraid. He told me that Mr. Olin had telephoned his boss and had told him to tell Harrison that I had planned to wait for him at the back entrance of the building at six o'clock and stab him. Harrison and I found it difficult to look at each other; we were upset and distrustful. We were not really angry at each other; we knew that the idea of murder had been planted in each of us by the white men who employed us. We told ourselves again and again that we did not agree with the white men; we urged ourselves to keep faith in each other. Yet there lingered deep down in each of us a suspicion that maybe one of us was trying to kill the other.

"I'm not angry with you, Harrison," I said.

"I don't wanna fight nobody," Harrsion said bashfully, but he kept his hand in his pocket on his knife.

Each of us felt the same shame, felt how foolish and weak we were in the face of the domination of the whites.

"I wish they'd leave us alone," I said.

"Me too," Harrison said.

"There are a million black boys like us to run errands," I said. "They wouldn't care if we killed each other."

"I know it," Harrison said.

Was he acting? I could not believe in him. We were toying with the idea of death for no reason that stemmed from our own lives, but because the men who ruled us had thrust the idea into our minds. Each of us depended upon the whites for the bread we ate, and we actually trusted the whites more than we did each other. Yet there existed in us a longing to trust men of our own color. Again Harrison and I parted, vowing not to be influenced by what our white boss men said to us.

The game of egging Harrison and me to fight, to cut each other, kept up for a week. We were afraid to tell the white men that we did not believe them, for that would have been tantamount to calling them liars or risking an argument that might have ended in violence being directed against us.

One morning a few days later Mr. Olin and a group of white men came to me and asked me if I was willing to settle my grudge with Harrison with gloves, according to boxing rules. I told them that, though I was not afraid of Harrison, I did not want to fight him and that I did not know how to box. I could feel now that they knew I no longer believed them.

When I left the factory that evening, Harrison yelled at me from down the block. I waited and he ran toward me. Did he want to cut me? I backed away as he approached. We smiled uneasily and sheepishly at each other. We spoke haltingly, weighing our words.

"Did they ask you to fight me with gloves?" Harrison asked.

"Yes," I told him. "But I didn't agree."

Harrison's face became eager.

"They want us to fight four rounds for five dollars apiece," he said. "Man, if I had five dollars, I could pay down on a suit. Five dollars is almost half a week's wages for me."

"I don't want to," I said.

"We won't hurt each other," he said.

"But why do a thing like that for white men?"

"To get that five dollars."

"I don't need five dollars that much."

"Aw, you're a fool," he said. Then he smiled quickly.

"Now, look here," I said. "Maybe you *are* angry with me . . ."

"Naw, I'm not." He shook his head vigorously.

"I don't want to fight for white men. I'm no dog or rooster."

I was watching Harrison closely and he was watching me closely. Did he really want to fight me for some reason of his own? Or was it the money? Harrison stared at me with puzzled eyes. He stepped toward me and I stepped away. He smiled nervously.

"I need that money," he said.

"Nothing doing," I said.

He walked off wordlessly, with an air of anger. Maybe he will stab me now, I thought. I got to watch that fool . . .

For another week the white men of both factories begged us to fight. They made up stories about what Harrison had said about me; and when they saw Harrison they lied to him in the same way. Harrison and I were wary of each other whenever we met. We smiled and kept out of arm's reach, ashamed of ourselves and of each other.

Again Harrison called to me one evening as I was on my way home.

"Come on and fight," he begged.

"I don't want to and quit asking me," I said in a voice louder and harder than I had intended.

Harrison looked at me and I watched him. Both of us still carried the knives that the white men had given us.

"I wanna make a payment on a suit of clothes with that five dollars," Harrison said.

"But those white men will be looking at us, laughing at us," I said.

"What the hell," Harrison said. "They look at you and laugh at you every day, nigger."

It was true. But I hated him for saying it. I ached to hit him in his mouth, to hurt him.

"What have we got to lose?" Harrison asked.

"I don't suppose we have anything to lose," I said.

"Sure," he said. "Let's get the money. We don't care."

"And now they know that we know what they tried to do to us," I said, hating myself for saying it. "And they hate us for it."

"Sure," Harrison said.

"So let's get the money. You can use five dollars, can't you?"

"Yes."

"Then let's fight for 'em."

"I'd feel like a dog."

"To them, both of us are dogs," he said.

"Yes," I admitted. But again I wanted to hit him.

"Look, let's fool them white men," Harrison said. "We won't hurt each other. We'll just pretend, see? We'll show 'em we ain't dumb as they think, see?"

"I don't know."

"It's just exercise. Four rounds for five dollars. You scared?"

"No."

"Then come on and fight."

"All right," I said. "It's just exercise. I'll fight."

Harrison was happy. I felt that it was all very foolish. But what the hell. I would go through with it and that would be the end of it. But I still felt a vague anger that would not leave.

When the white men in the factory heard that we had agreed to fight, their excitement knew no bounds. They offered to teach me new punches. Each morning they would tell me in whispers that Harrison was eating raw onions for strength. And—from Harrison—I heard that they told him I was eating raw meat for strength. They offered to buy me my meals each day, but I refused. I grew ashamed of what I had agreed to do and wanted to back out of the fight, but I was afraid that they would be angry if I tried to. I felt that if white men tried to persuade two black boys to stab each other for no reason save their own pleasure, then it would not be difficult for them to aim a wanton blow at a black boy in a fit of anger, in a passing mood of frustration.

The fight took place one Saturday afternoon in the basement of a Main Street building. Each white man who attended the fight dropped his share of the pot into a hat that sat on the concrete floor. Only white men were allowed in the basement; no women or Negroes were admitted. Harrison and I were stripped to the waist. A bright electric bulb glowed above our heads. As the gloves were tied on my hands, I looked at Harrison and saw his eyes watching me. Would he keep his promise? Doubt made me nervous.

We squared off and at once I knew that I had not thought sufficiently about what I had bargained for. I could not pretend to fight. Neither Harrison nor I knew enough about boxing to deceive even a child for a moment. Now shame filled me. The white men were smoking and yelling obscenities at us.

"Crush that nigger's nuts, nigger!"

"Hit that nigger!"

"Aw, fight, you goddamn niggers!"

"Sock 'im in his f-k-g piece!"

"Make 'im bleed!"

I lashed out with a timid left. Harrison landed high on my head and, before I knew it, I had landed a hard right on Harrison's mouth and blood came. Harrison shot a blow to my nose. The fight was on, was on against our will. I felt trapped and ashamed. I lashed out even harder, and the harder I fought the harder Harrison fought. Our plans and promises now meant nothing. We fought four hard rounds, stabbing, slugging, grunting, spitting, cursing, crying, bleeding. The shame and anger we felt for having allowed ourselves to be duped crept into our blows and blood ran into our eyes, half blinding us. The hate we felt for the men whom we had tried to cheat went into the blows we threw at each other. The white men made the rounds last as long as five minutes and each of us was afraid to stop and ask for time for fear of receiving a blow that would knock us out. When we were on the point of collapsing from exhaustion, they pulled us apart.

I could not look at Harrison. I hated him and I hated myself. I clutched my five dollars in my fist and walked home. Harrison and I avoided each other after that and we rarely spoke. The white men attempted to arrange other fights for us, but we had sense enough to refuse. I heard of other fights being staged between other black boys, and each time I heard those plans falling from the lips of the white men in the factory I eased out of earshot. I felt that I had done something unclean, something for which I could never properly atone.

RALPH ELLISON

THE BATTLE ROYAL

from *Invisible Man*

Everyone praised me and I was invited to give the speech at a gathering of the town's leading white citizens. It was a triumph for our whole community.

It was in the main ballroom of the leading hotel. When I got there I discovered that it was on the occasion of a smoker, and I was told that since I was to be there anyway I might as well take part in the battle royal to be fought by some of my schoolmates as part of the entertainment. The battle royal came first.

All of the town's big shots were there in their tuxedoes, wolfing down the buffet foods, drinking beer and whiskey and smoking black cigars. It was a large room with a high ceiling. Chairs were arranged in neat rows around three sides of a portable boxing ring. The fourth side was clear, revealing a gleaming space of polished floor. I had some misgivings over the battle royal, by the way. Not from a distaste for fighting, but because I didn't care too much for the other fellows who were to take part. They were tough guys who seemed to have no grandfather's curse worrying their minds. No one could mistake their toughness. And besides, I suspected that fighting a battle royal might detract from the dignity of my speech. In those pre-invisible days I visualized myself as a potential Booker T. Washington. But the other fellows didn't care too much for me either, and there were nine of them. I felt superior to them in my way, and I didn't like the manner in which we were all crowded together into the servants' elevator. Nor did they like my being there. In fact, as the warmly lighted floors flashed past the elevator we had words over the fact that I, by taking part in the fight, had knocked one of their friends out of a night's work.

We were led out of the elevator through a rococo hall into an anteroom and told to get into our fighting togs. Each of us was issued a pair of boxing gloves and ushered out into the big mirrored hall, which we entered looking cautiously about us and whispering, lest we might accidentally be heard above the noise of the room. It was foggy with cigar smoke. And already the whiskey was taking effect. I was shocked to see some of the most important men of the town quite tipsy. They were all there—bankers, lawyers, judges, doctors, fire chiefs, teachers, merchants. Even one of the more fashionable pastors. Something we could not see was going on up front. A clarinet was vibrating sensuously and the men were standing up and moving eagerly forward. We were a small tight group, clustered together, our bare upper bodies touching and shining with anticipatory sweat; while up front the big shots were becoming increasingly excited over something we still could not see. Suddenly I heard the school superintendent, who had told me to come, yell, "Bring up the shines, gentlemen! Bring up the little shines!"

We were rushed up to the front of the ballroom, where it smelled even more strongly of tobacco and whiskey. Then we were pushed into place. I almost wet my pants. A sea of faces, some hostile, some amused, ringed around us, and in the center, facing us, stood a magnificent blond—stark naked. There was dead silence. I felt a blast of cold air chill me. I tried to back away, but they were behind me and around me. Some of the boys stood with lowered heads, trembling. I felt a wave of irrational guilt and fear. My teeth chattered, my skin turned to goose flesh, my knees knocked. Yet I was strongly attracted and looked in spite of myself. Had the price of looking been blindness, I would have looked. The hair was yellow like that of a circus kewpie doll, the face heavily powdered and rouged, as though to form an abstract mask, the eyes hollow and smeared a cool blue, the color of a baboon's butt. I felt a desire to spit upon her as my eyes brushed slowly over her body. Her breasts were firm and round as the domes of East Indian temples, and I stood so close as to see the fine skin texture, and beads of pearly perspiration glistening like dew around the pink and erected buds of her nipples. I wanted at one and the same time to run from the room, to sink through the floor, or go to her and cover her from my eyes and the eyes of the others with my body; to feel the soft thighs, to caress her and destroy her, to love her and murder her, to hide from her, and yet to stroke where below the small American flag tattooed upon her belly her thighs formed a capital V. I had a notion that of all in the room she saw only me with her impersonal eyes.

And then she began to dance, a slow sensuous movement; the smoke of a hundred cigars clinging to her like the thinnest of veils. She seemed like a fair bird-girl girdled in veils calling to me from the angry surface of some gray and threatening sea. I was transported. Then I became aware of the clarinet playing and the big shots yelling at us. Some threatened us if we looked and others if we did not. On my right I saw one boy faint. And now a man grabbed a silver pitcher from a table and stepped close as he dashed ice water upon him and stood him up and forced two of us to support him as his head hung and moans issued from his thick bluish lips. Another boy began to plead to go home. He was the largest of the group, wearing dark red fighting trunks much too small to conceal the erection which projected from him as though in answer to the insinuating low-registered moaning of the clarinet. He tried to hide himself with his boxing gloves.

And all the while the blonde continued dancing, smiling faintly at the big shots who watched her with fascination, and faintly smiling at our fear. I noticed a certain merchant who followed her hungrily, his lips loose and drooling. He was a large man who wore diamond studs in a shirtfront which swelled with the ample paunch underneath, and each time the blonde swayed her undulating hips he ran his hand through the thin hair of his bald head and, with his arms upheld, his posture clumsy like that of an intoxicated panda, wound his belly in a slow and obscene grind. This creature was completely hypnotized. The music had quickened. As the dancer flung herself about with a detached expression on her face, the men began reaching out to touch her. I could see their beefy fingers sink into the soft flesh. Some of the others tried to stop them and she began to move around the floor in graceful circles, as they gave chase, slipping and sliding over the polished floor. It was mad. Chairs went crashing, drinks were spilt, as they ran laughing and howling after her. They caught her just as she reached a door, raised her from the floor, and tossed her as college boys are tossed at a hazing, and above her red, fixed-smiling lips I saw the terror and disgust in her eyes, almost like my own terror and that which I saw in some of the other boys. As I watched, they tossed her twice and her soft breasts seemed to flatten against the air and her legs flung wildly as she spun. Some of the more sober ones helped her to escape. And I started off the floor, heading for the anteroom with the rest of the boys.

Some were still crying and in hysteria. But as we tried to leave we were stopped and ordered to get into the ring. There was nothing to do but what we were told. All ten of us climbed under the ropes and allowed ourselves to be blindfolded with broad bands of white cloth. One of the men seemed to feel a bit sympathetic and tried to cheer us up as we stood with our backs against the ropes. Some of us tried to grin. "See that boy over there?" one of the men said. "I want you to run across at the bell and give it to him right in the belly. If you don't get him, I'm going to get you. I don't like his looks." Each of us was told the same. The blindfolds were put on. Yet even then I had been going over my speech. In my mind each word was as bright as flame. I felt the cloth pressed into place, and frowned so that it would be loosened when I relaxed.

But now I felt a sudden fit of blind terror. I was unused to darkness. It was as though I had suddenly found myself in a dark room filled with poisonous cottonmouths. I could hear the bleary voices yelling insistently for the battle royal to begin.

"Get going in there!"

"Let me at that big nigger!"

I strained to pick up the school superintendent's voice, as though to squeeze some security out of that slightly more familiar sound.

"Let me at those black sonsabitches!" someone yelled.

"No, Jackson, no!" another voice yelled. "Here, somebody, help me hold Jack."

"I want to get at that ginger-colored nigger. Tear him limb from limb," the first voice yelled.

I stood against the ropes trembling. For in those days I was what they called ginger-colored, and he sounded as though he might crunch me between his teeth like a crisp ginger cookie.

Quite a struggle was going on. Chairs were being kicked about and I could hear voices grunting as with a terrific effort. I wanted to see, to see more desperately than ever before. But the blindfold was as tight as a thick skin-puckering scab and when I raised my gloved hands to push the layers of white aside a voice yelled, "Oh, no you don't, black bastard! Leave that alone!"

"Ring the bell before Jackson kills him a coon!" someone boomed in the sudden silence. And I heard the bell clang and the sound of the feet scuffling forward.

A glove smacked against my head. I pivoted, striking out stiffly as someone went past, and felt the jar ripple along the length of my arm to my shoulder. Then it seemed as though all nine of the boys had turned upon me at once. Blows pounded me from all sides while I struck out as best I could. So many blows landed upon me that I wondered if I were not the only blindfolded fighter in the ring, or if the man called Jackson hadn't succeeded in getting me after all.

Blindfolded, I could no longer control my motions. I had no dignity. I stumbled about like a baby or a drunken man. The smoke had become thicker and with each new blow it seemed to sear and further restrict my lungs. My saliva became like hot bitter glue. A glove connected with my head, filling my mouth with warm blood. It was everywhere. I could not tell if the moisture I felt upon my body was sweat or blood. A blow landed hard against the nape of my neck. I felt myself going over, my head hitting the floor. Streaks of blue light filled the black world behind the blindfold. I lay prone, pretending that I was knocked out, but felt myself seized by hands and yanked to my feet. "Get going, black boy! Mix it up!" My arms were like lead, my head smarting from blows. I managed to feel my way to the ropes and held on, trying to catch my breath. A glove landed in my mid-section and I went over again, feeling as though the smoke had become a knife jabbed into my guts. Pushed this way and that by the legs milling around me, I finally pulled erect and discovered that I could see the black, sweat-washed forms weaving in the smoky-blue atmosphere like drunken dancers weaving to the rapid drum-like thuds of blows.

Everyone fought hysterically. It was complete anarchy. Everybody fought everybody else. No group fought together for long. Two, three, four, fought one, then turned to fight each other, were themselves attacked. Blows landed below the belt and in the kidney with the gloves open as well as closed, and with my eye partly opened now there was not so much terror. I moved carefully, avoiding blows, although not too many to attract attention, fighting from group to group. The boys groped about like blind, cautious crabs crouching to protect their mid-sections, their heads pulled in short against their shoulders, their arms stretched nervously before them, with their fists testing the smoke-filled air like the knobbed feelers of hypersensitive snails. In one corner I glimpsed a boy violently punching the air and heard him scream in pain as he smashed his hand against a ring post. For a second I saw him bent over holding his hand, then going down as a blow caught his unprotected head. I played one group against the other, slipping in and throwing a punch then stepping out of range while pushing the others into the melee to take the blows blindly aimed at me. The smoke was agonizing and there were no rounds, no bells at three minute intervals to relieve our exhaustion. The room spun round me, a swirl of lights, smoke, sweating bodies surrounded by tense white faces. I bled from both nose and mouth, the blood spattering upon my chest.

The men kept yelling, "Slug him, black boy! Knock his guts out!"

"Uppercut him! Kill him! Kill that big boy!"

Taking a fake fall, I saw a boy going down heavily beside me as though we were felled by a single blow, saw a sneaker-clad foot shoot into his groin as the two who had knocked him down stumbled upon him. I rolled out of range, feeling a twinge of nausea.

The harder we fought the more threatening the men became. And yet, I had begun to worry about my speech again. How would it go? Would they recognize my ability? What would they give me?

I was fighting automatically when suddenly I noticed that one after another of the boys was leaving the ring. I was surprised, filled with panic, as though I had been left alone with an unknown danger. Then I understood. The boys had arranged it among themselves. It was the custom for the two men left in the ring to slug it out for the winner's prize. I discovered this too late. When the bell sounded two men in tuxedoes leaped into the ring and removed the blindfold. I found myself facing Tatlock, the biggest of the gang. I felt sick at my stomach. Hardly had the bell stopped ringing in my ears than it clanged again and I saw him moving swiftly toward me. Thinking of nothing else to do I hit him smash on the nose. He kept coming, bringing the rank sharp violence of stale sweat. His face was a black blank of a face, only his eyes alive—with hate of me and aglow with a feverish terror from what had happened to us all. I became anxious. I wanted to deliver my speech and he came at me as though he meant to beat it out of me. I smashed him again and again, taking his blows as they came. Then on a sudden impulse I struck him lightly and as we clinched, I whispered, "Fake like I knocked you out, you can have the prize."

"I'll break your behind," he whispered hoarsely.

"For *them?*"

"For *me*, sonofabitch!"

They were yelling for us to break it up and Tatlock spun me half around with a blow, and as a joggled camera sweeps in a reeling scene, I saw the howling red faces crouching tense beneath the cloud of blue-gray smoke. For a moment the world wavered, unraveled, flowed, then my head cleared and Tatlock bounced before me. That fluttering shadow before my eyes was his jabbing left hand. Then falling forward, my head against his damp shoulder, I whispered,

"I'll make it five dollars more."

"Go to hell!"

But his muscles relaxed a trifle beneath my pressure and I breathed, "Seven?"

"Give it to your ma," he said, ripping me beneath the heart.

And while I still held him I butted him and moved away. I felt myself bombarded with punches. I fought back with hopeless desperation. I wanted to deliver my speech more than anything else in the world, because I felt that only these men could judge truly my ability, and now this stupid clown was ruining my chances. I began fighting carefully now, moving in to punch him and out again with my greater speed. A lucky blow to his chin and I had him going too—until I heard a loud voice yell, "I got my money on the big boy."

Hearing this, I almost dropped my guard. I was confused: Should I try to win against the voice out there? Would not this go against my speech, and was not this a moment for humility, for nonresistance? A blow to my head as I danced about sent my right eye popping like a jack-in-the-box and settled my dilemma. The room went red as I fell. It was a dream fall, my body languid and fastidious as to where to land, until the floor became impatient and smashed up to meet me. A moment later I came to. An hypnotic voice said FIVE emphatically. And I lay there, hazily watching a dark red spot of my own blood shaping itself into a butterfly, glistening and soaking into the soiled gray world of the canvas.

When the voice drawled TEN I was lifted up and dragged to a chair. I sat dazed. My eye pained and swelled with each throb of my pounding heart and I wondered if now I would be allowed to speak. I was wringing wet, my mouth still bleeding. We were grouped along the wall now. The other boys ignored me as they congratulated Tatlock and speculated as to how much they would be paid. One boy whimpered over his smashed hand. Looking up front, I saw attendants in white jackets rolling the portable ring away and placing a small square rug in the vacant space surrounded by chairs. Perhaps, I thought, I will stand on the rug to deliver my speech.

Then the M.C. called to us, "Come on up here boys and get your money."

We ran forward to where the men laughed and talked in their chairs, waiting. Everyone seemed friendly now.

"There it is on the rug," the man said. I saw the rug covered with coins of all dimensions and a few crumpled bills. But what excited me, scattered here and there, were the gold pieces.

"Boys, it's all yours," the man said. "You get all you grab."

"That's right, Sambo," a blond man said, winking at me confidentially.

I trembled with excitement, forgetting my pain. I would get the gold and the bills, I thought. I would use both hands. I would throw my body against the boys nearest me to block them from the gold.

"Get down around the rug now," the man commanded, "and don't anyone touch it until I give the signal."

"This ought to be good," I heard.

As told, we got around the square rug on our knees. Slowly the man raised his freckled hand as we followed it upward with our eyes.

I heard, "These niggers look like they're about to pray!"

Then, "Ready," the man said. "Go!"

I lunged for a yellow coin lying on the blue design of the carpet, touching it and sending a surprised shriek to join those rising around me. I tried frantically to remove my hand but could not let go. A hot, violent force tore through my body, shaking me like a wet rat. The rug was electrified. The hair bristled up on my head as I shook myself free. My muscles jumped, my nerves jangled, writhed. But I saw that this was not stopping the other boys. Laughing in fear and embarrassment, some were holding back and scooping up the coins knocked off by the painful contortions of the others. The men roared above us as we struggled.

"Pick it up, goddamnit, pick it up!" someone called like a bass-voiced parrot. "Go on, get it!"

I crawled rapidly around the floor, picking up the coins, trying to avoid the coppers and to get greenbacks and the gold. Ignoring the shock by laughing, as I brushed the coins off quickly, I discovered that I could contain the electricity—a contradiction, but it works. Then the men began to push us onto the rug. Laughing embarrassedly, we struggled out of their hands and kept after the coins. We were all wet and slippery and hard to hold. Suddenly I saw a boy lifted into the air, glistening with sweat like a circus seal, and dropped, his wet back landing flush upon the charged rug, heard him yell and saw him literally dance upon his back, his elbows beating a frenzied tattoo upon the floor, his muscles twitching like the flesh of a horse stung by many flies. When he finally rolled off, his face was gray and no one stopped him when he ran from the floor amid booming laughter.

"Get the money," the M.C. called. "That's good hard American cash!"

And we snatched and grabbed, snatched and grabbed. I was careful not to come too close to the rug now, and when I felt the hot whiskey breath descend upon me like a cloud of foul air I reached out and grabbed the leg of a chair. It was occupied and I held on desperately.

"Leggo, nigger! Leggo!"

The huge face wavered down to mine as he tried to push me free. But my body was slippery and he was too drunk. It was Mr. Colcord, who owned a chain of movie houses and "entertainment palaces." Each time he grabbed me I slipped out of his hands. It became a real struggle. I feared the rug more than I did the drunk, so I held on, surprising myself for a moment by trying to topple *him* upon the rug. It was such an enormous idea that I found myself actually carrying it out. I tried not to be obvious, yet when I grabbed his leg, trying to tumble him out of the chair, he raised up roaring with laughter, and, looking at me with soberness dead in the eye, kicked me viciously in the chest. The chair leg flew out of my hand and I felt myself going and rolled. It was as though I had rolled through a bed of hot coals. It seemed a whole century would pass before I would roll free, a century in which I was seared through the deepest levels of my body to the fearful breath within me and the breath seared and heated to the point of explosion. It'll all be over in a flash, I thought as I rolled clear. It'll all be over in a flash.

But not yet, the men on the other side were waiting, red faces swollen as though from apoplexy as they bent forward in their chairs. Seeing their fingers coming toward me I rolled away as a fumbled football rolls off the receiver's fingertips, back into the coals. That time I luckily sent the rug sliding out of place and heard the coins ringing against the floor and the boys scuffling to pick them up and the M.C. calling. "All right, boys, that's all. Go get dressed and get your money."

I was limp as a dish rag. My back felt as though it had been beaten with wires.

When we had dressed the M.C. came in and gave us each five dollars, except Tatlock, who got ten for being last in the ring. Then he told us to leave. I was not to get a chance to deliver my speech, I thought. I was going out into the dim alley in despair when I was stopped and told to go back. I returned to the ballroom, where the men were pushing back their chairs and gathering in groups to talk.

The M.C. knocked on a table for quiet. "Gentlemen," he said, "we almost forgot an important part of the program. A most serious part, gentlemen. This boy was brought here to deliver a speech which he made at his graduation yesterday . . ."

"Bravo!"

"I'm told that he is the smartest boy we've got out there in Greenwood. I'm told that he knows more big words than a pocket-sized dictionary."

Much applause and laughter.

"So now, gentlemen, I want you to give him your attention."

There was still laughter as I faced them, my mouth dry, my eye throbbing. I began slowly, but evidently my throat was tense, because they began shouting, "Louder! Louder!"

"We of the younger generation extol the wisdom of that great leader and educator," I shouted, "who first spoke these flaming words of wisdom: 'A ship lost at sea for many days suddenly sighted a friendly vessel. From the mast of the unfortuntate vessel was seen a signal: "Water, water; we die of thirst!" The answer from the friendly vessel came back: "Cast down your bucket where you are." The captain of the distressed vessel, at last heeding the injunction, cast down his bucket, and it came up full of fresh sparkling water from the mouth of the Amazon River.' And like him I say, and in his words, 'To those of my race who depend upon bettering their condition in a foreign land, or who underestimate the importance of cultivating friendly relations with the Southern white man, who is his next-door neighbor, I would say: "Cast down your bucket where you are"—cast it down in making friends in every manly way of the people of all races by whom we are surrounded . . .' "

TRACK AND FIELD

The trauma of time is a theme of A. E. Housman's "To an Athlete Dying Young." Perhaps the sporting act of racing against time is an especially useful metaphor for evoking the ancient *carpe diem* (seize the day) theme.

Housman's poem explores the meaning of the athlete dying at the height of his glory as opposed to the slow erosion of that early fame. Since so much of athletic success occurs early in life, this is a real predicament for the athlete, as we saw in Shaw's "The Eighty-Yard Run."

Grace Butcher is not only an accomplished poet but a runner and a motorcyclist as well. As a writer *and* an athlete, she well represents the spirit of this anthology. In her three poems, she sensitively evokes not only the external grace of action but that feeling of delight that comes from actually participating in sports as well.

A. E. HOUSMAN

TO AN ATHLETE DYING YOUNG

> The time you won your town the race
> We chaired you through the market-place;
> Man and boy stood cheering by,
> And home we brought you shoulder-high.

Today, the road all runners come,
Shoulder-high we bring you home,
And set you at your threshold down,
Townsman of a stiller town.

Smart lad, to slip betimes away
From fields where glory does not stay
And early though the laurel grows
It withers quicker than the rose.

Eyes the shady night has shut
Cannot see the record cut,
And silence sounds no worse than cheers
After earth has stopped the ears;

Now you will not swell the rout
Of lads that wore their honour out,
Runners whom renown outran
And the name died before the man.

So set, before its echoes fade,
The fleet foot on the sill of shade,
And hold to the low lintel up
The still defended challenge-cup.

And round that early-laurelled head
Will flock to gaze the strengthless dead
And find unwithered on its curls
The garland briefer than a girl's.

GRACE BUTCHER

RUNNER AT TWILIGHT

I move, shining, over dim hills.
The grass unwinds a blur of rivers
      on the bottom of the night;
I cross with no bridges.
My hair is heavy with fog,
and my breathing is the force
      that spins the universe.
There is more to the spectrum
      than was supposed:
beyond violet are endless miles
of impossible colors.

JAVELIN

He is the ultimate warrior,
with all the ancient killing
coiled beneath his ribs.
He threatens the earth;
the air splits along a silver seam.
Pinned to earth, ghosts die
to archetypal screaming.
The sun is fierce on his hair,
and there is the wild curve of his arm
against the sky.

POLE VAULT

The miracle lies in the strange awkward run
transformed to fantastic flight.
The confrontation is between
the man and the invisible mountain.
The glass whip flares, bends in the sun,
flings him to the top of his strength
and enough beyond.
He has time to smile
during his endless fall
through the defeated air.

HUNTING AND FISHING

Sport, as it appears so far in this anthology, usually takes place on carefully marked playing fields before crowds of enthralled spectators. The arena of civility implies the rules and values of a particular cultural context, and one may try to know a culture by examining its sport.

But there is another kind of sport with all outdoors as its playing field and with its code largely unwritten. From one perspective, hunting and fishing may be seen as less competitive than other kinds of sport. Certainly competition between persons is remarkably absent from hunting and fishing. Furthermore, one persistent appeal of hunting and fishing appears to be the quiet depth of contemplation which comes from living, however, temporarily, on a level deeper than the normal codifications of civilized society. This sense of primal reality comes through strongly in both Wang Wei's "A Green Stream," the poem by Chi Wu-ch'ien, and Barbara Howes' "Out Fishing." Robinson Jeffers' "Salmon Fishing" adds a harsher note; no matter how deep the contemplative satisfactions of hunting and fishing, the cruelty of these sports must also be considered. Far from being the ritualized combat of football or boxing, these outdoor sports are intended to conclude with an all too real, and not symbolic, death. The reality of death comes through in Jeffers' poem, and it is an important element of the poems by Elizabeth Bishop, Sonya Dorman, and Edna St. Vincent Millay, as well as Washington Irving's essay on the buffalo hunt.

Perhaps no one has ever written better about the contemplative pleasures to be found in fishing than Izaak Walton, and the selection printed here gives just a taste of that seventeenth-century classic, *The Compleat Angler*. But in all fairness, cruelty should be added to contemplation to complete the paradoxical opposites that are to be found in hunting and fishing and which may account for part of the depth of their attraction.

There has long been a tradition of wanting to write "the great American novel," but many fans of Herman Melville's great book would say that the great American novel has already been written and that its name is *Moby Dick*. The plot of this long and difficult book is really rather simple. Captain Ahab has had his leg taken off in a previous encounter with the white whale, and he now seeks to revenge himself.

As a monomaniac, a man of enormous ego to the point of insanity, Captain Ahab projects his personal animosity on the whale in a way which, from a pragmatic and sensible standpoint (represented in the book by Starbuck, the first mate), is wholly improper because it represents an arrogant assertion of self as being more important than nature.

Thus, Ahab suffers from the sin of pride and, in his tormented mind, the whale has become a symbol of naked evil. From other perspectives, the whale can be seen as a mere "magnified mouse" (as he seems to Stubb) or as an animal to be feared and respected but not invested with great meaning (as he is to Starbuck). At its most complex, the white whale can be seen as a symbol of the multi-faceted, constantly changing, and deeply frightening nature of reality itself. No one perspective is adequate to describe what the whale represents.

Ahab is doomed to failure because he tries to reduce and fix the dynamic nature of reality. Consequently, he is destined to collide with reality because he will make no concessions to its intrinsic qualities. It is somewhat as though a person were to assert equality with the Atlantic Ocean by courageously, yet obstinately, setting out to swim from New York to London. However magnificent the attempt, it would still be fatal. Thus the sport of the chase may be seen as an emblem of life itself—always ending in a death that is given meaning by the way in which a person has lived.

WANG WEI

A GREEN STREAM

I have come on the River of Yellow Flowers,
Borne by the current of a green stream
Rounding ten thousand turns through the mountains
To journey less than a hundred li.
Rapids hum on scattered stones,
Light is dim in the close pines,
The surface of an inlet sways with nut-horns,
Weeds are lush along the banks.
Down in my heart I have always been clear
As this clarity of waters.
Oh, to remain on a broad flat rock
And cast my fishing-line forever!

Translated by Witter Bynner and Kiang Kang-hu

CHI WU-CH'IEN

FLOATING ON THE JO WEH STREAM IN SPRING

Here is seclusion and stillness with nothing to break the
    spell;
We follow wherever the boat chooses to drift;
The evening wind wafts it on its way
Entering the mouth of the gorge between flowery paths,
As dusk falls we wind among the western ravines.
Through a break in the hills one can see the Southern
    Dipper.
The air is heavy with floating mist
The moon among the trees sinks at my back.
The life of the world of men is a boundless waste;
My wish is to spend my days here as a fisherman in wild
    places.

Translated by Soame Jenyns

BARBARA HOWES

OUT FISHING

We went out, early one morning,
Over the loud marches of the sea,
In our walnut-shell boat,
Tip-tilting over that blue vacancy.

Combering, coming in,
The waves shellacked us, left us breathless, ill;
Hour on hour, out
Of this emptiness no fish rose, until

The great one struck that twine-
Wrapped flying-fish hard, turned and bolted
Off through the swelling sea
By a twist of his shoulder, with me tied fast; my rod

Held him, his hook held me,
In tug-of-war—sidesaddle on the ocean
I rode out the flaring waves,
Rode till the great fish sounded; by his submersion

He snapped the line, we lost
All contact; north, south, west, my adversary
Storms on through his world
Of water: I do not know him: he does not know me.

ROBINSON JEFFERS

SALMON-FISHING

The days shorten, the south blows wide for showers now,
The south wind shouts to the rivers,
The rivers open their mouths and the salt salmon

Race up into the freshet.
In Christmas month against the smoulder and menace
Of a long angry sundown
Red ash of the dark solstice, you see the anglers,
Pitiful, cruel, primeval,
Like the priests of the people that built Stonehenge,
Dark silent forms, performing
Remote solemnities in the red shallows
Of the river's mouth at the year's turn,
Drawing landward their live bullion, the bloody mouths
And scales full of the sunset
Twitch on the rocks, no more to wander at will
The wild Pacific pasture nor wanton and spawning
Race up into fresh water.

SONYA DORMAN

HUNTERS

Where the owl
sheds a feather
I walk softly.
Across my back
is written the license
to kill.
If I love in the city
I'm lucky, but light
takes the long way down;
the street is a place
to die.
At night
the owl flies off to hunt.

I can hear the cry
of his catch
and a siren in the city,
where if you've no passion
for killing, nothing assuages
your hunger.
I keep to the forest,
my thought fletched
with a dark feather
aimed at the bird
I love.

ELIZABETH BISHOP

THE FISH

I caught a tremendous fish
and held him beside the boat
half out of water, with my hook
fast in a corner of his mouth.
He didn't fight.
He hadn't fought at all.
He hung a grunting weight,
battered and venerable
and homely. Here and there
his brown skin hung in strips
like ancient wall-paper,
and its pattern of darker brown
was like wall-paper:
shapes like full-blown roses
stained and lost through age.
He was speckled with barnacles,

fine rosettes of lime,
and infested
with tiny white sea-lice,
and underneath two or three
rags of green weed hung down.
While his gills were breathing in
the terrible oxygen
—the frightening gills,
fresh and crisp with blood,
that can cut so badly—
I thought of the coarse white flesh
packed in like feathers,
the big bones and the little bones,
the dramatic reds and blacks
of his shiny entrails,
and the pink swim-bladder
like a big peony.
I looked into his eyes
which were far larger than mine
but shallower, and yellowed,
the irises backed and packed
with tarnished tinfoil
seen through the lenses
of old scratched isinglass.
They shifted a little, but not
to return my stare.
—It was more like the tipping
of an object toward the light.
I admired his sullen face,
the mechanism of his jaw,
and then I saw
that from his lower lip
—if you could call it a lip—
grim, wet, and weapon-like,
hung five old pieces of fish-line,
or four and a wire leader

with the swivel still attached,
with all their five big hooks
grown firmly in his mouth.
A green line, frayed at the end
where he broke it, two heavier lines,
and a fine black thread
still crimped from the strain and snap
when it broke and he got away.
Like medals with their ribbons
frayed and wavering,
a five-haired beard of wisdom
trailing from his aching jaw.
I stared and stared
and victory filled up
the little rented boat,
from the pool of bilge
where oil had spread a rainbow
around the rusted engine
to the bailer rusted orange,
the sun-cracked thwarts,
the oarlocks on their strings,
the gunnels—until everything
was rainbow, rainbow, rainbow!
And I let the fish go.

EDNA ST. VINCENT MILLAY

HUNTSMAN, WHAT QUARRY?

"Huntsman, what quarry
On the dry hill
Do your hounds harry?

When the red oak is bare
And the white oak still

Rattles its leaves
In the cold air:
What fox runs there?"

"Girl, gathering acorns
In the cold autumn,
I hunt the hot pads
That ever run before,
I hunt the pointed mask
That makes no reply,
I hunt the red brush
Of remembered joy."

"To tame or to destroy?"

"To destroy."

"Huntsman, hard by
In a wood of grey beeches
Whose leaves are on the ground,
Is a house with a fire;
You can see the smoke from here.
There's supper and a soft bed
And not a soul around.
Come with me there;
Bide there with me;
And let the fox run free."

The horse that he rode on
Reached down its neck,
Blew upon the acorns,
Nuzzled them aside;
The sun was near setting;
He thought, "Shall I heed her?"
He thought, "Shall I take her
For a one-night's bride?"

He smelled the sweet smoke,

He looked the lady over;
Her hand was on his knee;
But like a flame from cover
The red fox broke—
And "Hoick! Hoick!" cried he.

WASHINGTON IRVING

THE GRAND PRAIRIE—A BUFFALO HUNT

After proceeding about two hours in a southerly direction, we emerged towards mid-day from the dreary belt of the Cross Timber, and to our infinite delight beheld "The Great Prairie," stretching to the right and left before us. We could distinctly trace the meandering course of the Main Canadian, and various smaller streams, by the strips of green forests that bordered them. The landscape was vast and beautiful. There is always an expansion of feeling in looking upon these boundless and fertile wastes; but I was doubly conscious of it after emerging from our "close dungeon of innumerous boughs."

From a rising ground Beatte pointed out the place where he and his comrades had killed the buffaloes; and we beheld several black objects moving in the distance, which he said were part of the herd. The Captain determined to shape his course to a woody bottom about a mile distant, and to encamp there for a day or two, by way of having a regular buffalo-hunt, and getting a supply of provisions. As the troop defiled along the slope of the hill towards the camping ground, Beatte proposed to my messmates and myself, that we should put ourselves under his guidance, promising to take us where we should have plenty of sport. Leaving the line of march, therefore, we diverged towards the prairie; traversing a small valley, and ascending a gentle swell of land. As we reached the summit, we beheld a gang of wild horses about a mile off. Beatte was immediately on the alert, and no longer thought of buffalo hunting. He was mounted on his powerful half wild horse, with a lariat coiled at the saddle-bow, and set off in pursuit; while we remained on a rising ground watching his manoeuvres with great solicitude. Taking advantage of a strip of woodland, he stole quietly along, so as to get close to them before he was perceived. The moment they caught sight of him a grand scamper took place. We watched him skirting along the horizon like a privateer in full chase of a merchantman; at length he passed over the brow of a ridge, and down a shallow valley; in a few moments he was on the opposite hill, and close upon one of the horses. He was soon head and head, and appeared to be trying to noose his prey; but they both disappeared again behind the hill, and we saw no more of them. It turned out afterwards that he had noosed a powerful horse, but could not hold him, and had lost his lariat in the attempt.

While we were waiting for his return, we perceived two buffalo descending a slope, towards a stream, which wound through a ravine fringed with trees. The young Count and myself endeavored to get near them under covert of the trees. They discovered us while we were yet three or four hundred yards off, and turning about, retreated up the rising ground. We urged our horses across the ravine, and gave chase. The immense weight of head and shoulders causes the buffalo to labor heavily up-hill; but it accelerates his descent. We had the advantage, therefore, and gained rapidly upon the fugitives, though it was difficult to get our horses to approach them, their very scent inspiring them with terror. The Count, who had a double-barrelled gun loaded with ball, fired, but it missed. The bulls now altered their course, and galloped down-hill with headlong rapidity. As they ran in different directions, we each singled one and separated. I was provided with a brace of veteran brass-barrelled pistols, which I had borrowed at Fort Gibson, and which had evidently seen some service. Pistols are very effective in buffalo hunting, as the hunter can ride up close to the animal, and fire it while at full speed; whereas the long heavy rifles used on the frontier, cannot be easily managed, nor discharged with accurate aim from horseback. My object, therefore, was to get within pistol-shot of the buffalo. This was no very easy matter. I was well mounted on a horse of excellent speed and bottom, that seemed eager for the chase, and soon overtook the game; but the moment he came nearly parallel, he would keep sheering off, with ears forked and pricked forward, and every symptom of aversion and alarm. It was no wonder. Of all animals, a buffalo, when close pressed by the hunter, has an aspect the most diabolical. His two short black horns curve out of a huge frontlet of shaggy hair; his eyes glow like coals; his mouth is open; his tongue parched and drawn up into a half crescent; his tail is erect, and tufted and whisking about in the air; he is a perfect picture of mingled rage and terror.

It was with difficulty I urged my horse sufficiently near, when, taking aim, to my chagrin both pistols missed fire. Unfortunately the locks of these veteran weapons were so much worn, that in the gallop the priming had been shaken out of the pans. At the snapping of the last pistol I was close upon the buffalo, when, in his despair, he turned round with a sudden snort, and rushed upon me. My horse wheeled about as if on a pivot, made a convulsive spring, and, as I had been leaning on one side with pistol extended, I came near being thrown at the feet of the buffalo.

Three or four bounds of the horse carried us out of the reach of the enemy, who, having merely turned in desperate self-defence, quickly resumed his flight. As soon as I could gather in my panic-stricken horse, and prime the pistols afresh, I again spurred in pursuit of the buffalo, who had slackened his speed to take breath. On my approach he again set off full tilt, heaving himself forward with a heavy rolling gallop, dashing with headlong precipitation through brakes and ravines, while several deer and wolves, startled from their coverts by his thundering career, ran helter-skelter to right and left across the waste.

A gallop across the prairies in pursuit of game is by no means so smooth a career as those may imagine who have only the idea of an open level plain. It is true, the prairies of the hunting ground are not so much entangled with flowering plants and long herbage as the lower prairies, and are principally covered with short buffalo-grass; but they are diversified by hill and dale, and where most level, are apt to be cut up by deep rifts and ravines, made by torrents after rains; and which, yawning from an even surface, are almost like pitfalls in the way of the hunter, checking him suddenly when in full career, or subjecting him to the risk of limb and life. The plains, too, are beset by burrowing-holes of small animals, in which the horse is apt to sink to the fetlock, and throw both himself and his rider. The late rain had covered some parts of the prairie, where the ground was hard, with a thin sheet of water, through which the horse had to splash his way. In other parts there were innumerable shallow hollows, eight or ten feet in diameter, made by the buffaloes, who wallow in sand and mud like swine. These being filled with water, shone like mirrors, so that the horse was continually leaping over them or springing on one side. We had reached, too, a rough part of the prairie, very much broken and cut up; the buffalo, who was running for life, took no heed to his course, plunging down break-neck ravines, where it was necessary to skirt the borders in search of a safer descent. At length we came to where a winter stream had torn a deep chasm across the whole prairie, leaving open jagged rocks, and forming a long glen bordered by steep crumbling cliffs of mingled stone and clay. Down one of these the buffalo flung himself, half tumbling, half leaping, and then scuttled along the bottom; while I, seeing all further pursuit useless, pulled up, and gazed quietly after him from the border of the cliff, until he disappeared amidst the windings of the ravine.

Nothing now remained but to turn my steed and rejoin my companions. Here at first was some little difficulty. The ardor of the chase had betrayed me into a long, heedless gallop. I now found myself in the midst of a lonely waste, in which the prospect was bounded by undulating swells of land, naked and uniform, where, from the deficiency of landmarks and distinct features, an inexperienced man may become bewildered, and lose his way as readily as in the wastes of the ocean. The day, too, was overcast, so that I could not guide myself by the sun; my only mode was to retrace the track my horse had made in coming, though this I would often lose sight of, where the ground was covered with parched herbage.

To one unaccustomed to it, there is something inexpressibly lonely in the solitude of a prairie. The loneliness of a forest seems nothing to it. There the view is shut in by trees, and the imagination is left free to picture some livelier scene beyond. But here we have an immense extent of landscape without a sign of human existence. We have the consciousness of being far, far beyond the bounds of human habitation; we feel as if moving in the midst of a desert world. As my horse lagged slowly back over the scenes of our late scamper, and the delirium of the chase had passed away, I was peculiarly sensible to these circumstances. The silence of the waste was now and then broken by the cry of a distant flock of pelicans, stalking like spectres about a shallow pool; sometimes by the sinister croaking of a raven in the air, while occasionally a scoundrel wolf would scour off from before me, and, having attained a safe distance, would sit down and howl and whine with tones that gave a dreariness to the surrounding solitude.

After pursuing my way for some time, I descried a horseman on the edge of a distant hill, and soon recognized him to be the Count. He had been equally unsuccessful with myself; we were shortly after rejoined by our worthy comrade, the Virtuoso, who, with spectacles on nose, had made two or three ineffectual shots from horseback.

We determined not to seek the camp until we had made one more effort. Casting our eyes about the surrounding waste, we descried a herd of buffalo about two miles distant, scattered apart, and quietly grazing near a small strip of trees and bushes. It required but little stretch of fancy to picture them so many cattle grazing on the edge of a common, and that the grove might shelter some lonely farm-house.

We now formed our plan to circumvent the herd, and by getting on the other side of them, to hunt them in the direction where we knew our camp to be situated: otherwise, the pursuit might take us to such a distance as to render it impossible to find our way back before night-fall. Taking a wide circuit, therefore, we moved slowly and cautiously, pausing occasionally when we saw any of the herd desist from grazing. The wind fortunately set from them, otherwise they might have scented us and have taken the alarm. In this way we succeeded in getting round the herd without disturbing it. It consisted of about forty head; bulls, cows, and calves. Separating to some distance from each other, we now approached slowly in a parallel line, hoping by degrees to steal near without exciting attention. They began, however, to move off quietly, stopping at every step or two to graze, when suddenly a bull, that, unobserved by us, had been taking his siesta under a clump of trees to our left, roused himself from his lair, and hastened to join his companions. We were still at a considerable distance, but the game had taken the alarm. We quickened our pace; they broke into a gallop, and now commenced a full chase.

As the ground was level, they shouldered along with great speed, following each other in a line; two or three bulls bringing up the rear, the last of whom, from his enormous size and venerable frontlet, and beard of sunburnt hair, looked like a patriarch of the herd, and as if he might long have reigned the monarch of the prairie.

There is a mixture of the awful and the comic in the look of these huge animals, as they bear their great bulk forwards, with an up and down motion of the unwieldy head and shoulders, their tail cocked up like the cue of a Pantaloon in a pantomime, the end whisking about in a fierce yet whimsical style, and their eyes glaring venomously with an expression of fright and fury.

For some time I kept parallel with the line, without being able to force my horse within pistol-shot, so much had he been alarmed by the assault of the buffalo in the preceding chase. At length I succeeded, but was again balked by my pistols missing fire. My companions, whose horses were less fleet and more wayworn, could not overtake the herd; at length Mr. L., who was in the rear of the line, and losing ground, levelled his double-barrelled gun, and fired a long raking shot. It struck a buffalo just above the loins, broke its backbone, and brought it to the ground. He stopped and alighted to dispatch his prey, when, borrowing his gun, which had yet a charge remaining in it, I put my horse to his speed, again overtook the herd which was thundering along, pursued by the Count. With my present weapon there was no need of urging my horse to such close quarters; galloping along parallel, therefore, I singled out a buffalo, and by a fortunate shot brought it down on the spot. The ball had struck a vital part; it could not move from the place where it fell, but lay there struggling in mortal agony, while the rest of the herd kept on their headlong career across the prairie.

Dismounting, I now fettered my horse to prevent his straying, and advanced to contemplate my victim. I am nothing of a sportsman; I had been prompted to this unwonted exploit by the magnitude of the game and the excitement of an adventurous chase. Now that the excitement was over, I could not but look with commiseration upon the poor animal that lay struggling and bleeding at my feet. His very size and importance, which had before inspired me with eagerness, now increased my compunction. It seemed as if I had inflicted pain in proportion to the bulk of my victim, and as if there were a hundred-fold greater waste of life than there would have been in the destruction of an animal of inferior size.

To add to these after-qualms of conscience, the poor animal lingered in his agony. He had evidently received a mortal wound, but death might be long in coming. It would not do to leave him here to be torn piecemeal while yet alive, by the wolves that had already snuffed his blood, and were skulking and howling at a distance, and waiting for my departure; and by the ravens that were flapping about, croaking dismally in the air. It became now an act of mercy to give him his quietus, and put him out of his misery. I primed one of the pistols, therefore, and advanced close up to the buffalo. To inflict a wound thus in cold blood, I found a totally different thing from firing in the heat of the chase. Taking aim, however, just behind the fore-shoulder, my pistol for once proved true; the ball must have passed through the heart, for the animal gave one convulsive throe and expired.

While I stood meditating and moralizing over the wreck I had so wantonly produced, with my horse grazing near me, I was rejoined by my fellow-sportman the Virtuoso, who, being a man of universal adroitness, and withal more experienced and hardened in the gentle art of "venerie," soon managed to carve out the tongue of the buffalo, and delivered it to me to bear back to the camp as a trophy.

IZAAK WALTON

THE COMPLEAT ANGLER

A Conference betwixt an Angler, a Falconer, and a Hunter, each commending his Recreation

PISCATOR, VENATOR, AUCEPS

PISCATOR. You are well overtaken, Gentlemen! A good morning to you both! I have stretched my legs up Tottenham Hill to overtake you, hoping your businss may occasion you towards Ware whither I am going this fine fresh May morning.

VENATOR. Sir, I, for my part, shall almost answer your hopes; for my purpose is to drink my morning's draught at the Thatched House in Hoddesden; and I think not to rest till I come thither, where I have appointed a friend or two to meet me: but for this gentleman that you see with me, I know not how far he intends his journey; he came so lately into my company, that I have scarce had time to ask him the question.

AUCEPS. Sir, I shall by your favour bear you company as far as Theobalds, and there leave you; for then I turn up to a friend's house, who mews a Hawk for me, which I now long to see.

VENATOR. Sir, we are all so happy as to have a fine, fresh, cool morning; and I hope we shall each be the happier in the others' company. And, Gentlemen, that I may not lose yours, I shall either abate or amend my pace to enjoy it, knowing that, as the Italians say, "Good company in a journey makes the way to seem the shorter."

AUCEPS. It may do so, Sir, with the help of good discourse, which, methinks, we may promise from you, that both look and speak so cheerfully: and for my part, I promise you, as an invitation to it, that I will be as free and open hearted as discretion will allow me to be with strangers.

VENATOR. And, Sir, I promise the like.

PISCATOR. I am right glad to hear your answers; and, in confidence you speak the truth, I shall put on a boldness to ask you, Sir, whether business or pleasure caused you to be so early up, and walk so fast? for this other gentleman hath declared he is going to see a hawk, that a friend mews for him.

VENATOR. Sir, mine is a mixture of both, a little business and more pleasure; for I intend this day to do all my business, and then bestow another day or two in hunting the Otter, which a friend, that I go to meet, tells me is much pleasanter than any other chase whatsoever: howsoever, I mean to try it; for to-morrow morning we shall meet a pack of Otter-dogs of noble Mr. Sadler's, upon Amwell Hill, who will be there so early, that they intend to prevent the sunrising.

PISCATOR. Sir, my fortune has answered my desires, and my purpose is to bestow a day or two in helping to destroy some of those villanous vermin: for I hate them perfectly, because they love fish so well, or rather, because they destroy so much; indeed so much, that, in my judgment all men that keep Otter-dogs ought to have pensions from the King, to encourage them to destroy the very breed of those base Otters, they do so much mischief.

VENATOR. But what say you to the Foxes of the Nation, would not you as willingly have them destroyed? for doubtless they do as much mischief as Otters do.

PISCATOR. Oh, Sir, if they do, it is not so much to me and my fraternity, as those base vermin the Otters do.

AUCEPS. Why, Sir, I pray, of what fraternity are you, that you are so angry with the poor Otters?

PISCATOR. I am, Sir, a Brother of the Angle, and therefore an enemy to the Otter: for you are to note, that we Anglers all love one another, and therefore do I hate the Otter both for my own, and their sakes who are of my brotherhood.

VENATOR. And I am a lover of Hounds; I have followed many a pack of dogs many a mile, and heard many merry Huntsmen make sport and scoff at Anglers.

AUCEPS. And I profess myself a Falconer, and have heard many grave, serious men pity them, it is such a heavy, contemptible, dull recreation.

PISCATOR. You know, Gentlemen, it is an easy thing to scoff at any art or recreation; a little wit mixed with ill nature, confidence, and malice, will do it; but though they often venture boldly, yet they are often caught, even in their own trap, according to that of Lucian, the father of the family of Scoffers:

> Lucian, well skilled in scoffing, this hath writ,
> Friend, that's your folly, which you think your wit:
> This you went oft, void both of wit and fear,
> Meaning another, when yourself you jeer.

If to this you add what Solomon says of Scoffers, that they are an abomination to mankind, let him that thinks fit scoff on, and be a Scoffer still; but I account them enemies to me and all that love Virtue and Angling.

And for you that have heard many grave, serious men pity Anglers; let me tell you, Sir, there be many men that are by others taken to be serious and grave men, whom we contemn and pity. Men that are taken to be grave, because nature hath made them of a sour complexion; money-getting men, men that spend all their time, first in getting, and next, in anxious care to keep it; men that are condemned to be rich, and then always busy or discontented: for these poor rich-men, we Anglers pity them perfectly, and stand in no need to borrow their thoughts to think ourselves so happy. No, no, Sir, we enjoy a contentedness above the reach of such dispositions, and as the learned and ingenuous Montaigne says, like himself, freely, "When my Cat and I entertain each other with mutual apish tricks, as playing with a garter, who knows but that I make my Cat more sport than she makes me? Shall I conclude her to be simple, that has her time to begin or refuse, to play as freely as I myself have? Nay, who knows but that it is a defect of my not understanding her language, for doubtless Cats talk and reason with one another, that we agree no better: and who knows but that she pities me for being no wiser than to play with her, and laughs and censures my folly, for making sport for her, when we two play together?"

Thus freely speaks Montaigne concerning Cats; and I hope I may take as great a liberty to blame any man, and laugh at him too, let him be never so grave, that hath not heard what Anglers can say in the justification of their Art and Recreation; which I may again tell you, is so full of pleasure, that we need not borrow their thoughts, to think ourselves happy.

VENATOR. Sir, you have almost amazed me; for though I am no Scoffer, yet I have, I pray let me speak it without offence, always looked upon Anglers, as more patient, and more simple men, than I fear I shall find you to be.

PISCATOR. Sir, I hope you will not judge my earnestness to be impatience: and for my simplicity, if by that you mean a harmlessness, or that simplicity which was usually found in the primitive Christians, who were, as most Anglers are, quiet men, and followers of peace; men that were so simply wise, as not to sell their consciences to buy riches, and with them vexation and a fear to die; if you mean such simple men as lived in those times when there were fewer lawyers; when men might have had a lordship safely conveyed to them in a piece of parchment no bigger than your hand, though several sheets will not do it safely in this wiser age; I say, Sir, if you take us Anglers to be such simple men as I have spoke of, then myself and those of my profession will be glad to be so understood: But if by simplicity you meant to express a general defect in those that profess and practise the excellent Art of Angling, I hope in time to disabuse you, and make the contrary appear so evidently, that if you will but have patience to hear me, I shall remove all the anticipations that discourse, or time, or prejudice, have possessed you with against that laudable and ancient Art; for I know it is worthy the knowledge and practice of a wise man.

o   o   o   o   o   o   o

PISCATOR. Well, now, Mr. Venator, you shall neither want time, nor my attention to hear you enlarge your discourse concerning hunting.

VENATOR. Not I, Sir: I remember you said that Angling itself was of great antiquity, and a perfect art, and an art not easily attained to; and you have so won upon me in your former discourse, that I am very desirous to hear what you can say further concerning those particulars.

PISCATOR. Sir, I did say so: and I doubt not but if you and I did converse together but a few hours, to leave you possessed with the same high and happy thoughts that now possess me of it; not only of the antiquity of Angling, but that it deserves commendations; and that it is an art, and an art worthy the knowledge and practice of a wise man.

VENATOR. Pray, Sir, speak of them what you think fit, for we have yet five miles to the Thatched House; during which walk, I dare promise you, my patience and diligent attention shall not be wanting. And if you shall make that to appear which you have undertaken, first, that it is an art, and an art worth the learning, I shall beg that I may attend you a day or two a-fishing, and that I may become your scholar, and be instructed in the art itself which you so much magnify.

PISCATOR. O, Sir, doubt not but that Angling is an art; is it not an art to deceive a Trout with an artificial Fly? a Trout! that is more sharp-sighted than any Hawk you have named, and more watchful and timorous than your high-mettled Merlin is bold? and yet, I doubt not to catch a brace or two to-morrow, for a friend's breakfast: doubt not therefore, Sir, but that angling is an art, and an art worth your learning. The question is rather, whether you be capable of learning it? for angling is somewhat like poetry, men are to be born so: I mean, with inclinations to it, though both may be heightened by discourse and practice: but he that hopes to be a good angler, must not only bring an inquiring, searching, observing wit, but he must bring a large measure of hope and patience, and a love and propensity to the art itself; but having once got and practised it, then doubt not but angling will prove to be so pleasant, that it will prove to be, like virtue, a reward to itself.

VENATOR. Sir, I am now become so full of expectation, that I long much to have you proceed, and in the order that you propose.

PISCATOR. Then first, for the antiquity of Angling, of which I shall not say much, but only this; some say it is as ancient as Deucalion's flood: others, that Belus, who was the first inventor of godly and virtuous recreations, was the first inventor of Angling: and some others say, for former times have had their disquisitions about the antiquity of it, that Seth, one of the sons of Adam, taught it to his sons, and that by them it was derived to posterity: others say that he left it engraven on those pillars which he erected, and trusted to preserve the knowledge of the mathematicks, musick, and the rest of that precious knowledge, and those useful arts, which by God's appointment or allowance, and his noble industry, were thereby preserved from perishing in Noah's flood.

These, Sir, have been the opinions of several men, that have possibly endeavoured to make angling more ancient than is needful, or may well be warranted; but for my part, I shall content myself in telling you, that angling is much more ancient than the incarnation of our Saviour; for in the Prophet Amos mention is made of fish-hooks; and in the book of Job, which was long before the days of Amos, for that book is said to have been written by Moses, mention is made also of fish-hooks, which must imply anglers in those times.

But, my worthy friend, as I would rather prove myself a gentleman, by being learned and humble, valiant and inoffensive, virtuous and communicable, than by any fond ostentation of riches, or, wanting those virtues myself, boast that these were in my ancestors; and yet I grant, that where a noble and ancient descent and such merit meet in nay man, it is a double dignification of that person; so if this antiquity of angling, which for my part I have not forced, shall, like an ancient family, be either an honour or an ornament to this virtuous art which I profess to love and practise, I shall be the gladder that I made an accidental mention of the antiquity of it, of which I shall say no more, but proceed to that just commendation which I think it deserves.

And for that, I shall tell you, that in ancient times a debate hath risen, and it remains yet unresolved, whether the happiness of man in this world doth consist more in contemplation or action? Concerning which, some have endeavoured to maintain their opinion of the first; by saying, that the nearer we mortals come to God by way of imitation, the more happy we are. And they say, that God enjoys himself only, by a contemplation of his own infiniteness, eternity, power, and goodness, and the like. And upon this ground, many cloisteral men of great learning and devotion, prefer contemplation before action. And many of the fathers seem to approve this opinion, as may appear in their commentaries upon the words of our Saviour to Martha.

And on the contrary, there want not men of equal authority and credit, that prefer action to be the more excellent; as namely, experiments in physick, and the application of it, both for the ease and prolongation of man's life; by which each man is enabled to act and do good to others, either to serve his country, or do good to particular persons: and they say also, that action is doctrinal, and teaches both art and virtue, and is a maintainer of human society; and for these, and other like reasons, to be preferred before contemplation.

Concerning which two opinions I shall forbear to add a third, by declaring my own; and rest myself contented in telling you, my very worthy friend, that both these meet together, and do most properly belong to the most honest, ingenuous, quiet, and harmless art of angling.

And first, I shall tell you what some have observed, and I have found it to be a real truth, that the very sitting by the river's side is not only the quietest and fittest place for contemplation, but will invite an angler to it: and this seems to be maintained by the learned Peter du Moulin, who, in his discourse of the fulfilling of Prophecies, observes, that when God intended to reveal any future events of high notions to his prophets, he then carried them either to the deserts, or the sea-shore, that having so separated them from amidst the press of people and business, and the cares of the world, he might settle their mind in a quiet repose, and there make them fit for revelation.

And this seems also to be imitated by the children of Israel, who having in a sad condition banished all mirth and musick from their pensive hearts, and having hung up their then mute harps upon the willow-trees growing by the rivers of Babylon, sat down upon those banks, bemoaning the ruins of Sion, and contemplating their own sad condition.

And an ingenious Spaniard says, that "rivers and the inhabitants of the watery element were made for wise men to contemplate, and fools to pass by without consideration". And though I will not rank myself in the number of the first, yet give me leave to free myself from the last, by offering to you a short contemplation, first of rivers, and then of fish; concerning which I doubt not but to give you many observations that will appear very considerable: I am sure they have appeared so to me, and made many an hour pass away more pleasantly, as I have sat quietly on a flowery bank by a calm river, and contemplated what I shall now relate to you.

And first concerning rivers; there be so many wonders reported and written of them, and of the several creatures that be bred and live in them, and those by authors of so good credit, that we need not to deny them an historical faith.

As namely of a river in Epirus that puts out any lighted torch, and kindles any torch that was not lighted. Some waters being drunk, cause madness, some drunkenness, and some laughter to death. The river Selarus in a few hours turns a rod or wand to stone: and our Camden mentions the like in England, and the like in Lochmere in Ireland. There is also a river in Arabia, of which all the sheep that drink thereof have their wool turned into a vermilion colour. And one of no less credit than Aristotle, tells us of a merry river, the river Elusina, that dances at the noise of musick, for with musick it bubbles, dances, and grows sandy, and so continues till the musick ceases, but then it presently returns to its wonted calmness and clearness. And Camden tells us of a well near to Kirby, in Westmoreland, that ebbs and flows several times every day: and he tells us of a river in Surrey, it is called Mole, that after it has run several miles, being opposed by hills, finds or makes itself a way under ground, and breaks out again so far off, that the inhabitants thereabout boast, as the Spaniards do of their river Anus, that they feed divers flocks of sheep upon a bridge. And lastly, for I would not tire your patience, one of no less authority than Josephus, that learned Jew, tells us of a river in Judea that runs swiftly all the six days of the week, and stands still and rests all their sabbath.

But I will lay aside my discourse of rivers, and tell you some things of the monsters, or fish, call them what you will, that they breed and feed in them. Pliny the philosopher says, in the third chapter of his ninth book, that in the Indian Sea, the fish called Balaena or Whirlpool, is so long and broad, as to take up more in length and breadth than two acres of ground; and, of other fish, of two hundred cubits long; and that in the river Ganges, there be Eels of thirty feet long. He says there, that these monsters appear in that sea, only when the tempestuous winds oppose the torrents of water falling from the rocks into it, and so turning what lay at the bottom to be seen on the water's top. And he says, that the people of Cadara, an island near this place, make the timber for their houses of those fish bones. He there tells us, that there are sometimes a thousand of these great Eels found wrapt or inter-woven together. He tells us there, that it appears that dolphins love musick, and will come when called for, by some men or boys that know, and use to feed them; and that they can swim as swift as an arrow can be shot out of a bow; and much of this is spoken concerning the dolphin, and other fish, as may be found also in the learned Dr. Casaubon's *Discourse of Credulity and Incredulity,* printed by him about the year 1670.

I know, we Islanders are averse to the belief of these wonders; but there be so many strange creatures to be now seen, many collected by John Tradescant, and others added by my friend Elias Ashmole, Esq., who now keeps them carefully and metho-dically at his house near to Lambeth, near London, as may get some belief of some of the other wonders I mentioned. I will tell you some of the wonders that you may now see, and not till then believe, unless you think fit.

You may there see the Hog-fish, the Dog-fish, the Dolphin, the Cony-fish, the Parrot-fish, the Shark, the Poison-fish, Sword-fish, and not only other incredible fish, but you may there see the Salamander, several sorts of Barnacles, of Solan-Geese, the Bird of Paradise, such sorts of Snakes, and such Birds'-nests, and of so various forms, and so wonderfully made, as may beget wonder and amusement in any beholder; and so many hundred of other rarities in that collection, as will make the other wonders I spake of, the less incredible; for, you may note, that the waters are Nature's store-house, in which she locks up her wonders.

HERMAN MELVILLE

THE CHASE

from *Moby Dick*

The Chase—First Day

That night, in the mid-watch, when the old man—as his wont at intervals—stepped forth from the scuttle in which he leaned, and went to his pivot-hole, he suddenly thrust out his face fiercely, snuffing up the sea air as a sagacious ship's dog will, in drawing nigh to some barbarous isle. He declared that a whale must be near. Soon that peculiar odor, sometimes to a great distance given forth by the living Sperm Whale, was palpable to all the watch; nor was any mariner surprised when, after inspecting the compass, and then the dog-vane, and then ascertaining the precise bearing of the odor as nearly as possible, Ahab rapidly ordered the ship's course to be slightly altered, and the sail to be shortened.

The acute policy dictating these movements was sufficiently vindicated at daybreak, by the sight of a long sleek on the sea directly and lengthwise ahead, smooth as oil, and resembling in the pleated watery wrinkles bordering it, the polished metallic-like marks of some swift tide-rip, at the mouth of a deep, rapid stream.

"Man the mast-heads! Call all hands!"

Thundering with the butts of three clubbed handspikes on the forecastle deck, Daggoo roused the sleepers with such judgment claps that they seemed to exhale from the scuttle, so instantaneously did they appear with their clothes in their hands.

"What d'ye see?" cried Ahab, flattening his face to the sky.

"Nothing, nothing, Sir!" was the sound hailing down in reply.

"T'gallant sails!—stunsails! alow and aloft, and on both sides!"

All sail being set, he now cast loose the life-line, reserved for swaying him to the main royal-mast head; and in a few moments they were hoisting him thither, when, while but two thirds of the way aloft, and while peering ahead through the horizontal vacancy between the main-top-sail and top-gallant-sail, he raised a gull-like cry in the air, "There she blows!—there she blows! A hump like a snow-hill! It is Moby Dick!"

Fired by the cry which seemed simultaneously taken up by the three look-outs, the men on deck rushed to the rigging to behold the famous whale they had so long been pursuing. Ahab had now gained his final perch, some feet above the other look-outs, Tashtego standing just beneath him on the cap of the top-gallant-mast, so that the Indian's head was almost on a level with Ahab's heel. From this height the whale was now seen some mile or so ahead, at every roll of the sea revealing his high sparkling hump, and regularly jetting his silent spout into the air. To the credulous mariners it seemed the same silent spout they had so long ago beheld in the moonlit Atlantic and Indian Oceans.

"And did none of ye see it before?" cried Ahab, hailing the perched men all around him.

"I saw him almost the same instant, Sir, that Captain Ahab did, and I cried out," said Tashtego.

"Not the same instant; not the same—no, the doubloon is mine, Fate reserved the doubloon for me. *I* only; none of ye could have raised the White Whale first. There she blows! there she blows!—there she blows! There again!—there again!" he cried, in long-drawn, lingering, methodic tones, attuned to the gradual prolongings of the whale's visible jets. "He's going to sound! In stunsails! Down top-gallant-sails! Stand by three boats. Mr. Starbuck, remember, stay on board, and keep the ship. Helm there! Luff, luff a point! So; steady, man, steady! There go flukes! No, no; only black water! All ready the boats there? Stand by, stand by! Lower me, Mr. Starbuck; lower, lower,—quick, quicker!" and he slid through the air to the deck.

"He is heading straight to leeward, Sir," cried Stubb, "right away from us; cannot have seen the ship yet."

"Be dumb, man! Stand by the braces! Hard down the helm!—brace up! Shiver her!—shiver her! So; well that! Boats, boats!"

Soon all the boats but Starbuck's were dropped; all the boat-sails set—all the paddles plying; with rippling swiftness, shooting to leeward; and Ahab heading the onset. A pale, death-glimmer lit up Fedallah's sunken eyes; a hideous motion gnawed his mouth.

Like noiseless nautilus shells, their light prows sped through the sea; but only slowly they neared the foe. As they neared him, the ocean grew still more smooth; seemed drawing a carpet over its waves; seemed a noon-meadow, so serenely it spread. At length the breathless hunter came so nigh his seemingly unsuspecting prey, that his entire dazzling hump was distinctly visible, sliding along the sea as if an isolated thing, and continually set in a revolving ring of finest, fleecy, greenish foam. He saw the vast, involved wrinkles of the slightly projecting head beyond. Before it, far out on the soft Turkish-rugged waters, went the glistening white shadow from his broad, milky forehead, a musical rippling playfully accompanying the shade; and behind, the blue waters interchangeably flowed over into the moving valley of his steady wake; and on either hand bright bubbles arose and danced by his side. But these were broken again by the light toes of hundreds of gay fowl softly feathering the sea, alternate with their fitful flight; and like to some flag-staff rising from the painted hull of an argosy, the tall but shattered pole of a recent lance projected from the White Whale's back; and at intervals one of the cloud of soft-toed fowls hovering, and to and fro skimming like a canopy over the fish, silently perched and rocked on this pole, the long tail feathers streaming like pennons.

A gentle joyousness—a mighty mildness of repose in swiftness, invested the gliding whale. Not the white bull Jupiter swimming away with ravished Europa clinging to his graceful horns; his lovely, leering eyes sideways intent upon the maid; with smooth bewitching fleetness, rippling straight for the nuptial bower in Crete; not Jove, not that great majesty Supreme! did surpass the glorified White Whale as he so divinely swam.

On each soft side—coincident with the parted swell, that but once leaving him, then flowed so wide away—on each bright side, the whale shed off enticings. No wonder there had been some among the hunters who namelessly transported and allured by all his serenity, had ventured to assail it; but had fatally found that quietude but the vesture of tornadoes. Yet calm, enticing calm, oh, whale! thou glidest on, to all who for the first time eye thee, no matter how many in that same way thou may'st have bejuggled and destroyed before.

And thus, through the serene tranquillities of the tropical sea, among waves whose hand-clappings were suspended by exceeding rapture, Moby Dick moved on, still withholding from sight the full terrors of his submerged trunk, entirely hiding the wrenched hideousness of his jaw. But soon the fore part of him slowly rose from the water; for an instant his whole marbleized body formed a high arch, like Virginia's Natural Bridge, and warningly waving his bannered flukes in the air, the grand god revealed himself, sounded, and went out of sight. Hoveringly halting, and dipping on the wing, the white sea-fowls longingly lingered over the agitated pool that he left.

With oars apeak, and paddles down, the sheets of their sails adrift, the three boats now stilly floated, awaiting Moby Dick's reappearance.

"An hour," said Ahab, standing rooted in his boat's stern; and he gazed beyond the whale's place, towards the dim blue spaces and wide wooing vacancies to leeward. It was only an instant; for again his eyes seemed whirling round in his head as he swept the watery circle. The breeze now freshened; the sea began to swell.

"The birds!—the birds!" cried Tashtego.

In long Indian file, as when herons take wing, the white birds were now all flying towards Ahab's boat; and when within a few yards began fluttering over the water there, wheeling round and round, with joyous, expectant cries. Their vision was keener than man's; Ahab could discover no sign in the sea. But suddenly as he peered down and down into its depths, he profoundly saw a white living spot no bigger than a white weasel, with wonderful celerity uprising, and magnifying as it rose, till it turned, and then there were plainly revealed two long crooked rows of white, glistening teeth, floating up from the undiscoverable bottom. It was Moby Dick's open mouth and scrolled jaw; his vast, shadowed bulk still half blending with the blue of the sea. The glittering mouth yawned beneath the boat like an open-doored marble tomb; and giving one sidelong sweep with his steering oar, Ahab whirled the craft aside from this tremendous apparition. Then, calling upon Fedallah to change places with him, went forward to the bows, and seizing Perth's harpoon, commanded his crew to grasp their oars and stand by to stern.

Now, by reason of this timely spinning round the boat upon its axis, its bow, by anticipation, was made to face the whale's head while yet under water. But as if perceiving this stratagem, Moby Dick, with that malicious intelligence ascribed to him, sidelingly transplanted himself, as it were, in an instant, shooting his pleated head lengthwise beneath the boat.

Through and through; through every plank and each rib, it thrilled for an instant, the whale obliquely lying on his back, in the manner of a biting shark, slowly and feelingly taking its bows full within his mouth, so that the long, narrow, scrolled lower jaw curled high up into the open air, and one of the teeth caught in a row-lock. The bluish pearl-white of the inside of the jaw was within six inches of Ahab's head, and reached higher than that. In this attitude the White Whale now shook the slight cedar as a mildly cruel cat her mouse. With unastonished eyes Fedallah gazed, and crossed his arms; but the tiger-yellow crew were tumbling over each other's heads to gain the uttermost stern.

And now, while both elastic gunwales were springing in and out, as the whale dallied with the doomed craft in this devilish way; and from his body being submerged beneath the boat, he could not be darted at from the bows, for the bows were almost inside of him, as it were; and while the other boats involuntarily paused, as before a quick crisis impossible to withstand, then it was that monomaniac Ahab, furious with this tantalizing vicinity of his foe, which placed him all alive and helpless in the very jaws he hated; frenzied with all this, he seized the long bone with his naked hands, and wildly strove to wrench it from its gripe. As now he thus vainly strove, the jaw slipped from him; the frail gunwales bent in, collapsed, and snapped, as both jaws, like an enormous shears, sliding further aft, bit the craft completely in twain, and locked themselves fast again in the sea, midway between the two floating wrecks. These floated aside, the broken ends drooping, the crew at the stern-wreck clinging to the gunwales, and striving to hold fast to the oars to lash them across.

At that preluding moment, ere the boat was yet snapped, Ahab, the first to perceive the whale's intent, by the crafty upraising of his head, a movement that loosed his hold for the time; at that moment his hand had made one final effort to push the boat out of the bite. But only slipping further into the whale's mouth, and tilting over sideways as it slipped, the boat had shaken off his hold on the jaw; spilled him out of it, as he leaned to the push; and so he fell flat-faced upon the sea.

Ripplingly withdrawing from his prey, Moby Dick now lay at a little distance, vertically thrusting his oblong white head up and down in the billows; and at the same time slowly revolving his whole spindled body; so that when his vast wrinkled forehead rose—some twenty or more feet out of the water—the now rising swells, with all their confluent waves, dazzlingly broke against it; vindictively tossing their shivered spray still higher into the air.° So, in a gale, the but half baffled Channel billows recoil from the base of the Eddystone, only triumphantly to overleap its summit with their scud.

But soon resuming his horizontal attitude, Moby Dick swam swiftly round and round the wrecked crew; sideways churning the water in his vengeful wake, as if lashing himself up to still another and more deadly assault. The sight of the splintered boat seemed to madden him, as the blood of grapes and mulberries cast before Antiochus's elephants in the book of Maccabees. Meanwhile Ahab, half smothered in the foam of the whale's insolent tail, and too much of a cripple to swim,—though he could still keep afloat, even in the heart of such a whirlpool as that; helpless Ahab's head was seen, like a tossed bubble which the least chance shock might burst. From the boat's fragmen-

° This motion is peculiar to the Sperm Whale. It receives its designation (pitchpoling) from its being likened to that preliminary up-and-down poise of the whale-lance, in the exercise called pitchpoling, previously described. By this motion the whale must best and most comprehensively view whatever objects may be encircling him.

tary stern, Fedallah incuriously and mildly eyed him; the clinging crew, at the other drifting end, could not succor him; more than enough was it for them to look to themselves. For so revolvingly appalling was the White Whale's aspect, and so planetarily swift the ever-contracting circles he made, that he seemed horizontally swooping upon them. And though the other boats, unharmed, still hovered hard by; still they dared not pull into the eddy to strike, lest that should be the signal for the instant destruction of the jeopardized castaways, Ahab and all; nor in that case could they themselves hope to escape. With straining eyes, then, they remained on the outer edge of the direful zone, whose centre had now become the old man's head.

Meantime, from the beginning all this had been descried from the ship's mast-heads; and squaring her yards, she had borne down upon the scene; and was now so nigh, that Ahab in the water hailed her;— "Sail on the"—but that moment a breaking sea dashed on him from Moby Dick, and whelmed him for the time. But struggling out of it again, and chancing to rise on a towering crest, he shouted,—"Sail on the whale!—Drive him off!"

The Pequod's prows were pointed; and breaking up the charmed circle, she effectually parted the White Whale from his victim. As he sullenly swam off, the boats flew to the rescue.

Dragged into Stubb's boat with blood-shot, blinded eyes, the white brine caking in his wrinkles; the long tension of Ahab's bodily strength did crack, and helplessly he yielded to his body's doom: for a time, lying all crushed in the bottom of Stubb's boat, like one trodden under foot of herds of elephants. Far inland, nameless wails came from him, as desolate sounds from out ravines.

But this intensity of his physical prostration did but so much the more abbreviate it. In an instant's compass, great hearts sometimes condense to one deep pang, the sum total of those shallow pains kindly diffused through feebler men's whole lives. And so, such hearts, though summary in each one suffering; still, if the gods decree it, in their life-time aggregate a whole age of woe, wholly made up of instantaneous intensities; for even in their pointless centres, those noble natures contain the entire circumferences of inferior souls.

"The harpoon," said Ahab, half way rising, and draggingly leaning on one bended arm—"is it safe?"

"Aye, Sir, for it was not darted; this is it," said Stubb, showing it.

"Lay it before me;—any missing men?"

"One, two, three, four, five;—there were five oars, Sir, and here are five men."

"That's good.—Help me, man; I wish to stand. So, so, I see him! there! there! going to leeward still; what a leaping spout!—Hands off from me! The eternal sap runs up in Ahab's bones again! Set the sail; out oars; the helm!"

It is often the case that when a boat is stove, its crew, being picked up by another boat, help to work that second boat; and the chase is thus continued with what is called double-banked oars. It was thus now. But the added power of the boat did not equal the added power of the whale, for he seemed to have treble-banked his every fin; swimming with a velocity which plainly showed, that if now, under these circumstances, pushed on, the chase would prove an indefinitely prolonged, if not a hopeless one; nor could any crew endure for so long a period, such an unintermitted, intense straining at the oar; a thing barely tolerable only in some one brief vicissitude. The ship itself, then, as it sometimes happens, offered the most promising intermediate means of overtaking the chase. Accordingly, the boats now made for her, and were soon swayed up to their cranes—the two parts of the wrecked boat having been previously secured by her—and then hoisting everything to her side, and stacking her canvas high up, and sideways outstretching it with stun-sails, like the double-jointed wings of an albatross; the Pequod bore down in the leeward wake of Moby Dick. At the well known, methodic intervals, the whale's glittering spout was regularly announced from the manned mast-heads; and when he would be reported as just gone down, Ahab would take the time, and then pacing the deck, binnacle-watch in hand, so soon as the last second of the allotted hour expired, his voice was heard.—"Whose is the doubloon now? D'ye see him?" and if the reply was, No, sir! straightway he commanded them to lift him to his perch. In this way the day wore on; Ahab, now aloft and motionless; anon, unrestingly pacing the planks.

As he was thus walking, uttering no sound, except to hail the men aloft, or to bid them hoist a sail still higher, or to spread one to a still greater breadth—thus to and fro pacing, beneath his slouched hat, at every turn he passed his own wrecked boat, which had been dropped upon the quarter-deck, and lay there reversed; broken bow to shattered stern. At last he paused before it; and as in an already over-clouded sky fresh troops of clouds will sometimes sail across, so over the old man's face there now stole some such added gloom as this.

Stubb saw him pause; and perhaps intended, not vainly, though, to evince his own unabated fortitude, and thus keep up a valiant place in his captain's mind, he advanced, and eyeing the wreck exclaimed —"The thistle the ass refused; it pricked his mouth too keenly, Sir; ha! ha!

"What soulless thing is this that laughs before a wreck? Man, man! did I not know thee brave as fearless fire (and as mechanical) I could swear thou wert a poltroon. Groan nor laugh should be heard before a wreck."

"Aye, Sir," said Starbuck drawing near, " 'tis a solemn sight; an omen, and an ill one."

"Omen? omen?—the dictionary! If the gods think to speak outright to man, they will honorably speak outright; not shake their heads, and give an old wives' darkling hint.—Begone! Ye two are the opposite poles of one thing; Starbuck is Stubb reversed, and Stubb is Starbuck; and ye two are all mankind; and Ahab stands alone among the millions of the peopled earth, nor gods nor men his neighbors! Cold, cold—I shiver!—How now? Aloft there! D'ye see him? Sing out for every spout, though he spout ten times a second!"

The day was nearly done; only the hem of his golden robe was rustling. Soon, it was almost dark, but the look-out men still remained unset.

"Can't see the spout now, Sir;—too dark"—cried a voice from the air.

"How heading when last seen?"

"As before, Sir,—straight to leeward."

"Good! he will travel slower now 'tis night. Down royals and top-gallant stun-sails, Mr. Starbuck. We must not run over him before morning; he's making a passage now, and may heave-to a while. Helm there! keep her full before the wind!—Aloft! come down!—Mr. Stubb, send a fresh hand to the foremast head, and see it manned till morning."—Then advancing towards the doubloon in the main-mast—"Men, this gold is mine, for I earned it; but I shall let it abide here till the White Whale is dead; and then, whosoever of ye first raises him, upon the day he shall be killed, this gold is that man's; and if on that day I shall again raise him, then, ten times its sum shall be divided among all of ye! Away now!—the deck is thine, Sir."

And so saying, he placed himself half way within the scuttle, and slouching his hat, stood there till dawn, except when at intervals rousing himself to see how the night wore on.

The Chase—Second Day

At day-break, the three mast-heads were punctually manned afresh.

"D'ye see him?" cried Ahab, after allowing a little space for the light to spread.

"See nothing, Sir."

"Turn up all hands and make sail! he travels faster than I thought for;—the top-gallant sails!—aye, they should have been kept on her all night. But no matter—'tis but resting for the rush."

Here be it said, that this pertinacious pursuit of one particular whale, continued through day into night, and through night into day, is a thing by no means unprecedented in the South Sea fishery. For such is the wonderful skill, prescience of experience, and invincible confidence acquired by some great natural geniuses among the Nantucket commanders; that from the simple observation of a whale when last descried, they will, under certain given circumstances, pretty accurately foretell both the direction in which he will continue to swim for a time, while out of sight, as well as his probable rate of progression during that period. And, in these cases, somewhat as a pilot, when about losing sight of a coast, whose general trending he well knows, and which he desires shortly to return to again, but at some further point; like as this pilot stands by his compass, and takes the precise bearing of the cape at present visible, in order the more certainly to hit aright the remote, unseen headland, eventually to be visited: so does the fisherman, at his compass, with the whale; for after being chased, and diligently marked, through several hours of daylight, then, when night obscures the fish, the creature's future wake through the darkness is almost as established to the sagacious mind of the hunter, as the pilot's coast is to him. So that to this hunter's wondrous skill, the proverbial evanescence of a thing writ in water, a wake, is to all desired purposes well nigh as reliable as the steadfast land. And as the mighty iron Leviathan of the modern railway is so familiarly known in its every pace, that, with watches in their hands, men time his rate as doctors that of a baby's pulse; and lightly say of it, the up train or the down train will reach such or such a spot, at such or such an hour; even so, almost, there are occasions when these Nantucketers time that other Leviathan of the deep, according to the observed humor of his speed; and say to themselves, so many hours hence this whale will have gone two hundred miles, will have about reached this or that degree of latitude or longitude. But to render this acuteness at all successful in the end, the wind and the sea must be the whaleman's allies; for of what present avail to the becalmed or wind-bound mariner is the skill that assures him he is exactly ninety-three leagues and a quarter from his port? Inferable from these statements, are many collateral subtile matters touching the chase of whales.

The ship tore on; leaving such a furrow in the sea as when a cannon-ball, missent, becomes a plough-share and turns up the level field.

"By salt and hemp!" cried Stubb, "but this swift motion of the deck creeps up one's legs and tingles at the heart. This ship and I are two brave fellows!—Ha! ha! Some one take me up, and launch me, spine-wise, on the sea,—for by live-oaks! my spine's a keel. Ha, ha! we go the gait that leaves no dust behind!"

"There she blows—she blows! she blows!—right ahead!" was now the mast-head cry.

"Aye, aye!" cried Stubb, "I knew it—ye can't escape—blow on and split your spout, O whale! the mad fiend himself is after ye! blow your trump—blister your lungs! Ahab will dam off your blood, as a miller shuts his water-gate upon the stream!"

And Stubb did but speak out for well nigh all that crew. The frenzies of the chase had by this time worked them bubblingly up, like old wine worked anew. Whatever pale fears and forebodings some of them might have felt before; these were not only now kept out of sight through the growing awe of Ahab, but they were broken up, and on all sides routed, as timid prairie hares that scatter before the bounding bison. The hand of Fate had snatched all their souls; and by the stirring perils of the previous day; the rack of the past night's suspense; the fixed, unfearing, blind, reckless way in which their wild craft went plunging towards its flying mark; by all these things, their hearts were bowled along. The wind that made great bellies of their sails, and rushed the vessel on by arms invisible as irresistible; this seemed the symbol of that unseen agency which so enslaved them to the race.

They were one man, not thirty. For as the one ship that held them all; though it was put together of all contrasting things—oak, and maple, and pine wood; iron, and pitch, and hemp—yet all these ran into each other in the one concrete hull, which shot on its way, both balanced and directed by the long central keel; even so, all the individualities of the crew, this man's valor, that man's fear; guilt and guiltiness, all varieties were welded into oneness, and were all directed to that fatal goal which Ahab their one lord and keel did point to.

The rigging lived. The mast-heads, like the tops of tall palms, were outspreadingly tufted with arms and legs. Clinging to a spar with one hand, some reached forth the other with impatient wavings; others, shading their eyes from the vivid sunlight, sat far out on the rocking yards; all the spars in full bearing of mortals, ready and ripe for their fate. Ah! how they still strove through that infinite blueness to seek out the thing that might destroy them!

"Why sing ye not out for him, if ye see him?" cried Ahab, when, after the lapse of some minutes since the first cry, no more had been heard. "Sway me up, men; ye have been deceived; not Moby Dick casts one odd jet that way, and then disappears."

It was even so; in their headlong eagerness, the men had mistaken some other thing for the whale-spout, as the event itself soon proved; for hardly had Ahab reached his perch; hardly was the rope belayed to its pin on deck, when he struck the key-note to an orchestra, that made the air vibrate as with the combined discharges of rifles. The triumphant halloo of thirty buckskin lungs was heard, as—much nearer to the ship than the place of the imaginary jet, less than a mile ahead— Moby Dick bodily burst into view! For not by any calm and indolent spoutings; not by the peaceable gush of that mystic fountain in his head, did the White Whale now reveal his vicinity; but by the far more wondrous phenomenon of breaching. Rising with his utmost velocity from the furthest depths, the Sperm Whale thus booms his entire bulk into the pure element of air, and piling up a mountain of dazzling foam, shows his place to the distance of seven miles and more. In those moments, the torn, enraged waves he shakes off, seem his mane; in some cases, this breaching is his act of defiance.

"There she breaches! there she breaches!" was the cry, as in his immeasurable bravadoes the White Whale tossed himself salmon-like to heaven. So suddenly seen in the blue plain of the sea, and relieved against the still bluer margin of the sky, the spray that he raised, for the moment, intolerably glittered and glared like a glacier; and stood there gradually fading and fading away from its first sparkling intensity, to the dim mistiness of an advancing shower in a vale.

"Aye, breach your last to the sun, Moby Dick!" cried Ahab, "thy hour and thy harpoon are at hand!—Down! down all of ye, but one man at the fore. The boats!—stand by!"

Unmindful of the tedious rope-ladders of the shrouds, the men, like shooting stars, slid to the deck, by the isolated back-stays and halyards; while Ahab, less dartlingly, but still rapidly was dropped from his perch.

"Lower away," he cried, so soon as he had reached his boat—a spare one, rigged the afternoon previous. "Mr. Starbuck, the ship is thine —keep away from the boats, but keep near them. Lower, all!"

As if to strike a quick terror into them, by this time being the first assailant himself, Moby Dick had turned, and was now coming for the three crews. Ahab's boat was central; and cheering his men, he told them he would take the whale head-and-head,—that is, pull straight up to his forehead,—a not uncommon thing; for when within a certain limit such a course excludes the coming onset from the whale's side-long vision. But ere that close limit was gained, the White Whale churning himself into furious speed, almost in an instant as it were, rushing among the boats with open jaws, and a lashing tail, offered appalling battle on every side; and heedless of the irons darted at him from every boat, seemed only intent on annihilating each separate plank of which those boats were made. But skilfully manoeuvred, incessantly wheeling like trained chargers in the field; the boats for a while eluded him; though, at times, but by a plank's breadth; while all the time, Ahab's unearthly slogan tore every other cry but his to shreds.

But at last in his untraceable evolutions, the White Whale so crossed and recrossed, and in a thousand ways entangled the slack of the three lines now fast to him, that they foreshortened, and, of themselves, warped the devoted boats towards the planted irons in him; though now for a moment the whale drew aside a little, as if to

rally for a more tremendous charge. Seizing that opportunity, Ahab
first paid out more line: and then was rapidly hauling and jerking in
upon it again—hoping that way to disencumber it of some snarls
—when lo!—a sight more savage than the embattled teeth of sharks!

Caught and twisted—corkscrewed in the mazes of the line, loose
harpoons and lances, with all their bristling barbs and points, came
flashing and dripping up to the chocks in the bows of Ahab's boat.
Only one thing could be done. Seizing the boat-knife, he critically
reached within—through—and then, without—the rays of steel;
dragged in the line beyond, passed it, inboard, to the bowsman, and
then, twice sundering the rope near the chocks—dropped the intercepted fagot of steel into the sea; and was all fast again. That instant,
the White Whale made a sudden rush among the remaining tangles of
the other lines; by so doing, irresistibly dragged the more involved
boats of Stubb and Flask towards his flukes; dashed them together like
two rolling husks on a surf-beaten beach, and then, diving down into
the sea, disappeared in a boiling maelstrom, in which, for a space, the
odorous cedar chips of the wrecks danced round and round, like the
grated nutmeg in a swiftly stirred bowl of punch.

While the two crews were yet circling in the waters, reaching out
after the revolving line-tubs, oars, and other floating furniture, while
aslope little Flask bobbed up and down like an empty vial, twitching
his legs upwards to escape the dreaded jaws of sharks; and Stubb was
lustily singing out for some one to ladle him up; and while the old
man's line—now parting—admitted of his pulling into the creamy pool
to rescue whom he could;—in that wild simultaneousness of a thousand concreted perils,—Ahab's yet unstricken boat seemed drawn up
towards heaven by invisible wires,—as, arrow-like, shooting perpen-
dicularly from the sea, the White Whale dashed his broad forehead
against its bottom, and sent it, turning over and over, into the air; till it
fell again—gunwale downwards—and Ahab and his men struggled out
from under it, like seals from a sea-side cave.

The first uprising momentum of the whale—modifying its direction
as he struck the surface—involuntarily launched him along it, to a
little distance from the centre of the destruction he had made; and
with his back to it, he now lay for a moment slowly feeling with his
flukes from side to side; and when ever a stray oar, bit of plank, the
least chip or crumb of the boats touched his skin, his tail swiftly drew

back, and came sideways smiting the sea. But soon, as if satisfied that his work for that time was done, he pushed his pleated forehead through the ocean, and trailing after him the intertangled lines, continued his leeward way at a traveller's methodic pace.

As before, the attentive ship having descried the whole fight, again came bearing down to the rescue, and dropping a boat, picked up the floating mariners, tubs, oars, and whatever else could be caught at, and safely landed them on her decks. Some sprained shoulders, wrists, and ankles; livid contusions; wrenched harpoons and lances; inextricable intricacies of rope; shattered oars and planks; all these were there; but no fatal or even serious ill seemed to have befallen any one. As with Fedallah the day before, so Ahab was now found grimly clinging to his boat's broken half, which afforded a comparatively easy float; nor did it so exhaust him as the previous day's mishap.

But when he was helped to the deck, all eyes were fastened upon him; as instead of standing by himself he still half-hung upon the shoulder of Starbuck, who had thus been the foremost to assist him. His ivory leg had been snapped off, leaving but one short sharp splinter.

"Aye, aye, Starbuck, 'tis sweet to lean sometimes, be the leaner who he will; and would old Ahab had leaned oftener than he has."

"The ferrule has not stood, Sir," said the carpenter, now coming up; "I put good work into that leg."

"But no bones broken, Sir, I hope," said Stubb with true concern.

"Aye! and all splintered to pieces, Stubb!—d'ye see it.—But even with a broken bone, old Ahab is untouched; and I account no living bone of mine one jot more me, than this dead one that's lost. Nor White Whale, nor man, nor fiend, can so much as graze old Ahab in his own proper and inaccessible being. Can any lead touch yonder floor, any mast scrape yonder roof?—Aloft there! which way?"

"Dead to leeward, Sir."

"Up helm, then; pile on the sail again, ship keepers! down the rest of the spare boats and rig them—Mr. Starbuck away, and muster the boat's crews."

"Let me first help thee towards the bulwarks, Sir."

"Oh, oh, oh! how this splinter gores me now! Accursed fate! that the unconquerable captain in the soul should have such a craven mate!"

"Sir?"

"My body, man, not thee. Give me something for a cane—there, that shivered lance will do. Muster the men. Surely I have not seen him yet. By heaven it cannot be!—missing?—quick! call them all."

The old man's hinted thought was true. Upon mustering the company, the Parsee was not there.

"The Parsee!" cried Stubb—"he must have been caught in—"

"The black vomit wrench thee!—run all of ye above, alow, cabin, forecastle—find him—not gone—not gone!"

But quickly they returned to him with the tidings that the Parsee was nowhere to be found.

"Aye, Sir," said Stubb—"caught among the tangles of your line—I thought I saw him dragging under."

"*My* line! *my* line? Gone?—gone? What means that little word?— What death-knell rings in it, that old Ahab shakes as if he were the belfry. The harpoon, too!—toss over the litter there,—d'ye see it?—the forged iron, men, the White Whale's—no, no, no,—blistered fool! this hand did dart it!—'tis in the fish!—Aloft there! Keep him nailed— Quick!—all hands to the rigging of the boats—collect the oars—harpooneers! the irons, the irons!—hoist the royals higher—a pull on all the sheets!—helm there! steady, steady for your life! I'll ten times girdle the unmeasured globe; yea and dive straight through it, but I'll slay him yet!"

"Great God! but for one single instant show thyself," cried Starbuck; "never, never wilt thou capture him, old man—In Jesus' name no more of this, that's worse than devil's madness. Two days chased; twice stove to splinters; thy very leg once more snatched from under thee; thy evil shadow gone—all good angels mobbing thee with warnings:—what more wouldst thou have?—Shall we keep chasing this murderous fish till he swamps the last man? Shall we be dragged by him to the bottom of the sea? Shall we be towed by him to the infernal world? Oh, oh,—Impiety and blasphemy to hunt him more!"

"Starbuck, of late I've felt strangely moved to thee; ever since that hour we both saw—thou know'st what, in one another's eyes. But in this matter of the whale, be the front of thy face to me as the palm of this hand—a lipless, unfeatured blank. Ahab is for ever Ahab, man. This whole act's immutably decreed. 'Twas rehearsed by thee and me a billion years before this ocean rolled. Fool! I am the Fates' lieutenant; I act under orders. Look thou, underling! that thou obeyest mine.—Stand round me, men. Ye see an old man cut down to the stump; leaning on a shivered lance; propped up on a lonely foot. 'Tis Ahab—his body's part; but Ahab's soul's a centipede, that moves upon a hundred legs. I feel strained, half stranded, as ropes that tow dismasted frigates in a gale; and I may look so. But ere I break, ye'll hear me crack; and till ye hear *that,* know that Ahab's hawser tows his purpose yet. Believe ye, men, in the things called omens? Then laugh aloud, and cry encore! For ere they drown, drowning things will twice rise to the surface; then rise again, to sink for evermore. So with Moby Dick—two days he's floated—to-morrow will be the third. Aye, men, he'll rise once more,—but only to spout his last! D'ye feel brave men, brave?"

"As fearless fire," cried Stubb.

"And as mechanical," muttered Ahab. Then as the men went forward, he muttered on:—"The things called omens! And yesterday I talked the same to Starbuck there, concerning my broken boat. Oh! how valiantly I seek to drive out of others' hearts what's clinched so fast in mine!—The Parsee—the Parsee! gone, gone? and he was to go before:—but still was to be seen again ere I could perish—How's that?—There's a riddle now might baffle all the lawyers backed by the ghosts of the whole line of judges:—like a hawk's beak it pecks my brain. *I'll, I'll* solve it, though!"

When dusk descended, the whale was still in sight to leeward.

So once more the sail was shortened, and everything passed nearly as on the previous night; only, the sound of hammers, and the hum of the grindstone was heard till nearly daylight, as the men toiled by lanterns in the complete and careful rigging of the spare boats and sharpening their fresh weapons for the morrow. Meantime, of the broken keel of Ahab's wrecked craft the carpenter made him another leg; while still as on the night before, slouched Ahab stood fixed within his scuttle; his hid, heliotrope glance anticipatingly gone backward on its dial; sat due eastward for the earliest sun.

The Chase—Third Day

The morning of the third day dawned fair and fresh, and once more the solitary night-man at the fore-mast-head was relieved by crowds of the daylight look-outs, who dotted every mast and almost every spar.

"D'ye see him?" cried Ahab; but the whale was not yet in sight.

"In his infallible wake, though; but follow that wake, that's all. Helm there; steady, as thou goest, and hast been going. What a lovely day again! were it a new-made world, and made for a summer-house to the angels, and this morning the first of its throwing open to them, a fairer day could not dawn upon that world. Here's food for thought, had Ahab time to think; but Ahab never thinks; he only feels, feels, feels; *that's* tingling enough for mortal man! to think's audacity. God only has that right and privilege. Thinking is, or ought to be, a coolness and a calmness; and our poor hearts throb, and our poor brains beat too much for that. And yet, I've sometimes thought my brain was very calm—frozen calm, this old skull cracks so, like a glass in which the contents turned to ice, and shiver it. And still this hair is growing now; this moment growing, and heat must breed it; but no, it's like that sort of common grass that will grow anywhere, between the earthy clefts of Greenland ice or in Vesuvius lava. How the wild winds blow it; they whip it about me as the torn shreds of split sails lash the tossed ship they cling to. A vile wind that has no doubt blown ere this through prison corridors and cells, and wards of hospitals, and ventilated them, and now comes blowing hither as innocent as fleeces. Out upon it!—it's tainted. Were I the wind, I'd blow no more on such a wicked, miserable world. I'd crawl somewhere to a cave, and slink there. And yet, 'tis a noble and heroic thing, the wind! who ever conquered it? In every fight it has the last and bitterest blow. Run tilting at it, and you but run through it. Ha! a coward wind that strikes stark naked men, but will not stand to receive a single blow. Even Ahab is a braver thing—a nobler thing than *that.* Would now the wind but had a body; but all the things that most exasperate and outrage mortal man, all these things are bodiless, but only bodiless as objects, not as agents. There's a most special, a most cunning, oh, a most malicious difference! And yet, I say again, and swear it now, that there's something all glorious and gracious in the wind. These warm Trade Winds, at least, that in the clear heavens blow straight on, in strong and steadfast, vigorous mildness; and veer not from their mark, however the baser currents of the sea may turn and tack, and mightiest Mississippies of the land swift and swerve about, uncertain where to go at last. And by the eternal Poles! these same Trades that so directly blow my good ship on; these Trades, or something like them—something so unchangeable, and full as strong, blow my keeled soul along! To it! Aloft there! Where d-ye see?"

"Nothing, Sir."

"Nothing! and noon at hand! The doubloon goes a-begging! See the sun! Aye, aye, it must be so. I've oversailed him. How, got the start? Aye, he's chasing *me* now; not I, *him*—that's bad; I might have known it, too. Fool! the lines—the harpoons he's towing. Aye, aye, I have run him by last night. About! about! Come down, all of ye, but the regular look outs! Man the braces!"

Steering as she had done, the wind had been somewhat on the Pequod's quarter, so that now being pointed in the reverse direction, the braced ship sailed hard upon the breeze as she rechurned the cream in her own white wake.

"Against the wind he now steers for the open jaw," murmured Starbuck to himself, as he coiled the new hauled mainbrace upon the rail. "God keep us, but already my bones feel damp within me, and from the inside wet my flesh. I misdoubt me that I disobey my God in obeying him!"

"Stand by to sway me up!" cried Ahab, advancing to the hempen basket. "We should meet him soon."

"Aye, aye, Sir," and straightway Starbuck did Ahab's bidding, and once more Ahab swung on high.

A whole hour now passed; gold-beaten out to ages. Time itself now held long breaths with keen suspense. But at last, some three points off the weather bow, Ahab descried the spout again, and instantly from the three mast-heads three shrieks went up as if the tongues of fire had voiced it.

"Forehead to forehead I meet thee, this third time, Moby Dick! On deck there!—brace sharper up; crowd her into the wind's eye. He's too far off to lower yet, Mr. Starbuck. The sails shake! Stand over that helmsman with a top-maul! So, so; he travels fast, and I must down. But let me have one more good round look aloft here at the sea; there's time for that. An old, old sight, and yet somehow so young; aye, and not changed a wink since I first saw it, a boy, from the sand-hills of Nantucket! The same!—the same!—the same to Noah as to me. There's a soft shower to leeward. Such lovely leewardings! They must lead somewhere—to something else than common land, more palmy than the palms. Leeward! the White Whale goes that way; look to wind-ward, then; the better if the bitterer quarter. But good bye, good bye, old mast-head! What's this?—green? aye, tiny mosses in these warped cracks. No such green weather stains on Ahab's head! There's the difference now between man's old age and matter's. But aye, old mast, we both grow old together; sound in our hulls, though, are we not, my ship? Aye, minus a leg, that's all. By heaven this dead wood has the better of my life flesh every way. I can't compare with it; and I've known some ships made of dead trees outlast the lives of men made of the most vital stuff of vital fathers. What's that he said? he should still go before me, my pilot; and yet to be seen again? But where? Will I have eyes at the bottom of the sea, supposing I descend those endless stairs? and all night I've been sailing from him, wherever he did sink to. Aye, aye, like many more thou told'st direful truth as touching thyself, O Parsee; but, Ahab, there thy shot fell short. Good by, mast-head—keep a good eye upon the whale, the while I'm gone. We'll talk to-morrow, nay, to-night, when the White Whale lies down there, tied by head and tail."

He gave the word; and still gazing round him, was steadily lowered through the cloven blue air to the deck.

In due time the boats were lowered; but as standing in his shallop's stern, Ahab just hovered upon the point of the descent, he waved to the mate,—who held one of the tackle-ropes on dick—and bade him pause.

"Starbuck!"

"Sir?"

"For the third time my soul's ship starts upon this voyage, Starbuck."

"Aye, Sir, thou wilt have it so."

"Some ships sail from their ports, and ever afterwards are missing, Starbuck!"

"Truth, Sir: saddest truth."

"Some men die at ebb tide; some at low water; some at the full of the flood;—and I feel now like a billow that's all one crested comb, Starbuck. I am old;—shake hands with me, man."

Their hands met; their eyes fastened; Starbuck's tears the glue.

"Oh, my captain, my captain!—noble heart—go not—go not!—see, it's a brave man that weeps; how great the agony of the persuasion then!"

"Lower away!"—cried Ahab, tossing the mate's arm from him. "Stand by the crew!"

In an instant the boat was pulling round close under the stern.

"The sharks! the sharks!" cried a voice from the low cabin-window there; "O master, my master, come back!"

But Ahab heard nothing; for his own voice was high-lifted then; and the boat leaped on.

Yet the voice spake true; for scarce had he pushed from the ship, when numbers of sharks, seemingly rising from out the dark waters beneath the hull, maliciously snapped at the blades of the oars, every time they dipped in the water; and in this way accompanied the boat with their bites. It is a thing not uncommonly happening to the whale-boats in those swarming seas; the sharks at times apparently following them in the same prescient way that vultures hover over the banners of marching regiments in the east. But these were the first sharks that had been observed by the Pequod since the White Whale had been descried; and whether it was that Ahab's crew were all such tiger-yellow barbarians, and therefore their flesh more musky to the senses of the sharks—a matter sometimes well known to affect them, —however it was, they seemed to follow that one boat without molesting the others.

"Heart of wrought steel!" murmured Starbuck gazing over the side, and following with his eyes the receding boat—"canst thou yet ring boldly to that sight?—lowering thy keel among ravening sharks, and followed by them, open-mouthed to the chase; and this the critical third day?—For when three days flow together in one continuous intense pursuit; be sure the first is the morning, the second the noon, and the third the evening and the end of that thing—be that end what it may. Oh! my God! what is this that shoots through me, and leaves me so deadly calm, yet expectant,—fixed at the top of a shudder! Future things swim before me, as in empty outlines and skeletons; all the past is somehow grown dim. Mary, girl! thou fadest in pale glories behind me; boy! I seem to see but thy eyes grown wondrous blue. Strangest problems of life seem clearing; but clouds sweep between —Is my journey's end coming? My legs feel faint; like his who has footed it all day. Feel thy heart,—beats it yet?—Stir thyself, Starbuck!—stave it off—move, move! speak aloud!—Mast-head there! See ye my boy's hand on the hill?—Crazed;—aloft there!—keep thy keenest eye upon the boats:—mark well the whale!—Ho! again!—drive off that hawk! see he pecks—he tears the vane"—pointing to the red flag flying at the main-truck—"Ha! he soars away with it!—Where's the old man now? See'st thou that sight, oh Ahab!—shudder, shudder!"

The boats had not gone very far, when by a signal from the mast-heads—a downward pointed arm, Ahab knew that the whale had sounded; but intending to be near him at the next rising, he held on his way a little sideways from the vessel; the becharmed crew maintaining the profoundest silence, as the head-beat waves hammered and hammered against the opposing bow.

"Drive, drive in your nails, oh ye waves! to their uttermost heads drive them in! ye but strike a thing without a lid; and no coffin and no hearse can be mine:—and hemp only can kill me! Ha! ha!"

Suddenly the waters around them slowly swelled in broad circles; then quickly upheaved, as if sideways sliding from a submerged berg of ice, swiftly rising to the surface. A low rumbling sound was heard; a subterraneous hum; and then all held their breaths; as bedraggled with trailing ropes, and harpoons, and lances, a vast form shot lengthwise, but obliquely from the sea. Shrouded in a thin drooping veil of mist, it hovered for a moment in the rainbowed air; and then fell swamping back into the deep. Crushed thirty feet upwards, the waters flashed for an instant like heaps of fountains, then brokenly sank in a shower of flakes, leaving the circling surface creamed like new milk round the marble trunk of the whale.

"Give way!" cried Ahab to the oarsmen, and the boats darted forward to the attack; but maddened by yesterday's fresh irons that corroded in him, Moby Dick seemed combinedly possessed by all the angels that fell from heaven. The wide tiers of welded tendons overspreading his broad white forehead, beneath the transparent skin, looked knitted together; as head on, he came churning his tail among the boats; and once more flailed them apart; spilling out the irons and lances from the two mates' boats, and dashing in one side of the upper part of their bows, but leaving Ahab's almost without a scar.

While Daggoo and Queequeg were stopping the strained planks; and as the whale swimming out from them, turned, and showed one entire flank as he shot by them again; at that moment a quick cry went up. Lashed round and round to the fish's back; pinioned in the turns upon turns in which, during the past night, the whale had reeled the involutions of the lines around him, the half torn body of the Parsee was seen; his sable raiment frayed to shreds; his distended eyes turned full upon old Ahab.

The harpoon dropped from his hand.

"Befooled, befooled!"—drawing in a long lean breath—"Aye, Parsee! I see thee again.—Aye, and thou goest before; and this, *this* then is the hearse that thou didst promise. But I hold thee to the last letter of thy word. Where is the second hearse? Away, mates, to the ship! those boats are useless now; repair them if ye can in time, and return to me; if not, Ahab is enough to die—Down, men! the first thing that but offers to jump from this boat I stand in, that thing I harpoon. Ye are not other men, but my arms and my legs; and so obey me.— Where's the whale? gone down again?"

But he looked too nigh the boat; for as if bent upon escaping with the corpse he bore, and as if the particular place of the last encounter had been but a stage in his leeward voyage, Moby Dick was now again steadily swimming forward; and had almost passed the ship,—which thus far had been sailing in the contrary direction to him, though for the present her headway had been stopped. He seemed swimming with his utmost velocity, and now only intent upon pursuing his own straight path in the sea.

"Oh! Ahab," cried Starbuck, "not too late is it, even now, the third day, to desist. See! Moby Dick seeks thee not. It is thou, thou, that madly seekest him!"

Setting sail to the rising wind, the lonely boat was swiftly impelled to leeward, by both oars and canvas. And at last when Ahab was sliding by the vessel, so near as plainly to distinguish Starbuck's face as he leaned over the rail, he hailed him to turn the vessel about, and follow him, not too swiftly, at a judicious interval. Glancing upwards, he saw Tashtego, Queequeg, and Daggoo, eagerly mounting to the three mast-heads; while the oarsmen were rocking in the two staved boats which had but just been hoisted to the side, and were busily at work in repairing them. One after the other, through the portholes, as he sped, he also caught flying glimpses of Stubb and Flask, busying themselves on deck among bundles of new irons and lances. As he saw all this; as he heard the hammers in the broken boats; far other hammers seemed driving a nail into his heart. But he rallied. And now marking that the vane or flag was gone from the main-mast-head, he shouted to Tashtego, who had just gained that perch, to descend again for another flag, and a hammer and nails, and so nail it to the mast.

Whether fagged by the three days' running chase, and the resistance to his swimming in the knotted hamper he bore; or whether it was some latent deceitfulness and malice in him: whichever was true, the White Whale's way now began to abate, as it seemed, from the boat so rapidly nearing him once more; though indeed the whale's last start had not been so long a one as before. And still as Ahab glided over the waves the unpitying sharks accompanied him; and so pertinaciously stuck to the boat; and so continually bit at the plying oars, that the blades became jagged and crunched, and left small splinters in the sea, at almost every dip.

"Heed them not! those teeth but give new rowlocks to your oars. Pull on! 'tis the better rest, the shark's jaw than the yielding water."

"But at every bite, Sir, the thin blades grow smaller and smaller!"

"They will last long enough! pull on!—But who can tell"—he muttered—"whether these sharks swim to feast on the whale or on Ahab?—But pull on! Aye, all alive, now—we near him. The helm! take the helm; let me pass,"—and so saying, two of the oarsmen helped him forward to the bows of the still flying boat.

At length as the craft was cast to one side, and ran ranging along with the White Whale's flank, he seemed strangely oblivious of its advance—as the whale sometimes will—and Ahab was fairly within the smoky mountain mist, which, thrown off from the whale's spout, curled round his great, Monadnock hump; he was even thus close to him; when, with body arched back, and both arms lengthwise highlifted to the poise, he darted his fierce iron, and his far fiercer curse into the hated whale. As both steel and curse sank to the socket, as if sucked into a morass, Moby Dick sideways writhed; spasmodically rolled his nigh flank against the bow, and, without staving a hole in it, so suddenly canted the boat over, that had it not been for the elevated part of the gunwale to which he then clung, Ahab would once more have been tossed into the sea. As it was, three of the oarsmen—who foreknew not the precise instant of the dart, and were therefore unprepared for its effects—these were flung out; but so fell, that, in an instant two of them clutched the gunwale again, and rising to its level on a combing wave, hurled themselves bodily inboard again; the third man helplessly dropping astern, but still afloat and swimming.

Almost simultaneously, with a mighty volition of ungraduated, instantaneous swiftness, the White Whale darted through the weltering sea. But when Ahab cried out to the steersman to take new turns with the line, and hold it so; and commanded the crew to turn round on their seats, and tow the boat up to the mark; the moment the treacherous line felt that double strain and tug, it snapped in the empty air!

"What breaks in me? Some sinew cracks!—'tis whole again; oars! oars! Burst in upon him!"

Hearing the tremendous rush of the sea-crashing boat, the whale wheeled round to present his blank forehead at bay; but in that evolution, catching sight of the nearing black hull of the ship; seemingly seeing in it the source of all his persecutions; bethinking it—it may be—a larger and nobler foe; of a sudden, he bore down upon its advancing prow, smiting his jaws amid fiery showers of foam.

Ahab staggered; his hand smote his forehead. "I grow blind; hands! stretch out before me that I may yet grope my way. Is't night?"

"The whale! The ship!" cried the cringing oarsmen.

"Oars! oars! Slope downwards to thy depths, O sea, that ere it be for ever too late, Ahab may slide this last, last time upon his mark! I see: the ship! the ship! Dash on, my men! Will ye not save my ship?"

But as the oarsmen violently forced their boat through the sledge-hammering seas, the before whale-smitten bow-ends of two planks burst through, and in an instant almost, the temporarily disabled boat lay nearly level with the waves; its half-wading, splashing crew, trying hard to stop the gap and bale out the pouring water.

Meantime, for that one beholding instant, Tashtego's mast-head hammer remained suspended in his hand; and the red flag, half-wrapping him as with a plaid, then streamed itself straight out from him, as his own forward-flowing heart; while Starbuck and Stubb, standing upon the bowsprit beneath, caught sight of the down-coming monster just as soon as he.

"The whale, the whale! Up helm, up helm! Oh, all ye sweet powers of air, now hug me close! Let not Starbuck die, if die he must, in a woman's fainting fit. Up helm, I say—ye fools, the jaw! the jaw! Is this the end of all my bursting prayers? all my life-long fidelities? Oh, Ahab, Ahab, lo, thy work. Steady! helmsman, steady. Nay, nay! Up helm again! He turns to meet us! Oh, his unappeasable brow drives on towards one, whose duty tells him he cannot depart. My God, stand by me now!"

"Stand not by me, but stand under me, whoever you are that will now help Stubb; for Stubb, too, sticks here. I grin at thee, thou grinning whale! Who ever helped Stubb, or kept Stubb awake, but Stubb's own unwinking eye? And now poor Stubb goes to bed upon a mattress that is all too soft; would it were stuffed with brushwood! I grin at thee, thou grinning whale! Look ye, sun, moon, and stars! I call ye assassins of as good a fellow as ever spouted up his ghost. For all that, I would yet ring glasses with ye, would ye but hand the cup! Oh, oh! oh, oh! thou grinning whale, but there'll be plenty of gulping soon! Why fly ye not, O Ahab! For me, off shoes and jacket to it; let Stubb die in his drawers! A most mouldy and over salted death, though;—cherries! cherries! cherries! Oh, Flask, for one red cherry ere we die!"

"Cherries? I only wish that we were where they grow. Oh, Stubb, I hope my poor mother's drawn my part-pay ere this; if not, few coppers will now come to her, for the voyage is up."

From the ship's bows, nearly all the seamen now hung inactive; hammers, bits of plank, lances, and harpoons, mechanically retained in their hands, just as they had darted from their various employments; all their enchanted eyes intent upon the whale, which from side to side strangely vibrating his predestinating head, sent a broad bank of overspreading semicircular foam before him as he rushed. Retribution, swift vengeance, eternal malice were in his whole aspect, and spite of all that mortal man could do, the solid white buttress of his forehead smote the ship's starboard bow, till men and timbers reeled. Some fell flat upon their faces. Like dislodged trucks, the heads of the harpooners aloft shook on their bull-like necks. Through the breach, they heard the waters pour, as mountain torrents down a flume.

"The ship! The hearse!—the second hearse!" cried Ahab from the boat; "its wood could only be American!"

Diving beneath the settling ship, the whale ran quivering along its keel; but turning under water, swiftly shot to the surface again, far off the other bow, but within a few yards of Ahab's boat, where, for a time, he lay quiescent.

"I turn my body from the sun. What ho, Tashtego! let me hear thy hammer. Oh! ye three unsurrendered spires of mine; thou uncracked keel; and only god-bullied hull; thou firm deck, and haughty helm, and Pole-pointed prow,—death-glorious ship! must ye then perish, and without me? Am I cut off from the last fond pride of meanest shipwrecked captains? Oh, lonely death on lonely life! Oh, now I feel my topmost greatness lies in my topmost grief. Ho, ho! from all your furthest bounds, pour ye now in, ye bold billows of my whole foregone life, and top this one piled comber of my death! Towards thee I roll, thou all-destroying but unconquering whale; to the last I grapple with thee; from hell's heart I stab at thee; for hate's sake I spit my last breath at thee. Sink all coffins and all hearses to one common pool! and since neither can be mine, let me then tow to pieces, while still chasing thee, though tied to thee, thou damned whale! *Thus*, I give up the spear!"

The harpoon was darted; the stricken whale flew forward; with igniting velocity the line ran through the groove;—ran foul. Ahab stooped to clear it; he did clear it; but the flying turn caught him round the neck, and voicelessly as Turkish mutes bowstring their victim, he was shot out of the boat, ere the crew knew he was gone. Next instant, the heavy eye-splice in the rope's final end flew out of the stark-empty tub, knocked down an oarsman, and smiting the sea, disappeared in its depths.

For an instant, the tranced boat's crew stood still; then turned, "The ship? Great God, where is the ship?" Soon they through dim, bewildering mediums saw her sidelong fading phantom, as in the gaseous Fata Morgana; only the uppermost masts out of water; while fixed by infatuation, or fidelity, or fate, to their once lofty perches, the pagan harpooners still maintained their sinking look-outs on the sea. And now, concentric circles seized the long boat itself, and all its crew, and each floating oar, and every lance-pole, and spinning, animate and inanimate, all round and round in one vortex, carried the smallest chip of the Pequod out of sight.

But as the last whelmings intermixingly poured themselves over the sunken head of the Indian at the main-mast, leaving a few inches of the erect spar yet visible, together with long steaming yards of the flag, which calmly undulated, with ironical coincidings, over the destroying billows they almost touched;—at that instant, a red arm and a hammer hovered backwardly uplifted in the open air, in the act of nailing the flag faster and yet faster to the subsiding spar. A sky-hawk that tauntingly had followed the main-truck downwards from its natural home among the stars, pecking at the flag, and incommoding Tashtego there; this bird now chanced to intercept its broad fluttering wing between the hammer and the wood; and simultaneously feeling that etherial thrill, the submerged savage beneath, in his death-gasp, kept his hammer frozen there; and so the bird of heaven, with archangelic shrieks and his imperial beak thrust upwards, and his whole captive form folded in the flag of Ahab, went down with his ship, which, like Satan, would not sink to hell till she had dragged a living part of heaven along with her, and helmeted herself with it.

Now small fowls flew screaming over the yet yawning gulf; a sullen white surf beat against its steep sides; then all collapsed, and the great shroud of the sea rolled on as it rolled five thousand years ago.

SPORTS MISCELLANY

Growing up American must sometimes create the impression that the world of sport is bounded by baseball, basketball, and football. But in this section we can read works that indicate just how parochial this view is. The house of sport has many mansions, and the skimpiness of the selections dealing with basketball and track indicates that not all sports are as frequent subjects of literature as are baseball, football, and, surprisingly perhaps, boxing.

One of the unanticipated discoveries made while compiling this anthology was that Robert Francis may well be our greatest poet of sport. We have here four more of his poems, which combine precise observation with subtle suggestions that sport can be understood in a more universal context. The moving last lines of "That Dark Other Mountain" would especially illustrate this point as would also the short story by Carson McCullers which takes horse racing as its subject.

Po Chu-I is quoted here as a representative of the T'ang Dynasty of China (A.D. 618–907), one of the great poetic periods in all history.

Special attention should be paid to "The Yachts" by William Carlos Williams, one of the most important modern American poets. Like the poems of Robert Francis, this one moves from close scrutiny of detail to more general observation, with the difference that, in this case, the details are put in a social rather than a cosmic context. Thus the pleasures of yachting are gradually seen to exist, almost as though in a nightmare, in the midst of a sea of agonized faces which Williams understands in a profoundly original way as, "the horror of the race [which] dawns staggering the mind. . . ."

The poems on swimming by Maxine W. Kumin, tennis by Gwendolyn Brooks, surfing by Judith Wright, and golf by John Betjeman may lack the depth of Williams' extraordinary poem, but they each convey the truth and pleasure of sports.

Lawrence Ferlinghetti returns us to the poetic strategy of moving from part to whole. In this instance the poet is like an acrobat, a "little charleychaplin man" trying his hardest to catch the abstraction, Beauty.

The most popular game in the world is soccer, known to most of the world as football. No other sport has as many fans; yet in the United States, soccer has only recently shown signs of sharing in this global popularity. Alan Sillitoe's "The Match" is concerned with the impact of the game on the fan. Sillitoe is anti-Establishment in his sympathies, and he writes mainly of the working class. The hard lot of the British working man creates a need for heroes and escape, but in this particular instance, the misery of Lennox is too great, and his life takes an agonizing turn for the worse.

Grace Butcher's recounting of her motorcycle odyssey is striking in its understated modesty. Also to be noted are her confident sense of herself as a woman (she allows her pigtails to stick out from her helmet) and the extreme awareness of her environment, which is so strong that it can only be called poetic.

Zen Buddhism would seem to have a tangential relationship, at best, to sport; and perhaps archery, as it is discussed in Gilbert Highet's essay, is not exactly what most people think of as sport. Nevertheless, the importance of the unconscious emerges in many sporting activities. Broken-field running in football would be an example. Or, the golf swing is notoriously difficult to perform when thought about consciously. When athletes act with tightly disciplined instinct, they are responding in a way that would please the most exacting Zen master, or coach.

ROBERT FRANCIS

HIGH DIVER

How deep is his duplicity who in a flash
Passes from resting bird to flying bird to fish,

Who momentarily is sculpture, then all motion,
Speed and splash, then climbs again to contemplation.

He is the archer who himself is bow and arrow.
He is the upper-under-world-commuting hero.

His downward going has the air of sacrifice
To some dark seaweed-bearded seagod face to face

Or goddess. Rippling and responsive lies the water
For him to contemplate, then powerfully to enter.

SAILBOAT, YOUR SECRET

Sailboat, your secret. With what dove-and-serpent
Craft you trick the old antagonist.
Trick and transpose, snaring him into sponsor.

The blusterer—his blows you twist to blessing.
Your tactics and your tack, O subtle one,
Your war, your peace—you who defer and win.

Not in obeisance, not in defiance you bow,
You bow to him, but in deep irony.
The gull's wing kisses the whitecap not more archly

Than yours. Timeless and motionless I watch
Your craftsmanship, your wiles, O skimmer-schemer,
Your losses to profit, your wayward onwardness.

SKIER

He swings down like the flourish of a pen
Signing a signature in white on white.

The silence of his skis reciprocates
The silence of the world around him.

Wind is his one competitor
In the cool winding and unwinding down.

On incandescent feet he falls
Unfalling, trailing white foam, white fire.

THAT DARK OTHER MOUNTAIN

My father could go down a mountain faster than I
Though I was first one up.
Legs braced or with quick steps he slid the gravel slopes
Where I picked cautious footholds.

Black, Iron, Eagle, Doublehead, Chocorua,
Wildcat, and Carter Dome—
He beat me down them all. And that last other mountain
And that dark other mountain.

CARSON McCULLERS

THE JOCKEY

The jockey came to the doorway of the dining room, then after a
moment stepped to one side and stood motionless, with his back to the
wall. The room was crowded, as this was the third day of the season
and all the hotels in the town were full. In the dining room bouquets of
August roses scattered their petals on the white table linen and from
the adjoining bar came a warm, drunken wash of voices. The jockey
waited with his back to the wall and scrutinized the room with
pinched, crêpy eyes. He examined the room until at last his eyes
reached a table in a corner diagonally across from him, at which three
men were sitting. As he watched, the jockey raised his chin and tilted
his head back to one side, his dwarfted body grew rigid, and his hands
stiffened so that the fingers curled inward like gray claws. Tense
against the wall of the dining room, he watched and waited in this
way.

He was wearing a suit of green Chinese silk that evening, tailored
precisely and the size of a costume outfit for a child. The shirt was
yellow, the tie striped with pastel colors. He had no hat with him and
wore his hair brushed down in a stiff, wet bang on his forehead. His
face was drawn, ageless, and gray. There were shadowed hollows at
his temples and his mouth was set in a wiry smile. After a time he was
aware that he had been seen by one of the three men he had been
watching. But the jockey did not nod; he only raised his chin still
higher and hooked the thumb of his tense hand in the pocket of his
coat.

The three men at the corner table were a trainer, a bookie, and a
rich man. The trainer was Sylvester—a large, loosely built fellow with
a flushed nose and slow blue eyes. The bookie was Simmons. The rich
man was the owner of a horse named Seltzer, which the jockey had
ridden that afternoon. The three of them drank whiskey with soda,
and a white-coated waiter had just brought on the main course of the
dinner.

It was Sylvester who first saw the jockey. He looked away quickly, put down his whiskey glass, and nervously mashed the tip of his red nose with his thumb. "It's Bitsy Barlow," he said. "Standing over there across the room. Just watching us."

"Oh, the jockey," said the rich man. He was facing the wall and he half turned his head to look behind him. "Ask him over."

"God no," Sylvester said.

"He's crazy," Simmons said. The bookie's voice was flat and without inflection. He had the face of a born gambler, carefully adjusted, the expression a permanent deadlock between fear and greed.

"Well, I wouldn't call him that exactly," said Sylvester. "I've known him a long time. He was O.K. until about six months ago. But if he goes on like this, I can't see him lasting another year. I just can't."

"It was what happened in Miami," said Simmons.

"What?" asked the rich man.

Sylvester glanced across the room at the jockey and wet the corner of his mouth with his red, fleshy tongue. "A accident. A kid got hurt on the track. Broke a leg and a hip. He was a particular pal of Bitsy's. A Irish kid. Not a bad rider, either."

"That's a pity," said the rich man.

"Yeah. They were particular friends," Sylvester said. "You would always find him up in Bitsy's hotel room. They would be playing rummy or else lying on the floor reading the sports page together."

"Well, those things happen," said the rich man.

Simmons cut into his beefsteak. He held his fork prongs downward on the plate and carefully piled on mushrooms with the blade of his knife. "He's crazy," he repeated. "He gives me the creeps."

All the tables in the dining room were occupied. There was a party at the banquet table in the center, and green-white August moths had found their way in from the night and fluttered about the clear candle flames. Two girls wearing flannel slacks and blazers walked arm in arm across the room into the bar. From the main street outside came the echoes of holiday hysteria.

"They claim that in August Saratoga is the wealthiest town per capita in the world." Silvester turned to the rich man. "What do you think?"

"I wouldn't know," said the rich man. "It may very well be so."

Daintily, Simmons wiped his greasy mouth with the tip of his forefinger. "How about Hollywood? And Wall Street—"

"Wait," said Sylvester. "He's decided to come over here."

The jockey had left the wall and was approaching the table in the corner. He walked with a prim strut, swinging out his legs in a half-circle with each step, his heels biting smartly into the red velvet carpet on the floor. On the way over he brushed against the elbow of a fat woman in white satin at the banquet table; he stepped back and bowed with dandified courtesy, his eyes quite closed. When he had crossed the room he drew up a chair and sat at a corner of the table, between Sylvester and the rich man, without a nod of greeting or a change in his set, gray face.

"Had dinner?" Sylvester asked.

"Some people might call it that." The jockey's voice was high, bitter, clear.

Sylvester put his knife and fork down carefully on his plate. The rich man shifted his position, turning sidewise in his chair and crossing his legs. He was dressed in twill riding pants, unpolished boots, and a shabby brown jacket—this was his outfit day and night in the racing season, although he was never seen on a horse. Simmons went on with his dinner.

"Like a spot of seltzer water?" asked Sylvester. "Or something like that?"

The jockey didn't answer. He drew a gold cigarette case from his pocket and snapped it open. Inside were a few cigarettes and a tiny gold penknife. He used the knife to cut a cigarette in half. When he had lighted his smoke he held up his hand to a waiter passing by the table. "Kentucky bourbon, please."

"Now, listen, Kid," said Sylvester.

"Don't Kid me."

"Be reasonable. You know you got to behave reasonable."

The jockey drew up the left corner of his mouth in a stiff jeer. His eyes lowered to the food spread out on the table, but instantly he looked up again. Before the rich man was a fish casserole, baked in a cream sauce and garnished with parsley. Sylvester had ordered eggs Benedict. There was asparagus, fresh buttered corn, and a side dish of wet black olives. A plate of French-fried potatoes was in the corner of the table before the jockey. He didn't look at the food again, but kept his pinched eyes on the centerpiece of full-blown lavender roses. "I don't suppose you remember a certain person by the name of McGuire," he said.

"Now, listen," said Sylvester.

The waiter brought the whiskey, and the jockey sat fondling the glass with his small, strong, callused hands. On his wrist was a gold link bracelet that clinked against the edge of the table. After turning the glass between his palms, the jockey suddenly drank the whiskey neat in two hard swallows. He set down the glass sharply. "No, I don't suppose your memory is that long and extensive," he said.

"Sure enough, Bitsy," said Sylvester. "What makes you act like this? You hear from the kid today?"

"I received a letter," the jockey said. "The certain person we were speaking about was taken out from the cast on Wednesday. One leg is two inches shorter than the other one. That's all."

Sylvester clucked his tongue and shook his head. "I realize how you feel."

"Do you?" The jockey was looking at the dishes on the table. His gaze passed from the fish casserole to the corn, and finally fixed on the plate of fried potatoes. His face tightened and quickly he looked up again. A rose shattered and he picked up one of the petals, bruised it between his thumb and forefinger, and put it in his mouth.

"Well, those things happen," said the rich man.

The trainer and the bookie had finished eating, but there was food left on the serving dishes before their plates. The rich man dipped his buttery fingers in his water glass and wiped them with his napkin.

"Well," said the jockey. "Doesn't somebody want me to pass them something? Or maybe perhaps you desire to reorder. Another hunk of beefsteak, gentlemen, or—"

"Please," said Sylvester. "Be reasonable. Why don't you go on upstairs?"

"Yes, why don't I?" the jockey said.

His prim voice had risen higher and there was about it the sharp whine of hysteria.

"Why don't I go up to my god-damn room and walk around and write some letters and go to bed like a good boy? Why don't I just—" He pushed his chair back and got up. "Oh, foo," he said. "Foo to you. I want a drink."

"All I can say is it's your funeral," said Sylvester. "You know what it does to you. You know well enough."

The jockey crossed the dining room and went into the bar. He ordered a Manhattan, and Sylvester watched him stand with his heels pressed tight together, his body hard as a lead soldier's, holding his little finger out from the cocktail glass and sipping the drink slowly.

"He's crazy," said Simmons. "Like I said."

Sylvester turned to the rich man. "If he eats a lamb chop, you can see the shape of it in his stomach a hour afterward. He can't sweat things out of him any more. He's a hundred and twelve and a half. He's gained three pounds since we left Miami."

"A jockey shouldn't drink," said the rich man.

"The food don't satisfy him like it used to and he can't sweat it out. If he eats a lamb chop, you can watch it tooching out in his stomach and it don't go down."

The jockey finished his Manhattan. He swallowed, crushed the cherry in the bottom of the glass with his thumb, then pushed the glass away from him. The two girls in blazers were standing at his left, their faces turned toward each other, and at the other end of the bar two touts had started an argument about which was the highest mountain in the world. Everyone was with somebody else; there was no other person drinking alone that night. The jockey paid with a brand-new fifty-dollar bill and didn't count the change.

He walked back to the dining room and to the table at which the three men were sitting, but he did not sit down. "No, I wouldn't presume to think your memory is that extensive," he said. He was so small that the edge of the table top reached almost to his belt, and when he gripped the corner with his wiry hands he didn't have to stoop. "No, you're too busy gobbling up dinners in dining rooms. You're too—"

"Honestly," begged Sylvester. "You got to behave reasonable."

"Reasonable! Reasonable!" The jockey's gray face quivered, then set in a mean, frozen grin. He shook the table so that the plates rattled, and for a moment it seemed that he would push it over. But suddenly he stopped. His hand reached out toward the plate nearest to him and deliberately he put a few of the French-fried potatoes in his mouth. He chewed slowly, his upper lip raised, then he turned and spat out the pulpy mouthful on the smooth red carpet which covered the floor. "Libertines," he said, and his voice was thin and broken. He rolled the word in his mouth, as though it had a flavor and a substance that gratified him. "You libertines," he said again, and turned and walked with his rigid swagger out of the dining room.

Sylvester shrugged one of his loose, heavy shoulders. The rich man sopped up some water that had been spilled on the tablecloth, and they didn't speak until the waiter came to clear away.

PO   CHÜ-I

HAVING CLIMBED TO THE TOPMOST PEAK
OF THE INCENSE-BURNER MOUNTAIN

Up and up, the Incense-burner Peak!
In my heart is stored what my eyes and ears perceived.
All the year—detained by official business;
To-day at last I got a chance to go.
Grasping the creepers, I clung to dangerous rocks;
My hands and feet—weary with groping for hold.
There came with me three or four friends,
But two friends dared not go further.
At last we reached the topmost crest of the Peak;
My eyes were blinded, my soul rocked and reeled.
The chasm beneath me—ten thousand feet;
The ground I stood on, only a foot wide.
If you have not exhausted the scope of seeing and hearing,
How can you realize the wideness of the world?
The waters of the River looked narrow as a ribbon,
P'ēn Castle smaller than a man's fist.
How it clings, the dust of the world's halter!
It chokes my limbs: I cannot shake it away.
Thinking of retirement, I heaved an envious sigh,
Then, with lowered head, came back to the Ants' Nest.

Translated by Arthur Waley

WILLIAM CARLOS WILLIAMS

THE YACHTS

contend in a sea which the land partly encloses
shielding them from the too-heavy blows
of an ungoverned ocean which when it chooses

tortures the biggest hulls, the best man knows
to pit against its beatings, and sinks them pitilessly.
Mothlike in mists, scintillant in the minute

brilliance of cloudless days, with broad bellying sails
they glide to the wind tossing green water
from their sharp prows while over them the crew crawls

ant-like, solicitously grooming them, releasing,
making fast as they turn, lean far over and having
caught the wind again, side by side, head for the mark.

In a well guarded arena of open water surrounded by
lesser and greater craft which, sycophant, lumbering
and flittering follow them, they appear youthful, rare

as the light of a happy eye, live with the grace
of all that in the mind is fleckless, free and
naturally to be desired. Now the sea which holds them

is moody, lapping their glossy sides, as if feeling
for some slightest flaw but fails completely.
Today no race. Then the wind comes again. The yachts

move, jockeying for a start, the signal is set and they
are off. Now the waves strike at them but they are too
well made, they slip through, though they take in canvas.

Arms with hands grasping seek to clutch at the prows.
Bodies thrown recklessly in the way are cut aside.
It is a sea of faces about them in agony, in despair

until the horror of the race dawns staggering the mind,
the whole sea become an entanglement of watery bodies
lost to the world bearing what they cannot hold. Broken,

beaten, desolate, reaching from the dead to be taken up
they cry out, failing, failing! their cries rising
in waves still as the skillful yachts pass over.

MAXINE W. KUMIN

400-METER FREE STYLE

THE GUN full swing the swimmer catapults and
   cracks

                                         s
                                          i

                                        x
feet away onto that perfect glass he catches at
a
n
  d
throws behind him scoop after scoop cunningly
   moving

                                         t
                                        h
                                        e
water back to move him forward. Thrift is his
   wonderful
  s
   e
   c
ret; he has schooled out all extravagance. No muscle

  r

                                                        i

                                                    p
    ples without compensation wrist cock to heel snap to
    h
i
    s

    mobile mouth that siphons in the air that nurtures
                                                    h

                                                        i

                                                    m
    at half an inch above sea level so to speak.
    T
h
    e

    astonishing whites of the soles of his feet rise
                                                    a

                                                        n

                                                    d
    salute us on the turns. He flips, converts, and is gone
    a
l
    l

    in one. We watch him for signs. His arms are steady
            at

                                                        t

                                                        h

                                                        e
    catch, his cadent feet tick in the stretch, they know
    t
h
    e

    lesson well. Lungs know, too; he does not list for
                                                    a

                                                        i

                                                    r
    he drives along on little sips carefully expended

    b

   u

    t

that plum red heart pumps hard cries hurt how soon

                                     i

                                      t

                                   s

near   one   more   and   makes   its   final   surge

                           TIME: 4:25:9

GWENDOLYN BROOKS

OLD TENNIS PLAYER

Refuses
To refuse the racket, to mutter No to the net.
He leans to life, conspires to give and get
Other serving yet.

JUDITH WRIGHT

THE SURFER

He thrust his joy against the weight of the sea,
climbed through, slid under those long banks of foam—
(hawthorn hedges in spring, thorns in the face stinging).
How his brown strength drove through the hollow and coil
of green-through weirs of water!
Muscle of arm thrust down long muscle of water.
And swimming so, went out of sight
where mortal, masterful, frail, the gulls went wheeling
in air, as he in water, with delight.

Turn home, the sun goes down; swimmer, turn home.
Last leaf of gold vanishes from the sea-curve.
Take the big roller's shoulder, speed and swerve.
Come to the long beach home like a gull diving.

For on the sand the grey-wolf sea lies snarling;
cold twilight wind splits the waves' hair and shows
the bones they worry in their wolf-teeth. O, wind blows,
and sea crouches on sand, fawning and mouthing;
drops there and snatches again, drops and again snatches
its broken toys, its whitened pebbles and shells.

JOHN BETJEMAN

SEASIDE GOLF

How straight it flew, how long it flew,
It cleared the rutty track
And soaring, disappeared from view
Beyond the bunker's back—
A glorious, sailing, bounding drive
That made me glad I was alive.

And down the fairway, far along
It glowed a lovely white;
I played an iron sure and strong
And clipp'd it out of sight,
And spite of grassy banks between
I knew I'd find it on the green.

And so I did. It lay content
Two paces from the pin;
A steady putt and then it went
Oh, most securely in.

The very turf rejoiced to see
That quite unprecedented three.

Ah! seaweed smells from sandy caves
And thyme and mist in whiffs,
In-coming tide, Atlantic waves
Slapping the sunny cliffs,
Lark song and sea sounds in the air
And splendor, splendor everywhere.

LAWRENCE FERLINGHETTI

CONSTANTLY RISKING ABSURDITY

Constantly risking absurdity
     and death
  whenever he performs
     above the heads
       of his audience
 the poet like an acrobat
    climbs on rime
     to a high wire of his own making
and balancing on eyebeams
    above a sea of faces
   paces his way
    to the other side of day
 performing entrechats
    and sleight-of-foot tricks
and other high theatrics
    and all without mistaking
   any thing
    for what it may not be
 For he's the super realist
     who must perforce perceive
   taut truth

before the taking of each stance or step
in his supposed advance
toward that still higher perch
where Beauty stands and waits
with gravity
to start her death-defying leap
And he
a little charleychaplin man
who may or may not catch
her fair eternal form
spreadeagled in the empty air
of existence

GRACE BUTCHER

SO MUCH DEPENDS UPON A RED TENT

The best part? There were a lot of best parts. Depends on my mood when I look back on the trip. But the very best part was being alone. I don't quite understand that about myself—this lifelong love of being alone. I suppose being an only child is a big part of it. I just grew up doing things alone. Feels natural now, as if that's how it's supposed to be. And besides, I get along with myself better than with anybody else I know.

Joyously riding alone, never having to ask someone, "Shall we stop here? Do you want to turn off up there? Are you ready to go now? Should we camp here?"—that was the best part of all.

And the riding! That's all I had to do, day after glorious day, my white BMW R60/6 under me humming quietly through the blue and green and golden world. The bike was new. I'd had it only long enough to put 1,200 miles on it and have it checked over before I took off. It was my second bike (my third, really, if you count the 125 Suzuki Challenger that I'd started racing several months before). But my second street bike.

I'd had my first lesson on a full-dress BMW R75/5 and had fallen in love with it. "When I get good enough," I said, "I'm going to have a BMW." In about a year, I figured. And I rode my little Suzuki GT 250 thousands of miles through the northeastern Ohio winter while people kept asking, "Gee, isn't it a little cold to be out on that thing?" I had to ride. I had to get good enough.

Gradually I got better. I had to get better than I was that first day in the last week of October '73. That was when I went out to the garage alone the first time to start up my first bike and ride it after an hour or so of lessons the day before in first and second gear, stopping, starting and turning (or rather, lurching, stalling and wobbling).

After 20 minutes of fumbling with switches, frantic and clumsy kicking, a call to the dealer to find out why it stalled every time I tried to put it in first gear ("Rev it up a bit," his wife said. "It's new; everything's tight"), drenched with sweat I got the bike out of the garage. Only stalled it three or four times (between the garage and the end of the driveway, that is). From there I managed to avoid going in the ditch on the far side of the road as I swung out with what I hoped would be flair and what ended up as a gigantic, lopsided wobble. I made a mental note to write the highway commissioner about widening the county roads. My self-image was in jeopardy.

But I rode over a hundred miles that day. And the next day. And the next. A week later, shivering violently in pouring rain and 45° temperatures, I took my riding test, passed and sang at the top of my voice all the 15 miles back home.

Carefully, intensely, I piled up the mileage. Carefully one day I rode far out into the country and on a deserted road red-lined it through the gears to learn what the bike could do. Carefully I puttered through shopping centers, got groceries, did errands, rode to class. Carefully I rode fast on the freeways and slowly in traffic, with interest over rain grooves and with fear over the open steel grillwork of bridges. I rode thousands of miles alone and once in a while with a friend. Carefully that following summer I learned to race motocross and won a couple of trophies in powder-puff events. Gradually I was starting to feel good enough.

And then one day I walked into the cycle shop and there stood a brand-new white BMW. I'd never seen a white one. And I said to myself (and to anyone else who would listen;). "O.K., Grace, I think you're ready for a BMW."

Two weeks later I took off on a 2,500-mile camping trip through New England and Canada. And the best thing of all was being alone with my bike the whole time. It just seemed as if that was how it was supposed to be.

I had camped once but I'd just stood and watched while a friend put up the tent, made the fire, cooked the meal and packed up afterward. So before I left I put up a red nylon tent in the orchard and practiced sleeping in it so it would seem like home on the road. Oh, I was far from the house—at least 50 yards. The rustlings in the bushes at night! Apples thunderously falling to the ground in the dark! Leaves crashing into the tent and sliding and scratching down the sides! Good thing I practiced. Zipping myself into the tent and then into the sleeping bag produced claustrophobia of alarming proportions.

But within a few days I was sleeping well. Once, when I was told it had rained the night before, I was incredulous. Hadn't heard a thing. And so, another best part of the trip was going to sleep once all the camp chores were done, feeling the earth under me. I used no mattress, just let my body melt down around any unevenness of ground under the tent. I'm Capricorn, an earth sign. If that means anything, maybe that's why sleeping on the ground felt so good. I felt as if the whole planet was under me, holding me. A secure feeling. And outside, the bike would be parked and chained as close to the tent as I could get it. It looked massive and comforting, white in the moonlight, wet with dew, chrome gleaming quietly.

Everything I needed was in one compact roll and two small saddlebags loaded up the night before I left. That morning when I came bounding out of the house in new leathers, feeling rather self-conscious, I got down to reality quickly enough when my first tug didn't even budge the loaded bike off its center stand. "Oh Lord," I said out loud, with a weak grin in case *Candid Camera* was watching.

But the second or third tug got the bike down, and I was ready to leave. Even as I coasted backward down the slight slope of the driveway into the turnaround spot, though, I realized that this bike, which was still unfamiliar and a hundred pounds heavier than my other one, would handle differently with the load it now carried.

As I rode through the town of Chardon on the way to the freeway I began to feel like a worldly biker—full leathers, a big bike and all my worldly goods (more or less) tied on behind. And when I reached Route 90 and swooped (yes, with flair even!) down the ramp, checking out traffic, sun and blue sky in one glance, I said (out loud to myself, of course), "Well, here I go!" Not an especially original line, but the situation was original enough to make up for it. I, who had never even put up a tent in all my 40 years till two weeks before—I, who had never gone on a long motorcycle trip—I who, hadn't even been riding a year—I was leaving on a 2,500-mile camping trip on my incredibly fine bike, alone. I sang Moody Blues' songs and was amazingly happy.

Like fragmented, colored pieces in a kaleidoscope, images of each day's ride turned, changed, fell through my mind as I sat those nights writing in my journal by the light of a candle lantern. I loved that piece of equipment. A candle burns with a most peaceful flame.

All the trip long, people in cars waved and smiled. Mostly kids and, strangely enough, old ladies. I wondered about that and finally decided that the gray-haired gadabouts had reached a point in their lives when they realized most strongly that what life is *for*, if it is for anything, is to find out what you do well, and then *do* it, for heaven's sake, before it's too late. One group of ladies passed me, giving me a real lift with their big smiles and their waves. And coincidentally, we happened to stop at the same restaurant farther down the road. As I was taking off my gloves and helmet and brushing out my wind-tangled hair, one came bustling over to where I still sat on the bike. "I just wanted to tell you that we think you're just the bravest thing!" she beamed. "I said to the girls, 'My, just think how the wind must be blowing in her face!' And here you are out here all by yourself. We think that's just wonderful!"

I smiled modestly accepting the Wonder Woman image, and made a long acceptance speech extolling the joys of being female and being alone, riding a motorcycle. I found myself giving the same speech many times during the following weeks, and I never tired of it.

And so it went. I'd wondered, frankly, if I'd get hassled along the way. Hell's Angels? Rape? But people were only friendly, curious, helpful, courteous, interested. The bike was such a conversation piece that I'd get into discussions at traffic lights about the virtues of a shaft-driven engine (very virtuous!); at stop signs about what those things were sticking out on the sides ("Those are the cylinders, sir"); about how ghostly quiet the bike was ("Hey, is that thing running?"), and why couldn't *all* motorcycles be that quiet.

Mostly I'd ride along not too fast, just murmuring "Oh!" and "Gee!" as I'd top another hill and be wonderstruck by the next panoramic view. Is there any more striking combination of trees than clusters of white birch, stark and chalky against dense pine forests? One day, camping by a mountain lake in Maine, I found several pieces of birch bark and wrote letters. I'd always wanted to write a letter on a piece of birch bark. I felt like the Indian I used to pretend I was when I was seven.

Beauty everywhere. Even asbestos mines in Quebec were amazingly beautiful. They looked almost like natural gray canyons, and the piled-up asbestos like white mountains. Posing themselves against the backdrop of one of these "mountains" were four boxcars—two brown, one red and one green—and before them a sweep of green and golden meadow. I just sat and looked. The beauty of the mining area was astonishing.

Sometimes I'd feel so full of the scenery that I'd stop looking at it for a while and just get into the rhythm of the road. Hills and curves, curves, curves. No, I wasn't scraping the foot pegs or the valve covers. But even now I remember the rhythm of those curves as I'd climb and plunge and letter-S through mile after mile, enclosed on both sides by deep pine forests of unforgettable scent.

Truly, I felt as if I had ridden into the pages of every motorcycle magazine I'd ever read. I could see myself—wine-red leathers, immaculate white bike, blue pack—against the pines, the startling silver-blue of lakes, red and brown and gray rock walls, the curves of flower-strewn meadows—moving through all the colors and textures.

What would I *do* with this trip, I wondered. How would I use it? What would it eventually mean to me? I pondered sometimes as I rode, or as I sat writing by candlelight, or as I washed my face with dew in the early mornings. How would I be different after I got home?

"But weren't you afraid?" People always asked that later.

No. Except once. Once in Quebec the road went off in two different directions. My way, or so I thought, went across a bridge. And the bridge was that biker's nightmare: an open metal grillwork, slippery as ice, that sends the front wheel of a bike off in every direction.

There's nothing to do but do nothing—to sit there, muscles frozen in an attitude of relaxation, hands holding the handlebars with a gentleness born of terror, for you must let the bike find its own way across.

Finally on the other side, I began to glory once more in the countryside, the road curving along a river lined with birches. But I started to notice that either the sun was going in the wrong direction or I was. After about 10 miles I stopped and checked my map. I had to go back over that damn bridge.

Quebec. How could I have forgotten that it is French-speaking? As I crossed the border I felt a combination of dismay, amusement and eagerness. I'd always thought I was pretty good in high school and college French. Now we'd see.

It was O.K. Vocabulary came rushing back. At one point, after I'd set up camp and walked away for a bit, I returned to find half a dozen adults around my bike. And I could talk to them with eagerness and enthusiasm (though probably sounding like a 6-year-old) about the mechanical wonders of the bike. *"Il n'y a pas de chaîne,"* I could say, gesturing at the chainless rear wheel and pointing out the enclosed drive shaft. I could answer questions about mileage, comfort, my route, my own brave self. *"Seule? Vous êtes seule? Vous êtes si brave!"* I liked to hear it in any language.

Once I chose a cabin instead of my tent. It was tiny, on the shore of the mighty St. Lawrence, 20 miles wide at that point and masquerading as the ocean, with tides and sea gulls and a fine driftwood tree washed up on the beach to lean against. I built a fireplace of stones, cooked, ate, then sat with a cup of my special mix of hot chocolate and coffee, watching the sun set and the tide come in.

I had been sitting in the dark, on the red-brown sand, my back against the water-washed smoothness of the tree trunk. But gradually I slumped farther and farther down till just my head was against the tree and my body relaxed in the sand. My fire was only embers, an orange crescent of moon had brightened with the approach of darkness, the tide had come to within a few yards of my feet. I lay there for a long time, scarcely moving. I could not have been more content.

There were times when I could escape my own observation. So often, perhaps because of my obsession with writing, I found myself mentally recording something I was in the process of doing as if I'd already done it, picturing myself telling someone about it in the future. It was hard sometimes not to feel as if I were constantly posing for some invisible photographer. It was hard to get away from *watching* myself at some beautiful spot, and simply *be* there.

But here, or on the night shore of a mountain lake listening to the loons, or wrapped in the sensuous golden day that seemed to pour itself down over the Vermont hills as I curved and flowed along the black and gray roads—here, on this trip was a kind of spontaneity that I'd never experienced. And my contentment had no particular structure other than knowing that I'd camp somewhere late in the afternoon and leave again sometime in the morning. No structure. No telephone ringing. No papers to grade. Nothing to do but tend to my bike and myself. Nothing to do day after shining blue day but ride. Except for a few calls home to my teen-age son, no one knew where I was. And for once, I didn't care that no one knew where to find me or when I'd be back.

I'd look down at the great silver sunbursts of my cylinders, feel the power waiting quietly under my right hand. Everything I could possibly need was in my blue pack, my black saddlebags. I could feel the sun through the leathers, smell the scent of pine for days.

My old aunt and uncle in their farmhouse on 150 acres in the Adirondacks. Hadn't seen them for years. Eighty-five years old he is, and his big-game-hunting license was on the dresser in the room where I slept. My aunt cooked for me and reminisced about my parents and made me feel loved. I rode away feeling I'd found part of my family again.

"Hi! Nice bike," said the guy at the stoplight somewhere in New Hampshire. "You should take those metal covers off your plugs because they'll short out in a rainstorm. Mine did when I took a trip back in '72."

"What part of Ohio you from? I'm from Cincinnati," said the boy wearing the cross-country T-shirt in the restaurant parking lot somewhere in western New York. So we talked about cross-country running and cross-country riding and how neat they both were.

"By cracky," said the white-haired, pleasant gentleman in the tiny post office in Somewhere, Maine (people *do* say "by cracky" in New England, by cracky). "I got me this son of a gun of a crick in my back yesterday morning—don't your back bother you on that machine?"

The people. That was another best part. One old couple outside an old inn, standing, looking at my bike. I spoke to them as I was leaving, and they offered to tear some pages out of their where-to-camp book for me. ("I have my own, thanks, but I sure do appreciate. . . .")

And the gas-station attendant in Quebec who answered my questions about the white "mountains" and sent his son inside to get me a piece of asbestos—shiny black rock with what looks like cotton fibers sticking out of it—so I could show it to my friends back home.

And the two little boys, whose grandparents ran the campgrounds, showing me the best, prettiest, most isolated spot by a stream to pitch my tent, and who ran along with me a mile or so as I jogged for a while that evening.

And the three adults who'd seen my bike in a restaurant parking lot and came in, looking for someone with a helmet who must belong to the bike so they could ask questions about how I liked it. "It's not your *husband's?* It's not your *boy friend's?* It's *yours?*"

How nicely tired I was each night after eight hours or so on the road. How early I went to bed, and how early I woke and with what eagerness! Moving carefully inside my red tent in the morning, drops of condensation clinging like rubies to the sides, gleaming in the morning light. Fold up the tent wet—it'd dry in my pack from the heat of the sun on that day's ride. I was glad the tent was red. Every morning started with a glow.

I washed and polished the bike when it needed it or when I felt the urge. Very soothing to rub and polish the long dazzling pipes, the plain clean lines of the tank and fenders. Changed plugs once. Changed the oil once. Had the steering-head bearings tightened once. Put air in the tires once or twice. The bike gave a lot and asked little.

I always had some what-ifs on my mind. What if the bike breaks down? New bikes don't break down. What if there are no gas stations? There are *always* gas stations. What if a runaway logging truck comes careening around a curve on the wrong side of the road up there in the middle of nowhere?

My long hair is always in pigtails when I ride, and sometimes they blow in my face because my windshield changes the airflow. I like motorists to know I am female, so I don't tuck my hair under my helmet. And as a result, I've never yet experienced any of the hostility that male bikers so often report. But one day I thought, "The heck with it. I'll just tie my hair back. It'll be out of the way." And shortly after that I stopped at a gas station to ask directions. Walked in without taking off my helmet and goggles as I nearly always do. And the station attendant said pleasantly enough, "Yes, sir, what can I do for you?" Back came the pigtails and my identity.

Some guy on a very noisy bike appeared alongside once and nodded and smiled as if he thought he'd found a traveling companion. I was annoyed. The noise of his engine compared to mine soon gave me a headache. And the last thing I wanted on my trip was company. Doing it alone was the whole point. Finally we rode in under the golden arches of that famous and ubiquitous restaurant, our first chance to talk since he'd joined me. "Hope you don't mind my boogieing along with you," he said. "Well," I answered, "as a matter of fact. . . ." And I just told him in a friendly way how it was with me. "Oh, O.K. That's cool," he said and went boogieing on his way. No problem.

As one man put it someplace where I stopped for gas, "To see a woman like you on a bike like that . . . well, you have all my respect. I can't imagine any guy would ever hassle you." And none ever did. I'm 5 feet 6 inches, 115 pounds. It wasn't my size that kept anyone from bothering me. It was something else. It was just what I was doing, I guess.

Busy, I sometimes felt very busy on my trip, once I'd stopped for the day. Unloading the bike, setting up camp, making a fire if I chose to, cooking, eating, cleaning up, arranging stuff in the tent, writing after all was taken care of—there seemed to be a great deal to do, and darkness seemed to come quickly. I was seldom awake after 10 P.M., seldom slept past five or six.

Making a fire that would burn right gave me great pleasure. I had to scrounge wood, and then stones with which to confine it. I had to be patient and not try to cook over the first high flames.

Once, I cooked a mixture of hamburger, hot dog, olives, cucumbers, egg and a can of pea soup, because that's what I had. It was delicious.

Once, by a river I found a thin flat stone to turn the fried eggs since I had no spatula. And I scoured the utensils with sand and dirt. It all made sense.

One thing I did not care for was threatening weather, riding with frequent glances up and around, checking the ominous clouds, always wondering if I should stop or keep going. But the weather was, on the whole, quite fine. I was rained in only one day, and that happened to be the time along the St. Lawrence that I had chosen the cabin instead of my tent.

I was quite happy at being rained in. The previous day's ride had covered only about 100 miles, all against a huge, hot wind, and I was glad for a cool rainy day. I'd ridden in a little rain to the nearby town and brought back enough food for six people. I lay on the bed, which nearly filled the one-room cabin, gazed out at the great river, whose endless sound filled my head, quieting me.

> *Gray sky, gray water,*
> *Creating no horizon.*
> *Where does the world end?*

I remembered a haiku I'd written years back. Sensuously, I ate, dozed, ate, wrote postcards, dozed, ate, wrote and finally slept. Everyone needs such days.

Sometimes I was disappointed to see what tourists call "camping." Camping at some sites I saw would have been like living in apartments, only outside. Numbered cubbyholes with bushes instead of walls. TV. Radio. Women walking around in bathrobes with their hair in rollers. Electric razors. I didn't stop at those places.

One beautiful warm, clear morning I just got up, put on shorts and a T-shirt and walked into the surprisingly warm water of a mountain lake in Quebec. It was just sunrise; no one was around. Briefly the thought entered my mind, "Should I go swimming here alone?" I answered myself, "Yes, do it. For once, be different. Forget about the shoulds and shouldn'ts for a while." I felt exhilarated and peaceful at the same time. I wish there were more lakes at sunrise in life.

When I came back across the border, feeling tense and excited at the crossing as if I were a spy, the friendly customs man talked bikes to me a bit as if to disarm me, then sprang *the* question: "What did you bring back with you that you didn't have when you came over?" I thought hard, desperately wanting to be honest. "Uh, two apples, two peaches, a can of chicken and a piece of asbestos." (Oh, Lord, I was transporting *minerals* across the border!) He laughed. "Well, you didn't do much for the Canadian economy," he said and motioned me on.

Wow! I was back in the States! I could speak English again. Vermont, I love you. I was surprised at how good that simple crossing felt. The lush small farms fit just right in the valleys of Vermont. It looked differently immediately. It was the United States.

It was a fine thing, all told, to be riding all day, every day, to be alone and silent, to lay a decent fire and cook a simple meal, to sit with my back against a white birch looking out over water with a cup of coffee in my hand as the sun went down, to be gently tired from the road and comfortable on the ground under a red roof.

The big white bike was always patiently nearby, forgiving of some of my early clumsiness, always starting at a touch, quietly humming over the hills and puttering through the towns, making friends wherever we went. I would look at it last thing at night before closing my tent and first thing in the morning. This trip was only the beginning. As William Carlos Williams might have put it,

So much depends upon
a red tent
glazed with dew
beside the white
motorcycle.

ALAN SILLITOE

THE MATCH

Bristol City had played Notts County and won. Right from the kick-off Lennox had somehow known that Notts was going to lose, not through any prophetic knowledge of each home-player's performance, but because he himself, a spectator, hadn't been feeling in top form. One-track pessimism had made him godly enough to inform his mechanic friend Fred Iremonger who stood by his side: "I knew they'd bleddy-well lose, all the time."

Towards the end of the match, when Bristol scored their winning goal, the players could only just be seen, and the ball was a roll of mist being kicked about the field. Advertising boards above the stands, telling of pork-pies, ales, whiskey, cigarettes, and other delights of Saturday night, faded with the afternoon visibility.

They stood in the one-and-threes, Lennox trying to fix his eyes on the ball, to follow each one of its erratic well-kicked movements, but after ten minutes going from blurred player to player he gave it up and turned to look at the spectators massed in the rising stands that reached out in a wide arc on either side and joined dimly way out over the pitch. This proving equally futile he rubbed a clenched hand into his weak eyes and squeezed them tight, as if pain would give them more strength. Useless. All it produced was a mass of grey squares dancing before his open lids, so that when they cleared his sight was no better than before. Such an affliction made him appear more phlegmatic at a football match than Fred and most of the others round about, who spun rattles, waved hats and scarves, opened their throats wide to each fresh vacillation in the game.

During his temporary blindness the Notts' forwards were pecking and weaving around the Bristol goal and a bright slam from one of them gave rise to a false alarm, an indecisive rolling of cheers roofed in by a grey heavy sky. " What's up?" Lennox asked Fred. "Who's scored? Anybody?"

Fred was a younger man, recently married, done up in his Saturday afternoon best of sports coat, gabardine trousers and rain-mac, dark hair sleeked back with oil. "Not in a month of Sundays," he laughed, "but they had a bleddy good try, I'll tell you that."

By the time Lennox had focused his eyes once more on the players the battle had moved to Notts' goal and Bristol were about to score. He saw a player running down the field, hearing in his imagination the thud of boots on damp introdden turf. A knot of adversaries dribbled out in a line and straggled behind him at a trot. Suddenly the man with the ball spurted forward, was seen to be clear of everyone as if, in a second of time that hadn't existed to any spectator or other player, he'd been catapulted into a hallowed untouchable area before the goal posts. Lennox's heart stopped beating. He peered between two oaken unmovable shoulders that, he thought with anger, had swayed in front purposely to stop him seeing. The renegade centre-forward from the opposing side was seen, like a puppet worked by someone above the low clouds, to bring his leg back, lunge out heavily with his booted foot. "No," Lennox had time to say. "Get on to him you dozy sods. Don't let him get it in."

From being an animal pacing within the prescribed area of his defended posts, the goalkeeper turned into a leaping ape, arms and legs outstretched, then became a mere stick that swung into a curve—and missed the ball as it sped to one side and lost itself in folds of net behind him.

The lull in the general noise seemed like silence for the mass of people packed about the field. Everyone had settled it in his mind that the match, as bad as it was, would be a draw, but now it was clear that Notts, the home team, had lost. A great roar of disappointment and joy, from the thirty thousand spectators who hadn't realized that the star of Bristol City was so close, or who had expected a miracle from their own stars at the last moment, ran up the packed embankments, overflowing into streets outside where groups of people, startled at the sudden noise of an erupting mob, speculated as to which team had scored.

Fred was laughing wildly, jumping up and down, bellowing something between a cheer and a shout of hilarious anger, as if out to get his money's worth on the principle that an adverse goal was better than no goal at all. "Would you believe it?" he called at Lennox. "Would you believe it? Ninety-five thousand quid gone up like Scotch mist!"

Hardly knowing what he was doing Lennox pulled out a cigarette, lit it. "It's no good," he cursed, "they've lost. They should have walked away with the game"—adding under his breath that he must get some glasses in order to see things better. His sight was now so bad that the line of each eye crossed and converged some distance in front of him. At the cinema he was forced down to the front row, and he was never the first to recognize a pal on the street. And it spelt ruination for any football match. He could remember being able to pinpoint each player's face, and distinguish every spectator around the field, yet he still persuaded himself that he had no need of glasses and that somehow his sight would begin to improve. A more barbed occurrence connected with such eyes was that people were beginning to call him Cock-eye. At the garage where he worked the men sat down to tea-break the other day, and because he wasn't in the room one of them said: "Where's owd Cock-eye? 'Is tea'll get cold."

"What hard lines," Fred shouted, as if no one yet knew about the goal. "Would you believe it?" The cheering and booing were beginning to die down.

"That goalie's a bloody fool," Lennox swore, cap pulled low over his forehead. "He couldn't even catch a bleeding cold."

"It was dead lucky," Fred put in reluctantly, "they deserved it, I suppose"—simmering down now, the full force of the tragedy seeping through even to his newly wedded body and soul. "Christ, I should have stayed at home with my missis. I'd a bin warm there, I know that much. I might even have cut myself a chunk of hearthrug pie if I'd have asked her right!"

The laugh and wink were intended for Lennox, who was still in the backwater of his personal defeat. "I suppose that's all you think of these days," he said wryly.

" 'Appen I do, but I don't get all that much of it, I can tell you." It was obvious though that he got enough to keep him in good spirits at a cold and disappointing football match.

"Well," Lennox pronounced, "all that'll alter in a bit. You can bet on that."

"Not if I know it," Fred said with a broad smile. "And I reckon it's better after a bad match than if I didn't come to one."

"You never said a truer word about bad," Lennox said. He bit his lip with anger. "Bloody team. They'd even lose at blow football." A woman behind, swathed in a thick woollen scarf coloured white and black like the Notts players, who had been screaming herself hoarse in support of the home team all the afternoon was almost in tears at the adverse goal. "Foul! Foul! Get the dirty lot off the field. Send 'em back to Bristol where they came from. Foul! Foul I tell yer."

People all around were stamping feet dead from the cold, having for more than an hour staved off its encroachment into their limbs by the hope of at least one home-team win before Christmas. Lennox could hardly feel his, hadn't the will to help them back to life, especially in face of an added force to the bitter wind, and a goal that had been given away so easily. Movement on the pitch was now desultory, for there were only ten minutes of play left to go. The two teams knotted up towards one goal, then spread out around an invisible ball, and moved down the field again, back to the other with no decisive result. It seemed that both teams had accepted the present score to be the final state of the game, as though all effort had deserted their limbs and lungs.

"They're done for," Lennox observed to Fred. People began leaving the ground, making a way between those who were determined to see the game out to its bitter end. Right up to the dull warbling blast of the final whistle the hard core of optimists hoped for a miraculous revival in the worn-out players.

"I'm ready when yo' are," Fred said.

"Suits me." He threw his cigarette-end to the floor and, with a grimace of disappointment and disgust, made his way up the steps. At the highest point he turned a last glance over the field, saw two players running and the rest standing around in deepening mist—nothing doing—so went on down towards the barriers. When they were on the road a great cheer rose behind, as a whistle blew the signal for a mass rush to follow.

Lamps were already lit along the road, and bus queues grew quickly in semi-darkness. Fastening up his mac Lennox hurried across the road. Fred lagged behind, dodged a trolley-bus that sloped up to the pavement edge like a man-eating monster and carried off a crowd of people to the city-centre with blue lights flickering from overhead wires. "Well," Lennox said when they came close, "after that little lot I only hope the wife's got summat nice for my tea."

"I can think of more than that to hope for," Fred said. "I'm not one to grumble about my grub."

" 'Course," Lennox sneered, "you're living on love. If you had Kit-E-Kat shoved in front of you you'd say it was a good dinner." They turned off by the recruiting centre into the heart of the Meadows, an ageing suburb of black houses and small factories. "That's what yo' think," Fred retorted, slightly offended yet too full of hope to really mind. "I'm just not one to grumble a lot about my snap, that's all."

"It wouldn't be any good if you was," Lennox rejoined, "but the grub's rotten these days, that's the trouble. Either frozen, or in tins. Nowt natural. The bread's enough to choke yer." And so was the fog: weighed down by frost it lingered and thickened, causing Fred to pull up his rain-mac collar. A man who came level with them on the same side called out derisively: "Did you ever see such a game?"

"Never in all my born days," Fred replied.

"It's always the same though," Lennox was glad to comment, "the best players are never on the field. I don't know what they pay 'em for."

The man laughed at his sound logic. "They'll 'appen get 'em on nex' wik. That'll show 'em."

"Let's hope so," Lennox called out as the man was lost in the fog. "It ain't a bad team," he added to Fred. But that wasn't what he was thinking. He remembered how he had been up before the gaffer yesterday at the garage for clouting the mash-lad who had called him Cock-eye in front of the office-girl, and the manager said that if it happened again he would get his cards. And now he wasn't sure that he wouldn't ask for them anyway. He'd never lack a job, he told himself, knowing his own worth and the sureness of his instinct when dissecting piston from cylinder, camshaft and connecting-rod and searching among a thousand-and-one possible faults before setting an engine bursting once more with life. A small boy called from the doorway of a house: "What's the score, mate?"

"They lost, two-one," he said curtly, and heard a loud clear-sounding doorslam as the boy ran in with the news. He walked with hands in pockets, and a cigarette at the corner of his mouth so that ash occasionally fell on to his mac. The smell of fish-and-chips came from a well-lit shop, making him feel hungry.

"No pictures for me tonight," Fred was saying. "I know the best place in weather like this." The Meadows were hollow with the clatter of boots behind them, the muttering voices hot in discussion about the lost match. Groups gathered at each corner, arguing and teasing any girl that passed, lighted gas-lamps a weakening ally in the fog. Lennox turned into an entry, where the cold damp smell of backyards mingled with that of dustbins. They pushed open gates to their separate houses.

"So long. See you tomorrow at the pub maybe."

"Not tomorrow," Fred answered, already at his back door. "I'll have a job on mending my bike. I'm going to gi' it a coat of enamel and fix in some new brake blocks. I nearly got flattened by a bus the other day when they didn't work."

The gate-latch clattered. "All right then," Lennox said, "see you soon"—opening the back door and going into his house.

He walked through the small living-room without speaking, took off his mac in the parlour. "You should mek a fire in there," he said, coming out. "It smells musty. No wonder the clo'es go to pieces inside six months." His wife sat by the fire knitting from two balls of electric-blue wool in her lap. She was forty, the same age as Lennox, but gone to a plainness and discontented fat, while he had stayed thin and wiry from the same reason. Three children, the eldest a girl of fourteen, were at the table finishing tea.

Mrs. Lennox went on knitting. "I was going to make one today but I didn't have time."

"Iris can mek one," Lennox said, sitting down at the table.

The girl looked up. "I haven't finished my tea yet, our dad." The wheedling tone of her voice made him angry. "Finish it later," he said with a threatening look. "The fire needs making now, so come on, look sharp and get some coal from the cellar."

She didn't move, sat there with the obstinacy of the young spoiled by a mother. Lennox stood up. "Don't let me have to tell you again." Tears came into her eyes. "Go on," he shouted. "Do as you're told." He ignored his wife's plea to stop picking on her and lifted his hand to settle her with a blow.

"All right. I'm going. Look"—she got up and went to the cellar door. So he sat down again, his eyes roaming over the well-set table before him, holding his hands tightly clenched beneath the cloth. "What's for tea, then?"

His wife looked up again from her knitting. "There's two kippers in the oven."

He did not move, sat morosely fingering a knife and fork. "Well?" he demanded. "Do I have to wait all night for a bit o' summat t'eat?"

Quietly she took a plate from the oven and put it before him. Two brown kippers lay steaming across it. "One of these days," he said, pulling a long strip of white flesh from the bone, "we'll have a change."

"That's the best I can do," she said, her deliberate patience no way to stop his grumbling—though she didn't know what else would. And the fact that he detected it made things worse.

"I'm sure it is," he retorted. The coal bucket clattered from the parlour where the girl was making a fire. Slowly, he picked his kippers to pieces without eating any. The other two children sat on the sofa watching him, not daring to talk. On one side of his plate he laid bones; on the other, flesh. When the cat rubbed against his leg he dropped pieces of fish for it on to the lino, and when he considered that it had eaten enough he kicked it away with such force that its head knocked against the sideboard. It leapt on to a chair and began to lick itself, looking at him with green surprised eyes.

He gave one of the boys sixpence to fetch a *Football Guardian.* "And be quick about it," he called after him. He pushed his plate away, and nodded towards the mauled kippers. "I don't want this. You'd better send somebody out for some pastries. And mash some fresh tea," he added as an afterthought, "that pot's stewed."

He had gone too far. Why did he make Saturday afternoon such hell on earth? Anger throbbed violently in her temples. Through the furious beating of her heart she cried out: "If you want some pastries you'll fetch 'em yourself. And you'll mash your own tea as well."

"When a man goes to work all week he wants some tea," he said, glaring at her. Nodding at the boy: "Send him out for some cakes."

The boy had already stood up. "Don't go. Sit down," she said to him. "Get 'em yourself," she retorted to her husband. "The tea I've already put on the table's good enough for anybody. There's nowt wrong wi' it at all, and then you carry on like this. I suppose they lost at the match, because I can't think of any other reason why you should have such a long face."

He was shocked by such a sustained tirade, stood up to subdue her. "You what?" he shouted. "What do you think you're on wi'?"

Her face turned a deep pink. "You heard," she called back. "A few home truths might do you a bit of good."

He picked up the plate of fish and, with exaggerated deliberation, threw it to the floor. "There," he roared. "That's what you can do with your bleeding tea."

"You're a lunatic," she screamed. "You're mental."

He hit her once, twice, three times across the head, and knocked her to the ground. The little boy wailed, and his sister came running in from the parlour. . . .

Fred and his young wife in the house next door heard a commotion through the thin walls. They caught the cadence of voices and shifting chairs, but didn't really think anything amiss until the shriller climax was reached. "Would you believe it?" Ruby said, slipping off Fred's knee and straightening her skirt. "Just because Notts have lost again. I'm glad yo' aren't like that."

Ruby was nineteen, plump like a pear not round like a pudding, already pregnant though they'd only been married a month. Fred held her back by the waist. "I'm not so daft as to let owt like that bother me."

She wrenched herself free. "It's a good job you're not; because if you was I'd bosh you one."

Fred sat by the fire with a bemused, Cheshire-cat grin on his face while Ruby was in the scullery getting them something to eat. The noise in the next house had died down. After a slamming of doors and much walking to and fro outside Lennox's wife had taken the children, and left him for the last time.

GILBERT HIGHET

THE MYSTERY OF ZEN

The mind need never stop growing. Indeed, one of the few experiences which never pall is the experience of watching one's own mind, and observing how it produces new interests, responds to new stimuli, and develops new thoughts, apparently without effort and almost independently of one's own conscious control. I have seen this happen to myself a hundred times; and every time it happens again, I am equally fascinated and astonished.

Some years ago a publisher sent me a little book for review. I read it, and decided it was too remote from my main interests and too highly specialized. It was a brief account of how a young German philosopher living in Japan had learned how to shoot with a bow and arrow, and how this training had made it possible for him to understand the esoteric doctrines of the Zen sect of Buddhism. Really, what could be more alien to my own life, and to that of everyone I knew, than Zen Buddhism and Japanese archery? So I thought, and put the book away.

Yet I did not forget it. It was well written, and translated into good English. It was delightfully short, and implied much more than it said. Although its theme was extremely odd, it was at least highly individual; I had never read anything like it before or since. It remained in my mind. Its name was *Zen in the Art of Archery*, its author Eugen Herrigel, its publisher Pantheon of New York. One day I took it off the shelf and read it again; this time it seemed even stranger than before and even more unforgettable. Now it began to cohere with other interests of mine. Something I had read of the Japanese art of flower arrangement seemed to connect with it; and then, when I wrote an essay on the peculiar Japanese poems called *haiku*, other links began to grow. Finally I had to read the book once more with care, and to go through some other works which illuminated the same subject. I am still grappling with the theme; I have not got anywhere near understanding it fully; but I have learned a good deal, and I am grateful to the little book which refused to be forgotten.

The author, a German philosopher, got a job teaching philosophy at the University of Tokyo (apparently between the wars), and he did what Germans in foreign countries do not usually do: he determined to adapt himself and to learn from his hosts. In particular, he had always been interested in mysticism—which, for every earnest philosopher, poses a problem that is all the more inescapable because it is virtually insoluble. Zen Buddhism is not the only mystical doctrine to be found in the East, but it is one of the most highly developed and certainly one of the most difficult to approach. Herrigel knew that there were scarcely any books which did more than skirt the edge of the subject, and that the best of all books on Zen (those by philosopher D. T. Suzuki) constantly emphasize that Zen can never be learned from books, can never be studied as we can study other disciplines such as logic or mathematics. Therefore he began to look for a Japanese thinker who could teach him directly.

At once he met with embarrassed refusals. His Japanese friends explained that he would gain nothing from trying to discuss Zen as a philosopher, that its theories could not be spread out for analysis by a detached mind, and in fact that the normal relationship of teacher and pupil simply did not exist within the sect, because the Zen masters felt it useless to explain things stage by stage and to argue about the various possible interpretations of their doctrine. Herrigel had read enough to be prepared for this. He replied that he did not want to dissect the teachings of the school, because he knew that would be useless. He wanted to become a Zen mystic himself. (This was highly intelligent of him. No one could really penetrate into Christian mysticism without being a devout Christian; no one could appreciate Hindu mystical doctrine without accepting the Hindu view of the universe.) At this, Herrigel's Japanese friends were more forthcoming. They told him that the best way, indeed the only way, for a European to approach Zen mysticism was to learn one of the arts which exemplified it. He was a fairly good rifle shot, so he determined to learn archery, and his wife co-operated with him by taking lessons in painting and flower arrangement. How any philosopher could investigate a mystical doctrine by learning to shoot with a bow and arrow and watching his wife arrange flowers, Herrigel did not ask. He had good sense.

A Zen master who was a teacher of archery agreed to take him as a pupil. The lessons lasted six years, during which he practiced every single day. There are many difficult courses of instruction in the world: the Jesuits, violin virtuosi, Talmudic scholars, all have long and hard training, which in one sense never comes to an end; but Herrigel's training in archery equaled them all in intensity. If I were trying to learn archery, I should expect to begin by looking at a target and shooting arrows at it. He was not even allowed to aim at a target for the first four years. He had to begin by learning how to hold the bow and arrow, and then how to release the arrow; this took ages. The Japanese bow is not like our sporting bow, and the stance of the archer in Japan is different from ours. We hold the bow at shoulder level, stretch our left arm out ahead, pull the string and the nocked arrow to a point either below the chin or sometimes past the right ear, and then shoot. The Japanese hold the bow above the head, and then pull the hands apart to left and right until the left hand comes down to eye level and the right hand comes to rest above the right shoulder; then there is a pause, during which the bow is held at full stretch, with the tip of the three-foot arrow projecting only a few inches beyond the bow; after that, the arrow is loosed. When Herrigel tried this, even without aiming, he found it was almost impossible. His hands trembled. His legs stiffened and grew cramped. His breathing became labored. And of course he could not possibly aim. Week after week he practiced this, with the Master watching him carefully and correcting his strained attitude; week after week he made no progress whatever. Finally he gave up and told his teacher that he could not learn: it was absolutely impossible for him to draw the bow and loose the arrow.

To his astonishment, the Master agreed. He said, "Certainly you cannot. It is because you are not breathing correctly. You must learn to breathe in a steady rhythm, keeping your lungs full most of the time, and drawing in one rapid inspiration with each stage of the process, as you grasp the bow, fit the arrow, raise the bow, draw, pause, and loose the shot. If you do, you will both grow stronger and be able to relax." To prove this, he himself drew his massive bow and told his pupil to feel the muscles of his arms: they were perfectly relaxed, as though he were doing no work whatever.

Herrigel now started breathing exercises; after some time he combined the new rhythm of breathing with the actions of drawing and shooting; and, much to his astonishment, he found that the whole thing, after this complicated process, had become much easier. Or rather, not easier, but different. At times it became quite unconscious. He says himself that he felt he was not breathing, but being breathed; and in time he felt that the occasional shot was not being dispatched by him, but shooting itself. The bow and arrow were in charge; he had become merely a part of them.

All this time, of course, Herrigel did not even attempt to discuss Zen doctrine with his Master. No doubt he knew that he was approaching it, but he concentrated solely on learning how to shoot. Every stage which he surmounted appeared to lead to another stage even more difficult. It took him months to learn how to loosen the bowstring. The problem was this. If he gripped the string and arrowhead tightly, either he froze, so that his hands were slowly pulled together and the shot was wasted, or else he jerked, so that the arrow flew up into the air or down into the ground; and if he was relaxed, then the bowstring and arrow simply *leaked* out of his grasp before he could reach full stretch, and the arrow went nowhere. He explained this problem to the Master. The Master understood perfectly well. He replied, "You must hold the drawn bowstring like a child holding a grownup's finger. You know how firmly a child grips; and yet when it lets go, there is not the slightest jerk—because the child does not think of itself, it is not self-conscious, it does not say, 'I will now let go and do something else,' it merely acts instinctively. That is what you must learn to do. Practice, practice, and practice, and then the string will loose itself at the right moment. The shot will come as effortlessly as snow slipping from a leaf." Day after day, week after week, month after month, Herrigel practiced this; and then, after one shot, the Master suddenly bowed and broke off the lesson. He said "Just then it shot. Not you, but *it*." And gradually thereafter more and more right shots achieved themselves; the young philosopher forgot himself, forgot that he was learning archery for some other purpose, forgot even that he was practicing archery, and became part of that unconsciously active complex, the bow, the string, the arrow, and the man.

Next came the target. After four years, Herrigel was allowed to shoot at the target. But he was strictly forbidden to aim at it. The Master explained that even he himself did not aim; and indeed, when he shot, he was so absorbed in the act, so selfless and unanxious, that his eyes were almost closed. It was difficult, almost impossible, for Herrigel to believe that such shooting could ever be effective; and he risked insulting the Master by suggesting that he ought to be able to hit the target blindfolded. But the Master accepted the challenge. That night, after a cup of tea and long meditation, he went into the archery hall, put on the lights at one end and left the target perfectly dark, with only a thin taper burning in front of it. Then, with habitual grace and precision, and with that strange, almost sleepwalking, selfless confidence that is the heart of Zen, he shot two arrows into the darkness. Herrigel went out to collect them. He found that the first had gone to the heart of the bull's eye, and that the second had actually hit the first arrow and splintered it. The Master showed no pride. He said, "Perhaps, with unconscious memory of the position of the target, *I* shot the first arrow; but the second arrow? *It* shot the second arrow, and *it* brought it to the center of the target."

At last Herrigel began to understand. His progress became faster and faster; easier, too. Perfect shots (perfect because perfectly unconscious) occurred at almost every lesson; and finally, after six years of incessant training, in a public display he was awarded the diploma. He needed no further instruction: he had himself become a Master. His wife meanwhile had become expert both in painting and in the arrangement of flowers—two of the finest of Japanese arts. (I wish she could be persuaded to write a companion volume, called *Zen in the Art of Flower Arrangement;* it would have a wider general appeal than her husband's work.) I gather also from a hint or two in his book that she had taken part in the archery lessons. During one of the most difficult periods in Herrigel's training, when his Master had practically refused to continue teaching him—because Herrigel had tried to cheat by *consciously* opening his hand at the moment of loosing the arrow—his wife had advised him against that solution, and sympathized with him when it was rejected. She in her own way had learned more quickly than he, and reached the final point together with him. All their effort had not been in vain: Herrigel and his wife had really acquired a new and valuable kind of wisdom. Only at this point, when he was about to abandon his lessons forever, did his Master treat him almost as an equal and hint at the innermost doctrines of Zen Buddhism. Only hints he gave; and yet, for the young philosopher who had now become a mystic, they were enough. Herrigel understood the doctrine, not with his logical mind, but with his entire being. He at any rate had solved the mystery of Zen.

Without going through a course of training as absorbing and as complete as Herrigel's, we can probably never penetrate the mystery. The doctrine of Zen cannot be analyzed from without: it must be lived.

But although it cannot be analyzed, it can be hinted at. All the hints that the adherents of this creed give us are interesting. Many are fantastic; some are practically incomprehensible, and yet unforgettable. Put together, they take us toward a way of life which is utterly impossible for westerners living in a western world, and nevertheless has a deep fascination and contains some values which we must respect.

The word Zen means "meditation." (It is the Japanese word, corresponding to the Chinese Ch'an and the Hindu Dhyana.) It is the central idea of a special sect of Buddhism which flourished in China during the Sung period (between A.D. 1000 and 1300) and entered Japan in the twelfth century. Without knowing much about it, we might be certain that the Zen sect was a worthy and noble one, because it produced a quantity of highly distinguished art, specifically painting. And if we knew anything about Buddhism itself, we might say that Zen goes closer than other sects to the heart of Buddha's teaching: because Buddha was trying to found, not a religion with temples and rituals, but a way of life based on meditation. However, there is something eccentric about the Zen life which is hard to trace in Buddha's teaching; there is an active energy which he did not admire, there is a rough grasp on reality which he himself eschewed, there is something like a sense of humor, which he rarely displayed. The gravity and serenity of the Indian preacher are transformed, in Zen, to the earthy liveliness of Chinese and Japanese sages. The lotus brooding calmly on the water has turned into a knotted tree covered with spring blossoms.

In this sense, "meditation" does not mean what we usually think of when we say a philosopher meditates: analysis of reality, a long-sustained effort to solve problems of religion and ethics, the logical dissection of the universe. It means something not divisive, but whole; not schematic, but organic; not long-drawn-out, but immediate. It means something more like our words "intuition" and "realization." It means a way of life in which there is no division between thought and action; none of the painful gulf, so well known to all of us, between the unconscious and the conscious mind; and no absolute distinction between the self and the external world, even between the various parts of the external world and the whole.

When the German philosopher took six years of lessons in archery in order to approach the mystical significance of Zen, he was not given direct philosophical instruction. He was merely shown how to breathe, how to hold and loose the bowstring, and finally how to shoot in such a way that the bow and arrow used him as an instrument. There are many such stories about Zen teachers. The strangest I know is one about a fencing master who undertook to train a young man in the art of the sword. The relationship of teacher and pupil is very important, almost sacred, in the Far East; and the pupil hardly ever thinks of leaving a master or objecting to his methods, however extraordinary they may seem. Therefore this young fellow did not at first object when he was made to act as a servant, drawing water, sweeping floors, gathering wood for the fire, and cooking. But after some time he asked for more direct instruction. The master agreed to give it, but produced no swords. The routine went on just as before, except that every now and then the master would strike the young man with a stick. No matter what he was doing, sweeping the floor or weeding in the garden, a blow would descend on him apparently out of nowhere; he had always to be on the alert, and yet he was constantly receiving unexpected cracks on the head or shoulders. After some months of this, he saw the master stooping over a boiling pot full of vegetables; and he thought he would have his revenge. Silently he lifted a stick and brought it down; but without any effort, without even a glance in his direction, his master parried the blow with the lid of the cooking pot. At last, the pupil began to understand the instinctive alertness, the effortless perception and avoidance of danger, in which his master had been training him. As soon as he had achieved it, it was child's play for him to learn the management of the sword: he could parry every cut and turn every slash without anxiety, until his opponent, exhausted, left an opening for his counterattack. (The same principle was used by the elderly samurai for selecting his comrades in the Japanese motion picture *The Magnificent Seven.*)

These stories show that Zen meditation does not mean sitting and thinking. On the contrary, it means acting with as little thought as possible. The fencing master trained his pupil to guard against every attack with the same immediate, instinctive rapidity with which our eyelid closes over our eye when something threatens it. His work was aimed at breaking down the wall between thought and act, at completely fusing body and senses and mind so that they might all work together rapidly and effortlessly. When a Zen artist draws a picture, he does it in a rhythm almost the exact reverse of that which is followed by a Western artist. We begin by blocking out the design and then filling in the details, usually working more and more slowly as we approach the completion of the picture. The Zen artist sits down very calmly; examines his brush carefully; prepares his own ink; smooths out the paper on which he will work; falls into a profound silent ecstasy of contemplation—during which he does not think anxiously of various details, composition, brushwork, shades of tones, but rather attempts to become the vehicle through which the subject can express itself in painting; and then, very quickly and almost unconsciously, with sure effortless strokes, draws a picture containing the fewest and most effective lines. Most of the paper is left blank; only the essential is depicted, and that not completely. One long curving line will be enough to show a mountainside; seven streaks will become a group of bamboos bending in the wind; and yet, though technically incomplete, such pictures are unforgettably clear. They show the heart of reality.

All this we can sympathize with, because we can see the results. The young swordsman learns how to fence. The intuitional painter produces a fine picture. But the hardest thing for us to appreciate is that Zen masters refuse to teach philosophy or religion directly, and deny logic. In fact, they despise logic as an artificial distortion of reality. Many philosophical teachers are difficult to understand because they analyze profound problems with subtle intricacy: such is Aristotle in his *Metaphysics*. Many mystical writers are difficult to understand because, as they themselves admit, they are attempting to use words to describe experiences which are too abstruse for words, so that they have to fall back on imagery and analogy, which they themselves recognize to be poor media, far coarser than the realities with which they have been in contact. But the Zen teachers seem to deny the power of language and thought altogether. For example, if you ask a Zen master what is the ultimate reality, he will answer without the slightest hesitation, "The bamboo grove at the foot of the hill" or "A branch of plum blossom." Apparently he means that these things, which we can see instantly without effort, or imagine in the flash of a second, are real with the ultimate reality; that nothing is more real than these; and that we ought to grasp ultimates as we grasp simple immediates. A Chinese master was once asked the central question, "What is the Buddha?" He said nothing whatever, but held out his index finger. What did he mean? It is hard to explain; but apparently he meant "Here. Now. Look and realize with the effortlessness of seeing. Do not try to use words. Do not think. Make no efforts toward withdrawal from the world. Expect no sublime ecstasies. Live. All *that* is the ultimate reality, and it can be understood from the motion of a finger as well as from the execution of any complex ritual, from any subtle argument, or from the circling of the starry universe."

In making that gesture, the master was copying the Buddha himself, who once delivered a sermon which is famous, but was hardly understood by his pupils at the time. Without saying a word, he held up a flower and showed it to the gathering. One man, one alone, knew what he meant. The gesture became renowned as the Flower Sermon.

In the annals of Zen there are many cryptic answers to the final question, "What is the Buddha?"—which in our terms means "What is the meaning of life? What is truly real?" For example, one master, when asked "What is Buddha?" replied, "Your name is Yecho." Another said, "Even the finest artist cannot paint him." Another said, "No nonsense here." And another answered, "The mouth is the gate of woe." My favorite story is about the monk who said to a Master, "Has a dog Buddha-nature too?" The Master replied, "Wu"—which is what the dog himself would have said.

Now, some critics might attack Zen by saying that this is the creed of a savage or an animal. The adherents of Zen would deny that—or more probably they would ignore the criticism, or make some cryptic remark which meant that it was pointless. Their position—if they could ever be persuaded to put it into words—would be this. An animal is instinctively in touch with reality, and so far is living rightly, but it has never had a mind and so cannot perceive the Whole, only that part with which it is in touch. The philosopher sees both the Whole and the parts, and enjoys them all. As for the savage, he exists only through the group; he feels himself as part of a war party or a ceremonial dance team or a ploughing-and-sowing group of the Snake clan; he is not truly an individual at all, and therefore is less than fully human. Zen has at its heart an inner solitude; its aim is to teach us to live, as in the last resort we do all have to live, alone.

A more dangerous criticism of Zen would be that it is nihilism, that its purpose is to abolish thought altogether. (This criticism is handled, but not fully met, by the great Zen authority Suzuki in his *Introduction to Zen Buddhism.*) It can hardly be completely confuted, for after all the central doctrine of Buddhism is—Nothingness. And many of the sayings of Zen masters are truly nihilistic. The first patriarch of the sect in China was asked by the emperor what was the ultimate and holiest principle of Buddhism. He replied, "Vast emptiness, and nothing holy in it." Another who was asked the searching question, "Where is the abiding-place for the mind?" answered, "Not in this dualism of good and evil, being and nonbeing, thought and matter." In fact, thought is an activity which divides. It analyzes, it makes distinctions, it criticizes, it judges, it breaks reality into groups and classes and individuals. The aim of Zen is to abolish that kind of thinking, and to substitute—not unconsciousness, which would be death, but a consciousness that does not analyze but experiences life directly. Although it has no prescribed prayers, no sacred scriptures, no ceremonial rites, no personal god, and no interest in the soul's future destination, Zen is a religion rather than a philosophy. Jung points out that its aim is to produce a religious conversion, a "transformation": and he adds, "The transformation process is incommensurable with intellect." Thought is always interesting, but often painful; Zen is calm and painless. Thought is incomplete; Zen enlightenment brings a sense of completeness. Thought is a process; Zen illumination is a state. But it is a state which cannot be defined. In the Buddhist scriptures there is a dialogue between a master and a pupil in which the pupil tries to discover the exact meaning of such a state. The master says to him, "If a fire were blazing in front of you, would you know that it was blazing?"

"Yes, master."

"And would you know the reason for its blazing?"

"Yes, because it had a supply of grass and sticks."

"And would you know if it were to go out?"

"Yes, master."

"And on its going out, would you know where the fire had gone? To the east, to the west, to the north, or to the south?"

"The question does not apply, master. For the fire blazed because it had a supply of grass and sticks. When it had consumed this and had no other fuel, then it went out."

"In the same way," replies the master, "no question will apply to the meaning of Nirvana, and no statement will explain it."

Such, then, neither happy nor unhappy but beyond all divisive description, is the condition which students of Zen strive to attain. Small wonder that they can scarcely explain it to us, the unilluminated.

SPORT AS A MICROCOSM OF SOCIETY

I s sport important, or is it merely the trivial playing of games? A bias exists, particularly in academic circles, against the idea that sport can be significant. The essays in this section, however, deal with issues that frequently come up in serious considerations of the role of sport in our society: excellence, sexism, racism, and heroism.

"Concern for Excellence," by Paul Weiss is a chapter from his book *The Philosophy of Sport*. Weiss, a distinguished philosopher, questions the reasons for the existence of sport. He asks the basic question, "Why does sport interest people?" He then goes on to ask why philosophers in general have not been concerned with sport; his answer suggests the bias against sport as a low-brow occupation has actually existed for centuries as a disdain for the commonplace.

Weiss concentrates on the youthful dimension of sport, a concern that has emerged time and again in other selections in this anthology. He views the athlete as an example of human excellence. Moreover, it is the only excellence which the young, because of inexperience, can hope to attain.

It might be objected that Weiss really means *manly* excellence, for it seems clear that sport has traditionally been considered more central to man's life than woman's. Marie Hart's essay delves into the role of women in sport and finds it distressing. In the first place, there is only a peripheral role for women in sport. In the second, when a woman does opt for participating in sport, her life is burdened to the point where she may well be forced to question her own identity as a woman. Because society tolerates the "tomboy" stereotype for only a limited time in girlhood, the female athlete of high school age or older finds herself severely disapproved of by many. The root of the situation appears to be that playing sports is active, hence the culturally preferred stereotype of passive femininity is called into question.

The selection from Robert Boyle's *Sport: Mirror of American Life* explores with incisive detail the nuances of being black in major league baseball. Although not quite contemporary, his essay covers the whole story of blacks in baseball from the beginnings to the early 1960s. It is a story of anguish and heroism. Much of the meaning of this story, both for sport and for society as a whole, is revealed in the anecdote of the team that did not put Latin American players on teams in the segregated South, so as not to sour them on the United States! One might spend some profitable moments contemplating all the meanings of that story. Whatever these meanings are, Boyle has vividly presented an important part of the American saga.

John Updike's essay, "Hub Fans Bid Kid Adieu," affectionately portrays the athlete as mythological hero. Updike explicitly deals with the theme by comparing Ted Williams to three Greek heroes: Jason, Achilles, and Nestor—the searching youth, the mature warrior, and the honored wise man. The essay concludes with Williams' magnificent last time at bat when he epitomized his entire career by hitting a memorable home run. Such legendary athletic feats make life a little less mean and enlarge our sense of human possibilities.

PAUL WEISS

CONCERN FOR EXCELLENCE

from *The Philosophy of Sport*

Excellence excites and awes. It pleases and it challenges. We are often delighted by splendid specimens whether they be flowers, beasts, or men. A superb performance interests us even more because it reveals to us the magnitude of what then can be done. Illustrating perfection, it gives us a measure for whatever else we do.

Unlike other beings we men have the ability to appreciate the excellent. We desire to achieve it. We want to share in it. Even though it may point up the fact that we are defective, less than we might have been, we like to look upon it. It is what ought to be.

There are many ways in which men are excellent. Some have great character. Their public acts serve as carriers for admirable, privately sustained virtues. Noble beings, they give private goods a public role. Other men achieve a stature far greater than the rest by making an art of living, and impressing this on the course of history. They are monumental beings, the great leaders and statesmen. Others are genuinely pious and infuse their relation to their fellows with sacred values. Teachers of mankind, they often outlast and outstrip those who rule nations and control armies. And others are truly wise, sages who embody what they know. Permeating their bodies with sound and wide-ranging knowledge, they ennoble those bodies and what those bodies do.

These excellent men are exceptions. Large enough for all of us to see, they are too large for most of us to imitate except at some remove. It is easier for most men to reach, not an excellence which requires them to first attain some perfection privately and then to impose it on a public body or world, but an excellence which results from a mastery of the body or of the things in the world. It is even easier, usually, to respect the rights of others, guided in part by what ethically ought to be. It is perhaps even easier, though no more common, to be a hero, having some impact on history. Almost any man, too, can assume leadership in some area for a time, limiting himself in the light of whatever eternal values he is able to discern. But young men find it easier to master their bodies than to be truly noble, monumental, pious, or wise. We have here one reason why they readily occupy themselves with sport.

Sport does not interest only the young; it interests almost everyone. The fact compels a pause. Why are so many so deeply involved, so caught up emotionally in athletic events? Are they in the grip of some basic drive? Do they only express some accidentally acquired cultural habit of admiration for successful violence? Are they really interested in perfection? Does it perhaps give them a special kind of pleasure?

These hard questions have philosophic import, dealing as they do—as we shall see—with what is close to the core of man, what he seeks, and what he does. Yet philosophers, as a rule have not looked carefully into the topic. They have neglected sport. Sport, of course, is not the only wide-spread activity that they have slighted. Sex, work, play, and worldly success never won the steady attention of eminent philosophers. They have given considerable thought to the nature and desirability of achieving pleasure; they have occupied themselves with the idea of excellence and with the desire for it; they have been appreciative of the fact that in many basic ways men everywhere are men, with similar natures and appetites. But this has not led them to devote their time and energy to studying some of the most universal occupations of men.

Why is it that certain widely dispersed and evidently attractive pursuits have not been extensively studied by the great, or even by the near-great philosophers who dot the history of thought? It is conceivable that these men believed that the activities expressed only some limited interest, some specialized concern for a particular good, and were therefore the proper topics of other enterprises. We will never know for certain whether or not this or some other is the reason for the neglect, for none of the philosophers has discussed the issue.

Let us go back toward the beginning of thought, as we know it in the Western world. We will find in the Greeks some good historically grounded explanations for the neglect of sport by philosophic minds, then and later. Despite their evident enjoyment of athletics, and their delight in speculating on the meaning of a hundred different human concerns, the Greek thinkers never dealt extensively with the nature, import, and reason for sport. Since Plato and his fellows formulated most of the issues that have occupied philosophers over the centuries, the Greek failure to provide a philosophical study became a norm for the rest. Whitehead goes too far when he says that "the safest general characterization of the European philosophic tradition is that it consists of a series of footnotes to Plato," but he does thereby make conspicuous the normative role that the Greeks assumed in Western thought. Whitehead's observation also points up the desirability of asking whether it is not time to write a new text; one overrun with footnotes should be discarded for another fresh account, granted, for the sake of accuracy, that it is Aristotle and not Plato who set the standards to which most Western philosophers subscribe.

Aristotle wrote brilliantly and extensively on logic, physics, biology, psychology, economics, politics, ethics, art, metaphysics, and rhetoric, but he says hardly a word about either history or religion, and nothing at all about sport. Since he was taken to be "the master of those who know" his position became paradigmatic for most of the thinkers who followed, even when they explicitly repudiated his particular claims. They tended, with him, to dismiss labor as an affair of low-class men, and to identify worldly success with political and princely power. The fact that these subjects are studied today by economists, psychologists, and sociologists has not yet sufficed to free them from many a philosopher's suspicion that they are low-grade subjects, not worthy of being pursued by men of large vision.

Aristotle extracted a grammar from learned discourse, a logic from skilled argument, and a political theory from the practices of statesmen. But he kept away from common discourse, common argument, and common practices. He and other masters of thought did not look for the structure and rationale of what occupies most men. They tacitly supposed that the popular could not be as philosophically important as the rare, solely because it was popular. What appealed to the many, it was thought, could not contain any significant truths. Following out that idea, one is tempted to conclude with Aristotle that God thinks only of what is noble and pure, and that we ought to try to follow his example. As Aristotle put it: "It must be of itself that the divine thought thinks since it is the most excellent of things." But we men are all imperfect, living in an impure world; we at least cannot and ought not avoid a study of the finite and the corrupt. It need no more corrupt us than a study of insanity will make us mad.

From its beginning until today, philosophy has been centrally occupied with the genteel and the respectable. We come upon this fact in surprising places. In a technical discussion by Plato, for example, we find Parmenides asking Socrates, "Are you also puzzled whether . . . hair or mud or dirt or any other trivial and undignified objects . . . have a separate Form?" and Socrates answering ". . . it would surely be too absurd to suppose that they have a Form." Socrates and his friends would have thought it equally absurd to suppose that sex, work, or sport had Forms of their own.

As befits the well-placed in a slave society, Aristotle and other Greek thinkers dealt mainly with what concerned the well-born. Later on, when the philosophers of history and religion (I refer here, of course, to the philosophers of religion of the West, for in the East they have been occupied with the issues for thousands of years) made their appearance, they too dealt primarily only with those topics that had been raised by leaders in act and thought.

The history of philosophy is a series of attempts to square the circle within which the privileged confine themselves. Among other things it neglects the history that is sweated through by ordinary men, and the life that they daily lead. It attends to dance and song only after they have made their way into the accredited theaters and concert halls. Some attention, to be sure, is paid to fate, luck, and freedom, which are certainly common concerns. But on the whole hardly anything is said about what grips mankind, what excites and overwhelms, what lures and confounds it—and therefore about what is important to the unwashed and uneducated.

Even if it be supposed that only what the upper classes do is worth reflecting on, a philosophic treatise on sports could have been written—and by the Greeks. In their athletic contests only free men were allowed to compete. There was presumably nothing low, therefore, to be contemplated in those contests, and presumably nothing untoward that would appear in the resulting reflection. The Greek thinkers did not write philosophic treatises on sport, perhaps because they thought that the kind of power and control that athletes exhibit was within the capacity of any and all men, and for that reason was intrinsically low-grade. Some of them did say that the athletes, though free, were inferior men. A strong, but not untypical expression of the contempt that aristocrats had for athletes is reported by Isocrates.

> Although in natural gifts and in strength of body he [Alcibiades]was inferior to none, he disdained the gymnastic contests, for he knew that some of the athletes were of low birth, inhabitants of petty states and of mean education, but turned to the breeding of race horses, which is possible only for the most blest by Fortune and not to be pursued by one of low estate.[1]

Veblen, characteristically, gives a more biting explanation for the aristocratic rejection of whatever the lower classes can do: "The canons of reputable living exclude from the scheme of life of the leisure class all activity that can not be classed as conspicuous leisure." [2] The sports of the rich, on this view, are necessarily different from those of the poor, but sufficiently close in spirit as to make well-off, reflective men shy away from thinking about them.

The typical philosopher disdains the common. He is justified when "common" means that which is beneath the interest of a civilized man. But "common" also means "what is widespread." No one has a right to move smoothly from the latter meaning to the former. But this is done when the common is dismissed as the vulgar—which itself was once a common term for "common."

For too many the common means little more than the brutish and the uncultivated. Let this be granted; it does not imply that a study of what is common must itself be demeaning. A clean science studies air pollution; it is a sober science that examines the history and causes of savage superstitions.

If philosophers did take the commonality of sport to be a sign of its insignificance, and then supposed that its character tainted the study of it, they committed a double blunder. The common can be good and desirable. And whether it be so or not, it can be dealt with carefully

---

1. *Isocrates,* Vol. III, trans. La Rue Van Hook, Loeb Classical Library (Cambridge, 1961), in "Concerning the Team of Horses," pp. 194–95.
2. Thorstein B. Veblen, *The Theory of the Leisure Class* (New York, 1931), p. 258.

and thoughtfully, and from a perspective not necessarily known or shared in by its participants.

Whatever the reason for the neglect, the opportunity to deal with sport philosophically was let slip away by the Greeks and their followers. From their time to our own, sports have not been taken seriously enough as a source or instance of large truths or first principles.

Both when participated in and when watched, sport quickly works on the emotions; it wins men's allegiance readily and often to a degree nothing else is able to do. Mankind's enthusiasm and devotion to it is remarkable, and deserves to be remarked upon. P. S. Fredrickson observes: "There is no society known to man which does not have games of the sort in which individuals set up purely artificial obstacles and get satisfaction from overcoming them." [3]

Art, science, and philosophy make larger contributions to civilization than sport does. They demand the use of an imagination and a mind within the power of only a small number—and those only when they willingly work in solitude, outside the borders of accepted beliefs, and with a power, range, daring, and persistence backed by maturity that only a fortunate few can attain.

Agriculture, manufacture, and business play a much larger role in our economy than is possible to sport, though, of course, sport is not without economic importance. The economically more important enterprises, however, do not often arouse the full attention of most men. Rarely do they enter into men's daily disputes or lay claim to basic loyalties in the way or to the degree that sport does. It is sport that catches the interest and elicits the devotion of both the young and the old, the wise and the foolish, the educated and the uneducated.

What is not immediately evident is why men in all walks and at all ages interest themselves in sport. We cannot take it to be a sure or a great source of pleasure, at least for the participants. It is too demanding, too onerous, and sometimes too dangerous to make its pursuit desirable for one who makes this his primary aim. Spectators may find sport to be a source of delight and exhilaration; the casual player may concern himself with sport in order to relax or to increase

3. P. S. Frederickson, "Sports and the Cultures of Man," *Science and Medicine of Exercise and Sports*, ed. Warren Russel Johnson (New York, 1960), p. 634.

his sense of well-being. But even here we find other and rather contrastive factors. Spectators and casual players are sometimes tensed and disappointed, angered and debilitated by what they confront.

Sport could be taken to answer to some driving common human need. But then we will have to face the question why comparatively few men vigorously devote themselves to sport. Why are most of them content to watch games, or to use them as occasions for release or for comradeship, and are unwilling to enter into them with utmost dedication? If sport is the product of a primal drive one would expect all men to exhibit that drive and therefore to engage in sport.

There is some justification in holding that there is a need for sport in men, which comes to clear expression only on some occasions and which has muted forms the rest of the time. On such a view spectators would be athletes manqué, and older men would be athletes who were unable to sustain their need physically.

This approach makes it possible to give a good account of the interest men have in sport. But a price would be paid. We would slight the fact that neither spectators nor older men want to do what the active athlete does. A plausible account of the appeal of sport should explain its insistent attraction for most, at the same time that it makes clear why all do not and need not actively participate in it. The wide spread is important if it is revelatory of man or nature, or of what is beyond them both. If a study of sport is to be of philosophic interest, it should show its relation to men's basic concerns. It will then be able to make evident why sport is pursued almost everywhere.

A philosophical account of sport can have no practical value beyond that of making one aware of basic distinctions, final boundaries, unnoticed connections, and neglected possibilities, and the place that sport has in the life of man. This, though, should be sufficient to make a theoretical, speculative study of some interest, even to those whose main stress is on the practical, the technical, and the immediate.

Educators, businessmen, and newspapers give a good deal of their time to sport, and often are deeply involved in it. Some men continue to be occupied with sport long past the time when they can participate in it with distinction or even with appreciable success. Some perform exceptionally well in middle age, though these are so few in number that almost every case awakens our wonder and admiration.

Most men have no athletic stature, but many of them participate in sports frequently and with great enthusiasm. It is the young men, though, who are most absorbed in sports. It is they who participate in it most passionately and most successfully.

Those who are young cannot do much to maintain or to contribute to culture; they are not experienced or developed enough to see or do things in the round. Most of them find it quite difficult to attend to the important for more than an occasional, short period, or to be much occupied with what is not relevant to the satisfaction of personal desires and short-run concerns. Most young men are largely unformed and undirected. No longer boys, they are not yet full adults, able to function as prime factors in society, state, or civilization. The best that most of them can do is to be good at sport. And that is a goal well worth their devotion.

Young men can distinguish themselves in sport to a degree they do not, on the whole attain elsewhere. A number of apparent exceptions come quickly to mind. Some youthful painters, novelists, poets, dancers, actors, and teachers are outstanding. They rightly awaken amazement and respect. Is this not due, though, to the fact that we see them as promising to move on to still greater heights, when they have matured? "Prodigy," our term for so many of them, is apt. It means "to foretell." If we use the term properly, we will not be so prone to confound a present evidence of promise with a likely eventuality.

When we attend to the athlete it is not his eventual success that we have in mind, but his present state and performance, for too often he has little or no future. While we expect our artistic prodigies to ripen with the years, and to continue to ripen long after the athlete has passed his prime, we realize that the athlete lives his life mainly in the present, frequently reaching his peak before he arrives at full manhood.

The athlete struggles to fulfill himself now; now is when he makes himself. It is now, and not later, that he seeks to, and can, attain the excellence which is possible to him. He does train and he can improve, but at his best he succeeds magnificently only when he is young. Unless perchance he is six years old and can run a hundred yards in ten seconds, he is no track prodigy. If he is an athlete it is because he now is well trained, though young.

A young man's emotions are more his master than his creatures. Quickly and unexpectedly they slip from his control, fluctuating wildly and without reference to the objective circumstances. Unprepared for and insistent, they fog his mind and confuse his actions. Rarely do young men envisage the major relevant possibilities, rarely do they see the bearing that remote factors have on what they would like to know. They need experience to teach them how to weigh probabilities, how to assess relevance, how to balance one bias with another.

Sometimes it is said that mathematicians and physicists make their mark when young or not at all. There are young poets whose thoughts have an incomparable fluidity and subtlety. But none shows much grasp of truths outside his special province. Like other young men each has a mind of only limited range.

A normal young man has much vitality, more than he knows how to utilize well. His energies spill over into a plurality of unfinished projects. Too often he follows sudden enthusiastic starts with sudden dismaying stops. Rarely can one credit him with more than a few skills, a little vision, episodic intelligence, and occasional good judgment. If he is fortunate, over the course of time he will become more and more skillful, his vision will widen, his intelligence will be steadied, and his judgment will become better informed and better directed. If singularly fortunate, he will spend his life using his energies to inquire, probe, discover, and create. But he can now, while young, gain satisfaction more readily by attending to those tasks that require the use of a well-prepared and well-toned body. In almost every other type of life it will normally take him decades before a similar satisfaction can be achieved.

It makes good sense for a young man to want to be a fine athlete; it is not unreasonable for him to suppose that through his body he can attain a perfection otherwise not possible to him. He has little hope of succeeding, however, if he is unwilling to pull his attention away from other tasks. He must hobble any desire that he might have to live an intellectual life to the full. An interest in a splendid body does not of course preclude thought. He who improves his body and uses it well must use his mind; he needs sound knowledge of fundamentals, good judgment of what a situation involves, and an understanding of what he, his teammates, and his opponents can and most likely will do. But this is not yet to say that he is one who devotes himself to a life of study or reflection.

An athlete strives to have a fine body and to use it well. Because different sports require the use of different organs, muscles, aptitudes, and training, he will arrive at his goal along one of many possible routes. How many routes are there? The answer depends on how sports are classified. Unfortunately, the subject still awaits its Linnaeus to provide it with its basic classifications. Not until he arrives will one know which new sports should be introduced, and which might be dropped because they differ too little from others which are more enriching or better established. We need this knowledge if we are to give young men the opportunity to make full creative use of their powers under the control of limiting but enabling conditions. We will then presumably be able to offer them a set of well-defined paths over which they can move expeditiously to arrive at the goal of being well-embodied men.

Though occasionally we may see a game in which there are more players than spectators, the reverse is usually the case. Despite man's great and widespread interest in sport, there are not many full-time athletes. With the advent of television, the number of the nonparticipants in sport has increased. And there are obviously far more indifferent players than there are major athletes, and far more major athletes than there are champions.

It is not necessary to suppose that all nonparticipants or even all players are imbued with a common desire. We need not suppose that they exhibit a drive that is characteristic of the most devoted and successful participant. But it is possible for them to see themselves in the players. An athlete carries out to completion one of the types of effort everyone occasionally makes to be or to become an excellent man.

All men would like to be perfected physically and mentally. Even those who dwell upon their misfortunes, who enjoy being pained and punished, or who would prefer not to be at the front of anything, aim at a state where they feel fulfilled, somehow completed. The defects they cherish are for them but opportunities for gaining a self-confidence or a social advantage; in effect those defects are agencies for reaching a mental or physical position of superiority (a not altogether reliable sign of a signal achievement). The self-defeated, like the rest of us, also seek perfection, even though they too often are content to rest uncritically with a faint simulacrum of it.

Few men work at becoming all they can be. Fewer still try to do this by achieving a disciplined mastery of their bodies. But all can, and occasionally some do, see the athlete as an expression of what man as such can be and do, in the special guise of this individual body and in these particular circumstances. In the athlete all can catch a glimpse of what one might be were one also to operate at the limit of bodily capacity.

So far as we see the athlete to be a splendid epitomization of man we look at him and his performance objectively, de-emphasizing what he is as an individual. At the same time we feel as though we ourselves had personally achieved something. By representing us, the athlete makes all of us be vicariously completed men. We cannot but be pleased by what such a representative man achieves.

The excellence that the athlete wants to attain is an excellence greater than that attained before. He wants to do better than he had; he would like to do better than anyone ever did. What he once achieved and what he might now achieve is an excellence relative to some particular period of time and circumstance. At another time and on another occasion, a superior state or performance will perhaps be produced, thereby making clear that man's final limits had not been reached before. This is a truth that will surely hold as long as men compete with one another. There is no reason, though, to believe that every record will be broken. Should we ever arrive at some limit of speed, endurance, accuracy, etc., however, we will undoubtedly use it as an occasion for modifying the circumstances, and thus for challenging man anew.

We cannot of course talk of records today with much feeling of confidence. An amazing number of what we once thought were the absolute limits of achievement have been discovered to be but momentary stops which better health, greater dedication, more favorable circumstance, more appropriate equipment, and new training methods have enabled men to pass beyond. Records, as we now understand them, are also comparatively new—hardly more than a hundred years old. Not only are the reports of performances of athletes before that time not reliable, but the conditions under which they were achieved are so dissimilar to our own that any comparison between them would be of little value. Heinz Schöbel reminds us that there were no such hard, springy, artificially laid-out tracks at Olympia as we have in our stadiums today; [4] that discuses varied in weight and size at different times and at different games; [5] and that wrestling at the Olympic Games was exclusively a stand-up fight, in which the aim was to pry the opponent loose and throw him to the ground three times.[6]

Unfortunately, many of the records we accept today are too often not definite enough to give us an adequate understanding of just what had been accomplished. Little or no account is taken of the difference which changes in rules, equipment, and circumstances make. We use such a different pole in the pole vault today that pole vaulting is actually a different sport from what it had been only a decade ago. Changes in shoes, turf, bats, balls, and other items have made it possible to attain results in running, jumping, baseball, basketball, and football that were impossible before.

Records not only record, but provide a means for comparing achievements at different places and at different times. Offering objective, public, and neutral accounts of the boundary beyond which no one could then pass, they tell us of the excellence that was possible at a certain place and time, and under certain circumstances, the limit beyond which it was not then possible to go. When the excellence exhibited is officially attributed to a team or an individual, it not only obscures the fact that it is man who is being tested, but the fact that everyone has had teachers, trainers, and foils, that all have been molded and directed in countless ways, and that the culture and environment have to be combined to make it possible for the athlete to develop and perform.

The athlete's answers to his challenges are measured and usually accredited to him if he takes part in a public, refereed game. There he presents himself, naked before the world, with his defenses down. He is not lax of course; on the contrary, he is readied in multiple ways, but this very fact means that he is, for the moment, unprotected with respect to anything other than what he is expected to meet in the game. All energy, all alertness, he is also relaxed, standing there exposed both as an individual and as a representative of all.

4. Heinz Schöbel, *The Ancient Olympic Games,* trans. Joan Becker (Princeton, N. J., 1966), p. 68.

5. Ibid., p. 87.

6. Ibid., p. 75.

The athlete, of course, is not the only man who represents or epitomizes the rest. We all represent one another when we make any statement about a matter of fact. When we say "The snow is falling" we are not giving public expression to a private surmise or belief; we are saying something that we think is true for any and every man: "There is snow there, look who will." But such judgments demand little effort or preparation. The more we are driven to be at our best, the better do we epitomize all, and the more worthily do we represent the rest. The athlete is matched here by the thinker, the artist, and the religious man. Without loss to their individuality, they too instantiate man in a splendid form, which the rest of us accept as an idealized portrait of ourselves. But the athlete shows us, as they do not, what we ideally are as bodies.

No one can separate out just what the individual athlete contributes and what is contributed by the past, his own and others', by his contemporaries, or by nature. The world's impersonal process has him as a focal point. He has, of course, a being and a will all his own; it is his prowess and virtues that are displayed. It is he who makes the judgments; it is he who struggles and strives; it is he who must contest. In the end it is the individual who must decide whether or not he is to continue beyond the point where others can or will perform. Yet the records he makes are only the records of man, showing what man can produce through his agency. It is because he is an outstanding instance of what man might do and be that an athlete is an outstanding man.

Sooner or later the athlete falls short. Eventually he reveals some failure of nerve, self-discipline, courage, insight, generosity, caution, or imagination. These limitations we treat somewhat in the way we deal with those that characterize thinkers, artists, and religious men. We tend to blame the failures on the individual, not on man, until we come to the point where we can confidently say that no one could have done better. We could have ascribed the failures to man and credited the successes to the individual, but that would stand in the way of our wanting to identify ourselves with the athlete, as one who is what a man ought to be.

Athletes are excellence in the guise of men. To be sure, there have been and are boastful athletes, and athletes who think mainly of themselves. Yet even they sometimes must surmise that the good they do lives on as an excellence which man achieved, and that they, just so far as they are superior to the rest of men, have but shown that they are worthy of representing them. The boasts and thoughts of these athletes ride on the surface of what they in fact are.

Long before they reached the stage of being full-fledged athletes, men had to prepare for it. Athletes have to discipline themselves, reorganize themselves, punish themselves. It is not easy to see why they were willing to do this. Why should young men want to be athletes, once account is taken of what they must become and do along the way? My answer has already been indicated: young men are attracted by athletics because it offers them the most promising means for becoming excellent. That answer, though, should not merely be stated, but won. This means it should be reached across the barrier of more obtrusive and apparently more plausible views.

MARIE HART

SPORT: WOMEN SIT IN THE BACK OF THE BUS

> Other things being equal, the man who has had the most experience in outdoor sports should be the best aviator. By the same token, women should be barred ... women have not the background of games of strength and skill that most men have. Their powers of correlation are correspondingly limited and their ability to cope with sudden emergency is inadequate.
>
> —Outing Magazine, November 1912

The roles of woman and successful female athlete are almost incompatible in the United States. The woman who wishes to participate in sports and remain "womanly" faces great stress. By choosing sport she usually places herself outside the social mainstream.

Today's new movements offer little support. What does Women's Lib have to say about freeing the woman athlete? Not much. If woman is to be more than mother, secretary and Miss America, we must reward her for sports achievement instead of stigmatizing her for it.

But the struggle focuses on other areas, such as dance. "Dance is a field for women, and male homosexuals," said *Women: A Journal of Liberation,* which described dance as one of the few ways to escape "Amerika's sick sexuality." And we seem to see sport as a field for men, and female homosexuals. Certainly, for a woman, sport intensifies sex-role problems. In most other parts of the Western world women coexist with men in sport as accepted and respected partners. Not in the United States. A female athlete meets more oppression than most other women in the American way of life.

Norms

Being female in this culture does not necessarily mean that one is perceived or accepted as feminine. Every culture has its social norms and sex roles. In the United States these seem to be especially rigid and narrow; women in sport do not fit our particular concept of femininity and those who persist in sport suffer for it.

Why has it been so difficult for women to remain "womanly" and yet be athletes, especially in games that require great physical skill? Games of physical skill are mostly associated with achievement and aggressiveness, which seem to make them the exclusive province of males. Women are more traditionally associated with obedience training and routine responsibility training and with games of strategy and games of chance. Conditioning begins early—in elementary school a girl feels pressure to select some games and avoid others if she is to be a "real" girl. If she is told often enough at 11 or 12 that sports are not ladylike, she may at that point make a choice between being a lady and being an athlete. This forced choice may create deep conflict that persists into adulthood. Sport is male territory; therefore participation of female intruders is a peripheral, noncentral aspect of sport. The sexually separate (and unequal) facilities and organizations in sport in the United States illustrate the subordination of women athletes.

Conflict

As a girl becomes more and more proficient in sport, her level of personal investment increases and the long hours of practice and limited associations may isolate her socially. Personal conflict and stress increase as it becomes necessary for her to convince others of her femininity. This tension and conflict may increase still more if a girl chooses a sport that most regard as exclusive male territory.

Chi Cheng, a student at California State Polytechnic College at Pomona who holds several world track records for women, was quoted as saying, "The public sees women competing and immediately thinks they must be manly—but at night, we're just like other women."

Why would a woman need to comment about herself in this way and how does this awareness of stigma affect her daily life? For Chi Cheng, one solution is "to give a lot of public appearances—where I can show off my femininity."

Hair

Numerous discussions with college groups over the past few years have convinced me that our society imposes a great burden on women who commit themselves to sport, as participants or as teachers. Several married women students majoring in physical education confided at one discussion group that they had wanted to cut their hair but felt they couldn't: they simply didn't want the stereotyped image. Even when general hair styles are short, women in sport are judged by a standard other than fashion. And if the married woman experiences anxiety over such things, one can imagine the struggle of the single woman.

When young women do enjoy sport, what activities are really open to them? In a 1963 study, 200 first- and second-year college women from four Southern California schools strongly recommended that girls not participate in track and field activities. The sports they did recommend were tennis, swimming, ice skating, diving, bowling, skiing and golf, all of which have esthetic social and fashion aspects. Physical strength and skill may be components of some but are not their primary identifications.

In startling contrast is the black woman athlete. In the black community, it seems, a woman can be strong and competent in sport and still not deny her womanliness. She can even win respect and status; Wilma Rudolph is an example.

Tomboy

Sport standards are male and the woman in sport is compared with men—not with other women. It starts early: *Wow, what a beautiful throw. You've got an arm like a guy. Look at that girl run; she could beat lots of boys.* Father comments, *Yes, she loves sports. She's our little tomboy.* It would seem strange to say of a small boy, *Oh, yes, he is our little marygirl.* (We have ways of getting messages to boys who don't fit the role, but we haven't integrated them into our language so securely.)

These comments carry the message of expected cultural behavior. When the girl has the message clearly she loses games to a boy on purpose. She knows that she may win the game and lose the boy.

Male performance standards and the attending social behavior have resulted in even more serious problems. In international sports events a woman must now pass a sex test of cells collected from inside of the cheek. In a normal woman, about 20 cells in every hundred contain Barr bodies (collections of chromatins). At the 1968 Olympic games, women whose tests showed Barr bodies in fewer than 10 cells in every hundred were barred from competition. Marion Lay, a Canadian swimmer, said that at those Olympics a long line of women awaiting the test in Mexico erupted in reactions that ranged from tension-releasing jokes to severe stress and upset. Some athletes suggested that if the doctor were good-looking enough, one might skip the test and prove her femininity by seducing him. Many were baffled, feeling that their honesty was in question along with their femininity.

There is also the problem of the use by some women performers of "steroid" drugs, male sex-hormone derivatives that tend to increase muscle size. There have been strong and continued warnings against the use of steroids by men because of their dangerous effects, but little has been published about the negative effects of male steriods on women. They are known to increase muscle size, to change fat distribution and also to produce secondary male characteristics such as increased face and body hair and lowered voice.

Why would a woman take such a drug? Because the values are on male records and performance and she will attempt to come as close to this goal as possible.

Bar

Social attitudes that limit sport choices for women have a long history. Here's an editorial from a 1912 issue of *Outing Magazine:*
"Other things being equal, the man who has had the most experience in outdoor sports should be the best aviator. By the same token, women should be barred ... Women have not the background of games of strength and skill that most men have. Their powers of correlation are correspondingly limited and their ability to cope with sudden emergency is inadequate."

In 1936 the editor of *Sportsman,* a magazine for the wealthy, commented of the Olympic Games that he was ". . . fed up to the ears with women as track and field competitors." He continued, "a woman's charms shrink to something less than zero" and urged the organizers to "keep them where they were competent. As swimmers and divers, girls are as beautiful and adroit as they are ineffective and unpleasing on the track."

More recent publications such as *Sports Illustrated* have not been as openly negative; but they sustain sexual bias by limiting their coverage of women in sport. The emphasis in periodicals is still largely on women as attractive objects rather than as skilled and effective athletes.

Muscles

Operating alongside sex bias to scare girls from sport have been such misunderstandings as the muscle myth—the fear that athletics will produce bulging muscles which imply masculinity. The fact, well documented by the exercise physiologists, Carl E. Klafs and Daniel D. Arnheim, is that "excessive development (muscle) is not a concomitant of athletic competition." They further report: "Contrary to lay opinion, participation in sports does not masculinize women. . . ." Some girl and women athletes are indeed muscular. Klafs and Arnheim explain: "Girls whose physiques reflect considerable masculinity are stronger per unit of weight than girls who are low in masculinity and boys who display considerable femininity of build. Those who are of masculine type often do enter sports and are usually quite successful because of the mechanical advantages possessed by the masculine structure. However, such types are the exception, and by far the greater majority of participants possess a feminine body build."

Opening

Myths die hard, but they do die. Today, gradually, women *have* begun to enter sport with more social acceptance and individual pride. In 1952, researchers from the Finnish Institute of Occupational Health who conducted an intensive study of the athletes participating in the Olympics in Helsinki predicted that "women are able to shake off civil disabilities which millennia of prejudice and ignorance have imposed upon them." The researchers found that the participation of women in sport was a significant indicator of the health and living standards of a country.

Simone de Beauvoir wrote in *The Second Sex* ". . . In sports the end in view is not success independent of physical equipment; it is rather the attainment of perfection within the limitations of each physical type; the featherweight boxing champion is as much of a champion as is the heavyweight; the woman skiing champion is not the inferior of the faster male champion; they belong to two different classes. It is precisely the female athletes who, being positively interested in their own game, feel themselves least handicapped in comparison with the male."

Americans seem to be still unable to apply to the woman in sport this view of "attainment of perfection within the limitations of each."

The experiencing of one's body in sport must not be denied to anyone in the name of an earlier century's image of femininity—a binding, limiting, belittling image. This is the age of the woman in space, and she demands her female space and identity in sport.

ROBERT BOYLE

A MINORITY GROUP: THE NEGRO BALL PLAYER

from *Sport: Mirror of American Life*

Sport has often served minority groups as the first rung on the social ladder. As such, it has helped further their assimilation into American life. It would not be far-fetched to say that it has done more in this regard than any other agency, including church and school. In *Organized Sport in Industrial America,* John R. Betts writes that nowhere is "the process of Americanization more in evidence than in sport." To Betts, it is significant that "the greatest fighter of recent decades was a Negro, the most spectacular ballplayer a German, and the most publicized wrestler a Greek, the most respected football coach a Norwegian, the most successful baseball manager an Irishman, the most highly paid jockey an Italian." [1]

Jews, for instance, have been among those to see the social benefit to be derived from sport. Speaking at a Zionist congress in 1901, Max Nordau, German scientist and publicist, called for the development of "muscular Judaism." The *Universal Jewish Encyclopedia* credits Daniel Mendoza, an eighteenth-century prize ring champion, with having been "a potent psychological influence in the liberation of the Jews of England some years later," and the encyclopedia goes on to say that the success of Jewish athletes in the twentieth-century United States "did more than any other single factor in convincing Americans that Jewish young men and women were no different from other youths."

In recent years, Negroes have come to occupy an increasingly prominent position in sport. Without doubt, they have achieved their most publicized success in major league baseball. During the 1959 season, fifty-seven of four-hundred-odd major league players were

1. Joe Louis, Babe Ruth, Jim Londos, Knute Rockne, Joe McCarthy and Eddie Arcaro.

Negroes, and they were paid a total salary of a little under a million dollars.[2] Thirteen years before, Jackie Robinson of the Brooklyn Dodgers was the only Negro in major league ball. He was paid five thousand dollars.[3]

The majority of these fifty-seven players showed a strong sense of group solidarity. "Negroes aren't supposed to stick together," said Brooks Lawrence, a relief pitcher on the Cincinnati Reds, "but the closest kind of adhesion I've ever known has been among Negro ballplayers." The Negro players had their own hangouts, such as the Sportsman Club in Los Angeles. "That's headquarters there," said one. "We won't be in town a half hour before we check in to see what's going on." They also had their own slang, which they guarded closely. "Why should I tell what they mean?" said Bill White of the St. Louis Cardinals when asked the meaning of "mullion" and "hog cutter." "Maybe they're secret words. Maybe we've got a code of our own. Ask someone else, not me. I'm not going to tell you." In addition to all this, the Negro players occupied a special position in Negro society at large. They were, as the late Professor E. Franklin Frazier, chairman of the Department of Sociology at Harvard University, phrased it, "an important part of the bourgeoisie elite."

The Color Line

Although it may surprise modern fans, the Negro's participation in baseball goes back to the 1860s, when Bud Fowler, the first Negro professional, began playing. Fowler had a remarkably long career by any standards; he lasted well into the 1890s, and he would have played longer but for the color line. The first Negroes to appear in a major league box score were the Walker brothers—Fleet, a catcher, and Welday Wilberforce, an outfielder—who both played briefly with Toledo of the American Association in 1884.[4] They had to quit when the team was threatened with mob violence in Richmond.

---

2. This chapter is based on a study made by the author at the end of the 1959 season.

3. At this writing, eighty-five of five hundred major leaguers are Negroes. They earn a total salary of almost two million. See "The Negro in Baseball: 1962: Year of the Big Money," *Ebony*, June 1962.

4. Between 1882 and 1891, the American Association ranked as a major league.

Fleet Walker went to Newark, where he caught George Stovey, a famous Negro pitcher, but in 1887 he and Stovey, who were known as the "Mulatto Battery," left baseball after Cap Anson of the White Stockings balked at playing against them in an exhibition game. The color line had been drawn.

In point of fact, a color bar had existed as early as 1867, when the National Association barred Negro players and clubs from membership, but some players managed to get by. In the Eighties and Nineties, however, an antipathy toward Negroes, instigated by white politicians in the South, set in throughout the country, and Negroes were driven not only from baseball but from such other fields as horse racing and barbering. Only in the prize ring did Negroes retain a foothold, and then many of them had to agree to lose before they could get a fight. Those were the days when Senator Benjamin Tillman of South Carolina plumped for the killing of thirty thousand Negroes in his home state, and a book called *The Negro a Beast* was a popular seller.

The prevailing attitude toward Negroes in baseball is best summed up by a story which appeared in *Sporting Life* in 1891:

Discovery of the Slide
THE FEET-FIRST SLIDE DUE TO A DESIRE TO CRIPPLE
COLORED PLAYERS

"No," said Ed Williamson, the once great shortstop the other day to a reporter, "ball players do not burn with a desire to have colored men on the team. It is, in fact, the deep-seated objection that most of them have for an Afro-American professional player that gave rise to the 'feet-first' slide. You may have noticed in a close play that the base-runner will launch himself into the air and take chances on landing on the bag. Some go head first, others with the feet in advance. Those who adopt the latter method are principally old-timers and served in the dark days prior to 1880. They learned the trick in the East. The Buffaloes—I think it was the Buffalo team—had a negro for second base. He was a few lines blacker than a raven, but he was one of the best players in the old Eastern League. The haughty Caucasians of the association were willing to permit darkies to carry water to them or guard the bat bag, but it made them sore to have the name of one on the batting list. They made a cabal against this man and incidentally introduced a new feature into the game. The players of the opposing teams made it their special business in life to 'spite' this brunette Buffalo. They would tarry at second when they might easily have made third, just to toy with the sensitive shins of the second baseman. The poor man played in two games out of five perhaps; the rest of the time he was on crutches. To give the frequent spiking of the darky an appearance of accident the 'feet first' slide was practiced. The negro got wooden armor for his legs and went into the field with the appearance of a man wearing nail kegs for stockings. The enthusiasm of opposition players would not let them take a bluff. They filed their spikes and the first man at second generally split the wooden half cylinders. The colored man seldom lasted beyond the fifth inning, as the base-runners became more expert. The practice survived long after the second baseman made his last trip to the hospital. 'And that's how Kelly learned to slide,' " concluded the reminiscent Ned.[5]

Barred from organized baseball, Negroes formed their own teams. Waiters at a smart Long Island hotel formed the first one. To get games, they called themselves the Cuban Giants, and on the field they spoke a gibberish that was supposed to be Spanish. Negro leagues followed shortly. Certainly some players were good enough to star in the majors—Josh Gibson, the home run hitting catcher, to name only one—but the color line held firm, though now and then it bent slightly. While managing Baltimore at the turn of the century, John McGraw signed Charlie Grant, a Negro second baseman, and claimed he was an Indian named Tokohoma. The ruse worked until Tokohoma went to

5. Williamson was no bully and his account is undoubtedly exaggerated, but he reflected the attitude of his times. The Negro player referred to was Frank Grant. He was known as the "Black Dunlap," an enormous compliment comparing him to Fred Dunlap, king of the second basemen. Joseph M. Overfield, authority on Buffalo baseball, says Grant seldom missed a game or retired in the middle of one.

Chicago for an exhibition game. Jubilant Negro fans jammed the stands, waving a banner: OUR BOY, CHARLIE GRANT.

Although Charlie Grant failed to stay, several light-skinned Negroes undoubtedly did "pass" into organized ball. In his later days, Bud Fowler said he knew of three or four. In the 1920s, Negro players gossiped that Babe Ruth himself was passing. "Look at his nose, his lips," an old-timer said. Told of this, Professor Frazier said that it was not uncommon for Negroes to lay claim to a celebrity who had features that might be Negroid. "The Negroes," said Frazier, "as with any people who have a low status and a negatively valued world, want to go ahead and neutralize that by claiming important people are Negroes."

Life in the Negro leagues was hard. A star might play in as many as three games a day and earn only four or five hundred dollars a month. But after Jackie Robinson broke in, major league clubs began to pick the Negro leagues clean. The Negro National League collapsed. At last report, the Negro American League limps on. In 1956, conditions were so bad that the West team, playing in the annual league all-star game in Chicago, went on strike. The players wound up getting nothing—except a fifty-dollar fine. Lonnie Harris of the Memphis Red Sox said: "Man, this is a rough league. In the South, if you're playing in a white town, you don't eat—unless there's a Dairy Queen. You can't get out of the bus. The secretary writes down all the stuff on a list and then hands it in the window, and then brings back the hamburgers and stuff. One night it was raining, and I went in for a cheese bit. You know, a little cheese bit. And the guy says to me, 'You wait outside, boy.' I said god damn to myself. It was raining like hell outside. I just got back in the damn bus.

"When we ride all night, they're supposed to give us an extra buck for food. But they just give you two dollars. One night we jumped from Greenwood, Mississippi, to Flint, Michigan, for a game. All we got was that two dollars."

Rufus Gibson of Memphis said: "Some of the guys eat steaks two or three times a week, but a guy can't eat steak like in organized baseball. Most of the guys eat on the run. Like us. Chicago today. Oklahoma City Tuesday. Muskogee, Oklahoma, Wednesday. From there to Little Rock to Memphis to New Orleans by Sunday. We ride all night. A whole lot of nights. If we get into town ten or twelve hours before game time, we usually get a hotel to sleep."

In all fairness, the owners could not be blamed for the meager salaries and backbreaking schedules. The Negro clubs scarcely made anything from the sale of players to the majors. The most any club got was the twenty thousand dollars the Kansas City Monarchs received for Ernie Banks. Dr. J. B. Martin, president of the Negro American League, took this all philosophically. "When Negro players got into the big leagues, people said it would hurt Negro baseball," he said. "I said, 'Let it hurt it.' When we had an entire Negro outfield—Henry Aaron, Frank Robinson, Willie Mays—on the National League team in the All Star game, well, my chest kind of poked out. I was happy to know it."

Negroes and Latins

In 1959–1960, the major league club with the most Negro players was the San Francisco Giants. Ten of the thirty-seven players on the Giants' winter roster were colored. The man mainly responsible was Alex Pompez, a sixty-seven-year-old Negro who had owned the New York Cubans in the Negro National League. Pompez, or "Pomp" as he is called, had played a part in the signing of almost every Negro then in the Giant organization. He got Willie Mays for ten thousand dollars, Willie Kirkland for two thousand and Willie McCovey for only five hundred. His job with the Giants was unique. First of all, he had charge of scouting all Negro and Latin-American players. Secondly, he had charge of all Negro and Latin prospects during spring training. He supervised their food, living quarters (he bunked Dominicans with Dominicans, Cubans with Cubans), manners (no hats on when eating) and dress. He gave them little pep talks.

"When they first start out," Pompez said, "I tell my boys, 'If you want to stay in organized baseball, you got to do things a little bit better. You got to fight, play hard and hustle.' And they do. They're more ambitious, and they're hungry. Every year we got the leading hitter, most valuable player, the big home run hitter." His most delicate task was explaining the color line to Latin Negroes new to the segregated South. "When they first come here, they don't like it," he said. "Some boys cry and want to go home. But after they stay and make big money, they accept things as they are. My main thing is to help them. They can't change the laws."

The segregation issue—in fact, the low status of the Negro in the United States—caused friction between the Latin Negro and American Negro players. With the exception of a few—for example, Felix Mantilla and Juan Pizarro of Milwaukee—Latin Negroes did not willingly mingle with American Negroes off the field. The reason was simple: to be a Negro in the United States was to be inferior. Therefore Latin Negroes were not Negroes, at least as far as they themselves were concerned. They were Cubans, Dominicans or Puerto Ricans.

For their part, American Negroes did not feel that the Latin Negroes should be compelled to associate with them, but what they often resented was the Latin Negro's attitude. "I don't think I'm any better than they are," said an American Negro, "but I'm not any worse, either. They think they're better than the colored guy." Another player said, "You could write a book about these guys. We never see them unless we happen to have some choice material or where they're uncertain about things." Told that Latin Negroes sometimes cry when they first encounter segregation, the player said, "I don't cry. We don't cry, and we have it a hell of a lot worse than they do. But we're conditioned, I guess." The player said that while he was in the minor leagues he roomed with a Latin Negro. "I showed him the ropes, how to order eggs and things." The player came back to the room one day and found that the Latin had moved out. The Latin tried to run around with the white players, but, said the American Negro, "they wouldn't tell him where they were having dinner," so he came back. "But I wouldn't take him. He didn't want me, so I didn't want him."

Mal Goode, a Negro advertising man and a member of the Pittsburgh Chapter of the National Association for the Advancement of Colored People, made it a practice to have Negro players home for dinner. Goode heard about a Latin Negro who was unhappy at not having been invited. "I invited him," Goode said. "After dinner he rubbed his skin and said, almost in tears, 'They say me no want to be colored, Mal. Look at me, Mal. What else can I be?' He said language was the barrier, but the players say differently, at least about the others."

Besides language, there were other barriers between the Latin and American Negro players. The Latin liked his food highly seasoned. He had his own customs and traditions. He was Roman Catholic while the American Negro was Protestant. Pompez recalled how he used a Cuban witch doctor, a *brujo,* to sign Minnie Minoso for the New York Cubans:

"I was in Havana, and I wanted to sign Minoso. But he wouldn't come. He wouldn't even talk to me. Then I heard about this hoodoo man, this *brujo.* He shined shoes in Havana. I was told to see him. So the first day I went there I say nothing. I have him shine my shoes, then I give him a half-dollar tip and go away. The next day I went back and do the same thing. The third day he says, 'Don't I know you?' I said, 'Maybe. My picture's in the paper. I'm Pompez of the New York Cubans.' He asks me, 'What are you doing in Havana?' I tell him I want to sign Minoso, but he won't sign. I ask the *brujo,* 'Do you know Minoso?' He laughs, ha, ha, ha, like he's going to fall down and says, 'Do I know Minoso!' I ask, 'Can you get Minoso to come to the United States to play ball?' He says, 'Yes.' I ask, 'How do you know that?' And he laughs again, and he says, 'If Minoso no go with you, his leg be broken!' I tell him, 'Okay, you get me Minoso, and I will bring you to the United States the year after next as coach.' He says okay, and I tell him where I will be the next night so Minoso can sign the contract.

"Sure enough, right at six o'clock, there's a knock on the door. It's Minoso. He doesn't say a word. I give him the pen, and he signs to play with the New York Cubans. That's it. Later I sold him to Cleveland for seventy-five hundred dollars.

"The next year" (and here Pomp's voice became hushed) "I bring the *brujo* to the United States as a coach. I give him a uniform. He is now my coach. Now in all my years in the Negro National League I have never won a pennant. The *brujo* comes up to me and he says, 'Hey, Pompez, is it true that you have never won the pennant?' I say, 'That's right. In all these years, I've never won the pennant.' You know what? The *brujo,* he looks at me and he says, 'Don't worry, Pompez. This year you win the pennant.' And you know what? I won the pennant! I won the pennant!"

Pomp became indignant when it was suggested that he was laying it on a bit. "That's the truth," he said seriously. "You know Mike Gonzalez" (a former St. Louis coach)? "You know why they say Gonzalez's team wins all the time in the Cuban League? Because he got a goat buried under second base!"

By the late 1950s, a few major league clubs were beginning to realize that the Latin and American Negro players come from vastly different worlds. The Giants, for instance, would put an American Negro on a farm team in the South, but they would not do that with a Latin Negro because they were "afraid that segregation might sour a foreign Negro on the United States as a whole." At the time, Latin Negroes were starting to outnumber American Negroes in the minor leagues. Of seventeen Negroes then in the Giants' farm system, ten were Latin; of thirty-one in the Cincinnati system, seventeen were Latin.

"Everybody Has Problems"

In the minors and the majors the American Negro players "hung kind of close." In some clubs there were leaders; in others there were not. There was, for instance, no leader in the Giants. "I think they're all leaders over there," said George Crowe of St. Louis, laughing. "It's like an army with all generals." (Mays, the logical leader, went his own way.) The main leaders were Bill Bruton on the Braves, Brooks Lawrence on the Reds, and Crowe. A budding leader was Bill White of St. Louis. Negro players expected White, a onetime premedical student, to become a "big man" once he got a couple more years' experience in the league.[6]

Crowe was the big man then. He was smart, level-headed, responsible and experienced. "Why, he's from the State of New York," said one player in awe. Before going to the Cardinals, Crowe had played for Cincinnati, and he had been the leader there. Vada Pinson, the Cincinnati center fielder, said that when he joined the Reds, Crowe "took me right under his wing. He came up to me and said, 'If there are any problems, you come to me. I'm your father, your big daddy up here.' He was serious." Later on, Pinson said:

"Something would come up about going somewhere, and he would

---

6. Crowe has since left the Cardinals, and White, as expected, has become the big man on the Cardinals, if not in the league, on matters of race. He and Bruton, now on the Tigers, have been the spokesmen for Negro players' complaints about spring training conditions in Florida.

say, 'You don't want to do that,' or 'We're supposed to be in bed then.'
He'd be around eavesdropping while another guy would be talking to
me, and after we were through talking, he'd come up to me and say,
'What did you think of what he said?' And I'd say it was good or bad,
and he'd tell me what he thought. He was the big daddy. When I see
him now I call him dad. We look up to him."

Asked about this, Crowe said, "I like to see everybody keep their
nose clean. And when you have fellows who are coming along who are
new to this, I'm glad to give guidance. So naturally I introduced
myself." Asked what sort of problems a youngster like Pinson would
have, Crowe spread his hands, smiled and said, "Everybody has
problems. Life itself is a problem."

Crowe was likely to do much the same thing for Negro youngsters
on other clubs. "If I knew a kid coming up with the Braves," he said,
"I'd say to Bruton, 'Look out for this kid. Show him the places to eat.
Don't leave him stand in the hotel. Take him to the movies. Find out
what he likes to do.' " Crowe had a sense of responsibility as a "race"
man. If, for example, the players were invited to make a public
appearance, he always tried to have a Negro player attend. If no one
else could, he went himself.

With such a sense of oneness, it was no wonder that the Negro
players had what might be called in informal code of behavior. For
example:

A Negro player did not get "the process"—that is, have his hair
straightened. Any player who was foolish enough to have this done
was ridiculed back into line. "That's for entertainers, not ballplayers."

A Negro player did not criticize another Negro player in front of a
white. "Whites talk about each other like dogs," said a Negro player.
"We don't. Don't you ever ask me about a colored ballplayer. I may
hate him, but that's none of your business."

Negro players shared with one another. "When you're on the road,
you never worry," said a player. "If you need anything, so-and-so will
give it to you. And there's no salary jealousy. The best-liked player is
Mays. He makes eighty-five thousand a year and every man is happy to
see him with it." Many players, the player went on, automatically
headed for Mays's home when they reached San Francisco. They had
dinner, then helped themselves to records, shirts or whatever else
Mays had received from admirers. Mays said, "A lot of colored guys
don't get that, so I give them to them."

Negro players did not fight each other. "You watch a fight," said one. "All the players will come out, and what we do is pick out one of us and run up and put it on. We're laughing and hugging, and the white guys are just slugging each other. We just hug. We don't try to harm each other. We got to make a living. You hardly ever see two colored guys fighting. It happens, but you hardly see it. Watch Mays in a fight. He's circling around, circling around, pretending he's looking for someone. Shucks, he's not looking for anyone. Unless it's a guy to pull away." This did not mean that Negroes did not play hard in a game, particularly against each other. "Negroes play harder against Negroes than against whites," said a Negro pitcher. "I'd rather anybody in the world get a hit off me than Mays or Aaron. If they hit, they tease me about it, and that doesn't go down well with me."

The only time Negro players loafed was on barnstorming tours. In the fall of 1959, a group of Negro major leaguers, led by Alex Pompez, toured the Southwest and Mexico playing against an all-white major league team. The whites were intent upon winning; the Negroes laughed and joked. "That white team hustles all the time," a Negro pitcher said. "We've laid down a hell of a lot. But not during the season. You know what would happen if we laid down during the season, don't you?" Another Negro player said, "The whites seem to really want to beat us. They get ahead, they really pour it on. I know that's true because all the guys have talked about it. We know we've got a better team, even though we may take it a little easy, and when we've got a big crowd, we'll beat them."

As a matter of fact, the Negro players took it so easy that they refused to allow Vada Pinson, a youngster who does not know how to stop hustling, to make the trip. Pinson was told, "It's best you don't go. You wouldn't know how to play it. You wouldn't know how to slow down." Pinson did not know how to slow down even when he hit a homer. Once during the 1959 season he sprinted all the way home even though he saw the ball clear the fence as he was rounding second base. When he got back to the bench, Frank Robinson, the Negro first baseman and left fielder, said, "Listen, kid, you'd better just stick to singles and leave those long balls for us cats who can act them out."

Hog Cutting

As with any intimate group, the Negro major leaguers had their own private nicknames for one another. A few of them were known to white players. Don Newcombe, for example, was Tiger to white and Negro players alike, and Mays was called Buck, not Willie, by Giants of both races. "Anyone who knows me well calls me Buck," said Mays. Among the Negroes themselves, George Crowe was Old Folks; Willie Kirkland, Kingfish; Bennie Daniels, Candyman; Charlie Neal, Snake ("He does things lower than a dog," said a Negro player, laughing); Elston Howard, Stellie; Vada Pinson and Frank Robinson, the T boys (both owned Thunderbirds; Robinson's name for Pinson was Bullet); Jim Pendleton, Road and Li'l James Artha; Gene Baker, the Fugitive; Bob Thurman, Cool Daddy; and Monte Irvin, Muggs. Two other Negro players had names that were so racial in origin that players refused to reveal them.

Charlie White, a catcher with Vancouver in the Pacific Coast League, was called the King of the Mullion Men. White, who was in the majors briefly, was a great favorite among Negro players because of his humor. When Negro players met, they often swapped the latest Charlie White story or began an outlandish phrase by saying, "As Chazz White used to say." Pompez would not think of barnstorming without taking White along. "He's very helpful in keeping the boys contented," Pomp said.

Slang in general was a rich field. The terms mullion, hog cutter, drinker and pimp apparently came from the Negro leagues. Drink and pimp barely survived in the majors by 1959. A pimp was a flashy dresser, and a drinker—so Jimmy Banks, a first baseman for the Memphis Red Sox in the Negro National League, once explained—was "a fielder who can pick it clean. He catches everything smooth. He can 'drink' it." Banks also said that a choo-choo papa was a sharp ballplayer, an acrobat was an awkward fielder, a monty was an ugly-looking ballplayer and a foxy girl was a good-looking girl.

Mullion and hog cutter were flexible terms. At first, mullion meant an ugly woman, but its range was extended to an ugly man "or even a child." The greeting "What say, mullion?" was standard among Negro major leaguers during the 1959 season. A hog cutter was a player who made a mistake. "Any mistake, that's a hog," said Crowe. "An error. Throwing to the wrong bag. Going into the bag without sliding. That's when you cut a hog." But, as another player explained, it was possible to cut a hog off the field:

"You cut a hog by saying something that you have no business saying. You can cut the hog with anybody, but it's how we feel if you cut the hog or not. For example, forgetting where you are. You'll be with whites, and you'll forget, and you'll sound off about a colored fellow, 'that black so-and-so.' And they say, 'Oh, he's cut that pig again.' Not much you can do except try to pass over it—the hog's cut then. No one has to say anything. You *know* you cut it. You can cut the hog at a social gathering when you do something very embarrassing. A big hog is when you have a lot of people, men and women, and everyone stops talking at once, and there you are. You're cussing and saying the *nastiest* things. Well, you've done it again with a king-sized hog. Hog cutting is filling the most embarrassing moment with the most embarrassing thing."

Asked who the hog cutters were, the player laughed and said, "A hog cutter is everywhere. He's more or less at large. How many of us did you say there were?"

"Fifty-seven."

"Then there are fifty-seven hog cutters," he said, still laughing.

"Are there different kinds of hog cutters?"

"Oh, yeah," he said. "Bruton and Monte Irvin were the quiet hog cutters. We called Monte sneaky. We'd be talking in a group, and you'd look up and he'd be gone. You'd say, 'Well, he's gone to cut one of those pigs.' "

"How about Brooks Lawrence?"

"Diplomatic-type hog cutter, the sneaking kind."

"Bill White?"

"Not a hog cutter. Only one who isn't."

"Does Newcombe cut a hog?"

"Elephants!"

"Frank Robinson?"

"King-size!"

"Pinson?"

"Just a little pig cutter, but he's learning."

"Covington?"

"He cuts it—both ways."

"Banks?"

"Not any more. He's quiet. But he can cut the hog before you find out the pig has been sliced."

Hog cutter should not be confused with hot dog, another baseball term. A hot dog was a showboat, a player who called attention to himself, either through his actions or his attitude. It was a white expression, although Negroes used it. Although only Negroes were hog cutters, anyone could be a hot dog, though Latin players had a sort of monopoly in the field. "You automatically assume any Latin is a hot dog until he proves himself otherwise," said a white pitcher. Another white word was flaky; it meant eccentric. Occasionally, Negroes and whites would share in the use of an expression. One expression reflected poorly on mother love, and several years ago, a Cub—a white, by the way—used it so freely that he caused a semantic crisis. Warren Giles, president of the National League, was so distraught that he dispatched a memo to each club forbidding its use, particularly toward umpires, under pain of a five-hundred-dollar fine. In his memo, Giles noted that the expression had been recently introduced into baseball. A Negro player saw this and nudged a buddy, saying proudly, "That means we brought it." The players were faced with the considerable problem of what to use instead.

Negroes and whites alike debated the point. "What are you going to say if the umpire is one?" asked a player plaintively. Finally the Negroes decided upon two substitutes: "You're one of those things!" and "You're five hundred dollars' worth!"

Race itself was responsible for much slang. Among the Negro players, whites were called ofays (generally shortened to fays), gray boys, paddies, them people, those people, the other side, squares, triangles, and blow-hair boys. Why triangle? "A triangle is a square in search of a corner," said a Negro player. Why blow-hair boy? "When the wind blows, your hair moves and mine doesn't."

Number Two

Among themselves, the Negro players referred to one another as scobes (derogatory), skokies (also derogatory), Indians and club members. The last was much in favor. A Negro player said,

"We'll get into a town and look around and not see many Negroes, and I might say, 'Hm, this looks like a poor place for club members.' "

Asked how St. Louis, a city with a Southern attitude toward racial matters, was for club members, the player said, "A good town for club members. Lot of club members there."

"And Milwaukee?"

"That's a lousy town for club members. But that's a lousy town for anybody."

Other expressions used by Negroes to denote a Negro were Number Two and M Two. The latter was a corruption of the former. Why Number Two? "Well, we're not Number One!" A word used only by Negro players was road. It meant another Negro player, usually, but not necessarily, on the same team. It was supposed to be short for road buddy. "Hey, road, what's doing?" was a common greeting. Road was a new word. "I called a guy road," said a Negro player, "and he thought I said rogue and he got mad." Earl Robinson, a Dodger bonus player with St. Paul in the American Association, said that when the 1959 season began, only Negroes on the Saints used the term road. Then it began to spread. "Once I was standing on second base after a pretty good double," he said, "and the second baseman on the other team said, 'Hey, road, where did you get all that power from?' "

According to Earl Robinson, Negro slang was freely minted in the minors. He and other Negroes on the Saints began calling one another berries. In short order, one player became young berry, another old berry and so on. Thus, old berry might come into the clubhouse and shout, "Hey, young berry, where's thin berry?" Young berry would reply, "Don't know, old berry. Might be with fat berry." Other slang in use at St. Paul was three bells for .300. To hit the ball "full in the face" or "sit on it" was to hit the ball hard. In night games, a Negro batter going for the long ball would say of the opposing pitcher, "I'm going to hit this guy in the night somewhere," or, "I'm going the night with him." Earl Robinson was of the opinion that "most Caucasian ballplayers are not aware that these things are going on."

Negro players joked about race in veiled terms in front of whites. When the Giants fielded seven Negroes for a game, the Negro players on the opposing bench joked, "Look at that big cloud rolling toward us! It's got to rain today!" and, "Look at those mullion men. Be more hog cutting than you can shake a stick at. They *can't* do right." In a situation like this, a Negro player said, "All the colored guys will be laughing, and the whites won't know anything about it. And we feel that's the way it should be."

Negro players seemingly did not care if a white player avoided them. "I'm not up here to make friends," said Harry Simpson of the A's. "I'm here to play baseball. Any team I've been on, I've made friends. But maybe a guy doesn't want to be friends. Well, it's a free country, and that's his privilege." A number of Negro players said that they generally got along better with white Southerners than white Northerners. "The Southern white knows he has to play with you," said Don Newcombe, "and because he is Southern, he is going to try to keep trouble down. He's more cautious of what he has to say." Another pitcher said, "A couple of years ago, the bullpen catcher told me, 'I don't care for colored players.' I said, 'I don't care for whites.' Then he showed me what I was doing wrong." The pitcher added, "White guys from the South are better. You know where they stand. I don't mind a guy telling me he doesn't like me. I don't want to impose my time on him."

There was little racial abuse from the stands. The same pitcher said, "You get those farmers that come out in St. Louis. That's the only place you expect to hear it. I was warming up one time, and a guy said, 'Hey, snowball, I wish I could pitch like you.' It didn't bother me. I went on pitching, but I had heard it. When I sat down on the bench, the other guys didn't say anything, but they knew I had heard it."

On the other hand, Don Newcombe said, "I can't honestly say that anyone has called me a name. Oh, they've called me a big bum, but that's an honest opinion, and the fan who yelled that may be a hell of a fan."

On occasion, it has been charged that white pitchers have deliberately hit or knocked down Negro batters because of race. Although this may have been true in the early 1950s, the feeling among both white and Negro players was that if more Negro batters were hit, it was because the Negroes were the "hot hitters" on a club. A Cincinnati Negro player said, "When Frank Robinson was knocked down by Cub pitchers, the Reds sent word to the Cubs that they would knock down Banks. Not because Banks is a Negro, but because he was their hot hitter. So Purkey" (Bob Purkey, a white pitcher) "threw four balls around him and under him." A Negro pitcher on another National

League club said, "Sure, I'll brush back a colored player. I've got to make a living. You've got to brush them back. The manager says, 'He's got to go.' You've got to when the guy digs in."

Off the Field

A peculiar thing about the Negro-white relationship off the field was that if a Negro offered an invitation to a white—and this was not common—it was likely to be accepted. But if the white offered the invitation to the Negro, it was unlikely to be accepted. For example, Jim Brosnan, a white pitcher on Cincinnati, sat in the bullpen with Brooks Lawrence. They discussed race, progressive jazz, in which they had a mutual interest, religion—in short, any subject that happened to come up. Yet when Brosnan invited Lawrence to a party at his home in a Chicago suburb, Lawrence refused the invitation. "Brooks said he couldn't make it," Brosnan said. "He said, 'Don't bug me about it.' " When Lawrence was asked why he had refused the invitation, he said, "The basic reason goes back long before baseball. It's our environment. If white people come bearing gifts, you're leary. It's probably your subconscious, but you're wondering if the invitation is real. What's his reason? Why? You wonder, 'Why's he doing this? What's he want?' "

There were other factors which kept the Negro player from intimate association with whites. One was women. "You have to ignore them," said a Negro player. "You don't see them. You don't hear them. Boy, you're playing with fire with that, and we all know it." Players who have played with fire have been sent down.

Tension was another factor. "You don't realize the problems we have," said a Negro player. "You can go anywhere, do anything, but we have terrific tensions. We feel good among our own people. What bothers me is when I, well, pay taxes for something like a school, and I can't go there." This player frankly said that he had "a chip on my shoulder about this wide"—and here he held his hands about a foot apart—about the race problem. "What annoys me most is to see a Negro woman with a white man," he said.

At times this player felt the race problem to be such an intolerable burden that he purposely avoided whites, even in his home town, a Northern industrial city. He said: "Sure I've had invitations to speak, but these people didn't want me before. Now that I'm a major league ball player they want me. But I won't go. I stay with my people. I go down to Pine Street and see my friends, my people. Some are poor and some may drink, but they're my people and my friends. It's a funny thing, but in any Negro section I've ever been in, there's a Pine Street. Always a Pine Street. That's where I go when I'm home. You know, I really didn't know I was a Negro until I was in junior high school. Before, when someone had a birthday party, we'd have it in our home room, and everybody would know. But in junior high school I noticed that I didn't know about the birthday parties any more, and that at the school dances they were on one side of the room and we were on the other."

Another Negro player said that he "found out what it was to be a Negro" when he was eight. "Each class was having a basketball team," he said, "and so I brought in fifty cents for uniform money. But the teacher said, 'Oh, we're not letting colored play this year.' I'll tell you, I waited. There were two high schools in town, one mostly white and one mostly colored. I chose the colored one, and I played every sport I could."

Asked how he did against the white high school, he said, "I wrecked them." [7]

As an adult, this player had what might be called a conciliatory attitude toward whites (he could by no means be called an Uncle Tom), although he was wary on occasion. He said:

"I have the most interesting life in the world. Why? Just being a Negro. I know that when I wake up in the morning and look in the mirror I have a challenge. Where can I find the humor in it? That's

7. See "On the Supremacy of the Negro Athlete in White Athletic Competition," *Psychoanalytic Review*, Vol. 30, 1943, in which Laynard L. Holloman, M.D., of Provident Hospital, Chicago, cites revenge, compensation and a desire to identify with the white race as the motivating factors behind the Negro's success in athletics. It is nonsense to attribute this success to anything physical. American Negroes are largely a mixture of Negro, Indian, and white stock, principally British, and although they differ from whites in some respects—for instance, they are less heavily bearded—they have no physical characteristics that would give them an advantage over white athletic competitors. For examinations of this, see M. F. Ashley Montagu, "The Physical Anthropology of the American Negro," *Psychiatry*, February 1944; "Physical Characteristics of the American Negro," *Scientific Monthly*, July 1944; and Montague Cobb, "Race and Runners," *Journal of Health and Physical Education*, Vol. 7, 1936.

what I try to do. It's so ridiculous you have to find the humor in it. If you didn't you'd go crazy.

"My brother-in-law says he has the toughest job in the world being a Negro. But I look at the other side, look for the humor in it, and I think being Negro's quite a job—especially when you can't get out of it."

On occasion, Negro and white players would attempt to bridge the gulf of race by kidding about it in almost bizarre fashion. "We sit around the clubhouse and joke about the Ku Klux Klan, which isn't a joke at all to a Negro," said a Negro player. "Things like that ease tension."

If Negro players had any complaints about the major leagues, they were:

Lack of advertising endorsements. "Negro players shave, too."

Having their lockers all in a row in the clubhouse. "It seems that clubhouse attendants stress 'togetherness' too much. They keep us all together too much."

Training in the segregated South. Many Negro players refuse to bring their wives. "The first thing I thought of when I was traded," said one player, "was not the club I was going to, but the fact that they trained in Florida. I don't like Florida." One player said he planned to hold out in the spring so he could "miss three weeks of Florida." Another player said, "Latin Americans are always late. They always try to miss spring training."

The feeling that they had to be "better" than white players to stay up in the majors. A Negro pitcher said, "If two players are the same, and one is white and one is colored and one has to go, nine out of ten times the colored guy will be the guy." A side to this that the Negro players did not always see was the outright discrimination against them. American League clubs were far slower to take Negroes than were National League teams. Of the fifty-seven Negroes in the majors a few years ago, forty-one were in the National League. "I haven't been told not to take Negroes," a scout for an American League club said. "The only thing is, you want a good one. Know what I mean? There's still a little taint. Know what I mean?" [8]

8. An official of one of the new major league clubs set up in the recent expansion said that his club wanted no more than five or six Negroes on the squad. The feeling was that "too many" Negroes might hurt the gate, particularly if the team was a losing one, as a new one was bound to be.

Lower, much lower, bonuses. Earl Robinson got "in excess of $50,000" from the Dodgers to sign, but he was a rarity. "I signed for four thousand dollars," said a Negro player, "and if I'd been white, I could have signed for thirty or maybe forty thousand. A lot of white ballplayers I played with in high school got far more than I did, and I was twice the ballplayer they were."

Even the fairest major league front offices admitted that the Negroes did not get the big bonus. "If the kid were another Willie Mays, yes," said a farm system supervisor, "but generally we would have to think twice about a big bonus. There's a limited number of places he can play, and so it's harder to develop him. Negroes can't play in the Southern Association or the Alabama-Florida League. If I went to make a working agreement with a club in either league, I would be told they can't take Negro players."

The farm supervisor went on to say that minor league clubs that did take Negroes did not set a strict quota as such, but "You'll be told by a certain town, 'Don't bring in more than four. That's about all we can handle.' Or, 'Two is about the saturation point here.' Of course that's sometimes due to the fact that there may be only one Negro family in town that could board them. Also, the bulk of the fans are white, and you have to consider their reactions."

Symbols of Achievement

Away from baseball, the Negro major leaguers had a higher status in their own communities than white players did in theirs. The minimum major league salary was seventy-five hundred a year, and only one half of one per cent of the seventeen million Negroes in the United States then made more than five thousand a year. "The Negro ballplayers have become symbols of achievement, symbols of Negro participation in a white world," Professor Frazier said, "and with their high incomes and conspicuous consumption they are an important part of the bourgeoisie elite."

Negro ballplayers were much in the mind of the Negro in general, and at times they were regarded with awe, although a big name would no longer "sell" a business. When Don Newcombe walked into a faculty cafeteria at Howard, everyone arose except for a professor of anthropology who did not know who Newcombe was. After he found out, he still refused to stand up. Later he complained to Frazier, "Imagine professors standing up for a ballplayer!"

Frazier placed sports, with baseball in the lead, as the number one topic of conversation among Negroes, and in *Black Bourgeoisie*, he wrote:

> Once the writer heard a Negro doctor who was prominent "socially" say that he would rather lose a patient than have his favorite baseball team lose a game. This was an extreme expression of the relative value of professional work and recreation among the black bourgeoisie. At the same time, it is indicative of the value which many Negro professional men and women, including college professors, place upon sports. Except when they are talking within the narrow field of their professions, their conversations are generally limited to sports—baseball and football. They follow religiously the scores of the various teams and the achievements of all the players. For hours they listen to the radio accounts of sports and watch baseball and football games on television.

Wilson Record, a sociologist at Sacramento State College, said that when he was doing field research in Chicago, Negroes who played the numbers game, an illegal lottery usually based on pari-mutuel returns at race tracks, would keep tabs on a special box the *Chicago Daily Defender* carried listing the batting averages of all Negro hitters. "From this," said Record, "they would get a number to play."

A curious, but perhaps valid, insight into the Negro regard for baseball might be obtained by consulting the various dream books sold to numbers players in Harlem and other Negro communities. These books interpret the subject matter of a dream and give the reader a number to play. Some subjects are good luck, others bad.

The Lucky Star Dream Book, by a Professor Konje, carried this entry on baseball: "To dream that you play this game denotes safety of your affairs and a happy reunion among your neighbors. 100." In *The Success Dream Book*, by a Professor De Herbert, was this entry: "To dream of playing base-ball is a sign that you will live to a good old age, and then die happily. 945. To see others play this game is a sign of peace and satisfaction. 567." The symbolism is obvious.

Generally speaking, the Negro ballplayers, unlike some Negro entertainers who were quick to express hostility to the Negro world below them, were "race" men. Mal Goode said: "The Negro players do accept responsibility as race men. Fifteen of them are buying or already have bought life memberships in the NAACP. That's five hundred dollars. Also, many of them have made special contributions to the NAACP. When the NAACP was fighting in the Supreme Court, the NAACP would send telegrams asking players for money. I've only heard one [Negro] ballplayer make a derogatory remark. He said, 'Don't you think the NAACP stirs up trouble?' I said, 'Do me a favor. Never say anything like that again.' "

Professor Frazier was not surprised at the ballplayers' being race men. "A baseball player is attached to conventional worlds," he said. "An entertainer isn't." As he saw it, the entertainer dwelt in "the House of Satan," so to speak, where anything went and ties were broken in the process. But the ballplayer did not. After all, said Frazier, "Baseball is an American sport with American respectability."

JOHN UPDIKE

HUB FANS BID KID ADIEU

Fenway Park, in Boston, is a lyric little bandbox of a ballpark. Everything is painted green and seems in curiously sharp focus, like the inside of an old-fashioned peeping-type Easter egg. It was built in 1912 and rebuilt in 1934, and offers, as do most Boston artifacts, a compromise between Man's Euclidean determinations and Nature's beguiling irregularities. Its right field is one of the deepest in the American League, while its left field is the shortest; the high leftfield wall, three hundred and fifteen feet from home plate along the foul line, virtually thrusts its surface at right-handed hitters. On the afternoon of Wednesday, September 28th, 1960, as I took a seat behind third base, a uniformed groundkeeper was treading the top of this wall, picking batting-practice home runs out of the screen, like a mushroom gatherer seen in Wordsworthian perspective on the verge of a cliff. The day was overcast, chill, and uninspirational. The Boston team was the worst in twenty-seven seasons. A jangling medley of incompetent youth and aging competence, the Red Sox were finishing in seventh place only because the Kansas City Athletics had locked them out of the cellar. They were scheduled to play the Baltimore Orioles, a much nimbler blend of May and December, who had been dumped from pennant contention a week before by the insatiable Yankees. I, and 10,453 others, had shown up primarily because this was the Red Sox's last home game of the season, and therefore the last time in all eternity that their regular left fielder, known to the headlines as TED, KID, SPLINTER, THUMPER, TW, and, most cloyingly, MISTER WONDERFUL, would play in Boston. "WHAT WILL WE DO WITHOUT TED? HUB FANS ASK" ran the headline on a newspaper being read by a bulb-nosed cigar smoker a few rows away. Williams' retirement had been announced, doubted (he had been threatening retirement for years), confirmed by Tom Yawkey, the Red Sox owner, and at last widely accepted as the sad but probable truth. He was forty-two and had redeemed his abysmal season of 1959 with a—considering his advanced age—fine one. He had been giving away his gloves and bats and had grudgingly consented to a sentimental ceremony today. This was not necessarily his last game; the Red Sox were scheduled to travel to New York and wind up the season with three games there.

I arrived early. The Orioles were hitting fungos on the field. The day before, they had spitefully smothered the Red Sox, 17-4, and neither their faces nor their drab gray visiting-team uniforms seemed very gracious. I wondered who had invited them to the party. Between our heads and the lowering clouds a frenzied organ was thundering through, with an appositeness perhaps accidental, "You *maaaade* me love you, I didn't wanna do it, I didn't wanna do it. . . ."

The affair between Boston and Ted Williams was no mere summer romance; it was a marriage composed of spats, mutual disappointments, and, toward the end, a mellowing hoard of shared memories. It fell into three stages, which may be termed Youth, Maturity, and Age; or Thesis, Antithesis, and Synthesis; or Jason, Achilles, and Nestor.

First there was the by now legendary epoch[1] when the young bridegroom came out of the West and announced "All I want out of life is that when I walk down the street folks will say 'There goes the greatest hitter who ever lived.' " The dowagers of local journalism attempted to give elementary deportment lessons to this child who spake as a god, and to their horror were themselves rebuked. Thus began the long exchange of backbiting, bat-flipping, booing, and spitting that has distinguished Williams' public relations.[2] The spit-

1. This piece was written with no research materials save an outdated record book and the Boston newspapers of the day; and Williams' early career preceded the dawning of my *Schlagballewusstsein* (Baseball-consciousness). Also for reasons of perspective was my account of his beginnings skimped. Williams first attracted the notice of a major-league scout—Bill Essick of the Yankees—when he was a fifteen-year-old pitcher with the San Diego American Legion Post team. As a pitcher-outfielder for San Diego's Herbert Hoover High School, Williams recorded averages of .586 and .403. Essick balked at signing Williams for the $1,000 his mother asked; he was signed instead, for $150 a month, by the local Pacific Coast League franchise, the newly created San Diego Padres. In his two seasons with this team, Williams hit merely .271 and .291, but his style and slugging (23 home runs the second year) caught the eye of, among others, Casey Stengel, then with the Boston Braves, and Eddie Collins, the Red Sox general manager. Collins bought him for the Padres for $25,000 in cash and $25,000 in players. Williams was then nineteen. Collins' fond confidence in the boy's potential matched Williams' own. Williams reported to the Red Sox training camp in Sarasota in 1938 and, after showing more volubility than skill, was shipped down to the Minneapolis Millers, the top Sox farm team. It should be said, perhaps, that the parent club was equipped with an excellent, if mature, outfield, mostly purchased from Connie Mack's dismantled A's. Upon leaving Sarasota, Williams is supposed to have told the regular outfield of Joe Vosmik, Doc Cramer, and Ben Chapman that he would be back and would make more money than the three of them put together. At Minneapolis he hit .366, batted in 142 runs, scored 130, and hit 43 home runs. He also loafed in the field, jabbered at the fans, and smashed a water cooler with his fist. In 1939 he came north with the Red Sox. On the way, in Atlanta, he dropped a foul fly, accidentally kicked it away in trying to pick it up, picked it up, and threw it out of the park. It would be nice if, his first time up in Fenway Park, he had hit a home run. Actually, in his first Massachusetts appearance, the first inning of an exhibition game against Holy Cross at Worcester, he *did* hit a home run, a grand slam. The Red Sox season opened in Yankee Stadium. Facing Red Ruffing, Williams struck out and, the next time up, doubled for his first major-league hit. In the Fenway Park opener, against Philadelphia, he had a single in five trips. His first home run came on April 23, in that same series with the A's. Williams was then twenty, and played *right* field. In his rookie season he hit .327; in 1940, .344.

2. See *Ted Williams,* by Ed Linn (Sport Magazine Library), Chapter 6, "Williams vs. the Press." It is Linn's suggestion that Williams walked into a circulation war among the seven Boston newspapers, who in their competitive zeal headlined incidents that the New York papers, say, would have minimized, just as they minimized the less genial side of the moody and aloof DiMaggio and smoothed Babe Ruth into a folk hero. It is also Linn's thought, and an interesting one, that Williams thrived on even adverse publicity, and needed a hostile press to elicit, contrariwise, his defiant best. The statistics (espe-

ting incidents of 1957 and 1958 and the similar dockside courtesies that Williams has now and then extended to the grandstand should be judged against his background: the left-field stands at Fenway for twenty years have held a large number of customers who have bought their way in primarily for the privilege of showering abuse on Williams. Greatness necessarily attracts debunkers, but in Williams' case the hostility has been systematic and unappeasable. His basic offense against the fans has been to wish that they weren't there. Seeking a perfectionist's vacuum, he has quixotically desired to sever the game from the ground of paid spectatorship and publicity that supports it. Hence his refusal to tip his cap [3] to the crowd or turn the other cheek to newsmen. It has been a costly theory—it has probably cost him, among other evidences of good will, two Most Valuable Player awards, which are voted by reporters [4]—but he has held to it. While his critics, oral and literary, remained beyond the reach of his discipline, the opposing pitchers were accessible, and he spanked them to the tune of .406 in 1941.[5] He slumped to .356 in 1942 and went off to war.

---

cially of the 1958 season, when he snapped a slump by spitting in all directions, and inadvertently conked an elderly female fan with a tossed bat) seem to corroborate this. Certainly Williams could have had a truce for the asking, and his industrious perpetuation of the war, down to his last day in uniform, implies its usefulness to him. The actual and intimate anatomy of the matter resides in locker rooms and hotel corridors fading from memory. When my admiring account was printed, I received a letter from a sports reporter who hated Williams with a bitter and explicit immediacy. And even Linn's hagiology permits some glimpses of Williams' locker-room manners that are not pleasant.

3. But he did tip his cap, high off his head, in at least his first season, as cartoons from that period verify. He also was extravagantly cordial to taxi-drivers and stray children. See Linn, Chapter 4, "The Kid Comes to Boston": "There has never been a ballplayer—anywhere, anytime—more popular than Ted Williams in his first season in Boston." To this epoch belongs Williams' prankish use of the Fenway scoreboard lights for rifle practice, his celebrated expressed preference for the life of a fireman, and his determined designation of himself as "The Kid."

4. In 1947 Joe DiMaggio and in 1957 Mickey Mantle, with seasons inferior to Williams', won the MVP award because sportswriters, who vote on ballots with ten places, had vengefully placed Williams ninth, tenth, or nowhere at all. The 1941 award to Joe DiMaggio, even though this was Williams' .406 year, is more understandable, since this was also *annus miraculorum* when DiMaggio hit safely in 56 consecutive games.

5. The sweet saga of this beautiful decimal must be sung once more. Williams, after hitting above .400 all season, had cooled to .39955 with one doubleheader left to play, in Philadelphia. Joe Cronin, then managing the Red Sox, offered to bench him to safeguard

In 1946, Williams returned from three years as a Marine pilot to the second of his baseball avatars, that of Achilles, the hero of incomparable prowess and beauty who nevertheless was to be found sulking in his tent while the Trojans (mostly Yankees) fought through to the ships. Yawkey, a timber and mining maharajah, had surrounded his central jewel with many gems of slightly lesser water, such as Bobby Doerr, Dom DiMaggio, Rudy York, Birdie Tebbetts, and Johnny Pesky. Throughout the late forties, the Red Sox were the best paper team in baseball, yet they had little three-dimensional to show for it, and if this was a tragedy, Williams was Hamlet. A succinct review of the indictment—and a fair sample of appreciative sports-page prose—appeared the very day of Williams' valedictory, in a column by Huck Finnegan in the Boston *American* (no sentimentalist, Huck):

> Williams' career, in contrast [to Babe Ruth's], has been a series of failures except for his averages. He flopped in the only World Series he every played in (1946) when he batted only .200. He flopped in the playoff game with Cleveland in 1948. He flopped in the final game of the 1949 season with the pennant hinging on the outcome (Yanks 5, Sox 3). He flopped in 1950 when he returned to the lineup after a two-month absence and ruined the morale of a club that seemed pennant-bound under Steve O'Neill. It has always been Williams' records first, the team second, and the Sox non-winning record is proof enough of that.

There are answers to all this, of course. The fatal weakness of the great Sox slugging teams was not-quite-good-enough pitching rather than Williams' failure to hit a home run every time he came to bat. Again, Williams' depressing effect on his teammates has never been

---

his average, which was exactly .400 when rounded to the third decimal place. Williams said (I forget where I read this) that he did not want to become a .400 hitter with just his toenails over the line. He played the first game and singled, homered, singled, and singled. With less to gain than to lose, he elected to play the second game and got two more hits, including a double that dented a loudspeaker horn on the top of the right-field wall, giving him six-for-eight on the day and a season's average that, in the forty years between Rogers Hornsby's .403 (1925) and the present, stands as unique.

proved. Despite ample coaching to the contrary, most insisted that they *liked* him. He has been generous with advice to any player who asked for it. In an increasingly combative baseball atmosphere, he continued to duck beanballs docilely. With umpires he was gracious to a fault. This courtesy itself annoyed his critics, whom there was no pleasing. And against the ten crucial games (the seven World Series games with the St. Louis Cardinals, the 1948 playoff with the Cleveland Indians, and the two-game series with the Yankees at the end of the 1949 season, when one victory would have given the Red Sox the pennant) that make up the Achilles' heel of Williams' record, a mass of statistics can be set showing that day in and day out he was no slouch in the clutch.[6] The correspondence columns of the Boston papers now and then suffer a sharp flurry of arithmetic on this score; indeed, for Williams to have distributed all his hits so they did nobody else any good would constitute a feat of placement unparalleled in the annals of selfishness.

Whatever residue of truth remains of the Finnegan charge those of us who love Williams must transmute as best we can, in our own personal crucibles. My personal memories of Williams began when I was a boy in Pennsylvania, with two last-place teams in Philadelphia to keep me company. For me, "W'ms, lf" was a figment of the box scores who always seemed to be going 3-for-5. He radiated, from afar, the hard blue glow of high purpose. I remember listening over the radio to the All-Star Game of 1946, in which Williams hit two singles and two home runs, the second one off a Rip Sewell "blooper" pitch; it was like hitting a balloon out of the park. I remember watching one of his home runs from the bleachers of Shibe Park; it went over the first baseman's head and rose methodically along a straight line and was still rising when it cleared the fence. The trajectory seemed qualitatively different from anything anyone else might hit. For me, Williams is the classic ballplayer of the game on a hot August weekday, before a small crowd, when the only thing at stake is the tissue-thin difference between a thing well done and a thing done ill. Baseball is a game of the long season, of relentless and gradual averaging-out. Irrelevance

6. For example: In 1948, the Sox came from behind to tie the Indians by winning three straight; in those games Williams went two for two, two for two; and two for four. In 1949, the Sox overtook the Yankees by winning nine in a row; in that streak, Williams won four games with home runs.

—since the reference point of most individual contests is remote and statistical—always threatens its interest, which can be maintained not by the occasional heroics that sportswriters feed upon by players who always *care;* who care, that is to say, about themselves and their art. Insofar as the clutch hitter is not a sportswriter's myth, he is a vulgarity, like a writer who writes only for money. It may be that, compared to such managers' dreams as the manifestly classy Joe DiMaggio and the always helpful Stan Musial, Williams was an icy star. But of all team sports, baseball, with its graceful intermittences of action, its immense and tranquil field sparsely settled with poised men in white, its dispassionate mathematics, seems to me best suited to accommodate, and be ornamented by, a loner. It is an essentially lonely game. No other player visible to my generation concentrated within himself so much of the sport's poignance, so assiduously refined his natural skills, so constantly brought to the plate that intensity of competence that crowds the throat with joy.

By the time I went to college, near Boston, the lesser stars Yawkey had assembled around Williams had faded, and his rigorous pride of craftsmanship had become itself a kind of heroism. This brittle and temperamental player developed an unexpected quality of persistence. He was always coming back—back from Korea, back from a broken collarbone, a shattered elbow, a bruised heel, back from drastic bouts of flu and ptomaine poisoning. Hardly a season went by without some enfeebling mishap, yet he always came back, and always looked like himself. The delicate mechanism of timing and power seemed sealed, shockproof, in some case deep within his frame.[7] In addition to injuries, there was a heavily publicized divorce, and the usual storms with the press, and the Williams Shift—the maneuver, custom-built by Lou Boudreau of the Cleveland Indians, whereby three infielders were concentrated on the right side of the

7. Two reasons for his durability may be adduced. A non-smoker, non-drinker, habitual walker, and year-round outdoorsman, Williams spared his body the vicissitudes of the seasonal athlete. And his hitting was in large part a mental process; the amount of cerebration he devoted to such details as pitchers' patterns, prevailing winds, and the muscular mechanics of swinging a bat would seem ridiculous, if it had not paid off. His intellectuality, as it were, perhaps explains the quickness with which he adjusted, after the war, to the changed conditions—the night games, the addition of the slider to the standard pitching repertoire, the new cry for the long ball. His reaction to the Williams Shift, then, cannot be dismissed as unconsidered.

infield.[8] Williams could easily have learned to punch singles through the vacancy on his left and fattened his average hugely. This was what Ty Cobb, the Einstein of average, told him to do. But the game had changed since Cobb; Williams believed that his value to the club and to the league was as a slugger, so he went on pulling the ball, trying to blast it through three men, and paid the price of perhaps fifteen points of lifetime average. Like Ruth before him, he bought the occasional home run at the cost of many directed singles—a calculated sacrifice certainly not, in the case of a hitter as average-minded as Williams, entirely selfish.

After a prime so harassed and hobbled, Williams was granted by the relenting fates a golden twilight. He became at the end of his career perhaps the best *old* hitter of the century. The dividing line falls between the 1956 and the 1957 seasons. In September of the first year, he and Mickey Mantle were contending for the batting championship. Both were hitting around .350, and there was no one else near them. The season ended with a three-game series between the Yankees and the Sox, and, living in New York then, I went up to the Stadium. Williams was slightly shy of the four hundred at-bats needed to qualify; the fear was expressed that the Yankee pitchers would walk him to protect Mantle. Instead, they pitched to him. It was wise. He looked terrible at the plate, tired and discouraged and unconvincing. He never looked very good to me in the Stadium.[9] The final outcome in 1956 was Mantle .353, Williams .345.

The next year, I moved from New York to New England, and it made all the difference. For in September of 1957, in the same situation, the story was reversed. Mantle finally hit .365; it was the best season of his career. But Williams, though sick and old, had run away

8. Invented, or perpetrated (as a joke?) by Boudreau on July 14, 1946, between games of a doubleheader. In the first game of the doubleheader, Williams had hit three homers and batted in eight runs. The shift was not used when men were on base and, had Williams bunted or hit late against it immediately, it might not have spread, in all its variations, throughout the league. The Cardinals used it in the lamented World Series of that year. Toward the end, in 1959 and 1960, rather sadly, it had faded from use, or degenerated to the mere clockwise twitching of the infield customary against pull hitters.

9. Shortly after his retirement, Williams, in *Life*, wrote gloomily of the Stadium, "There's the bigness of it. There are those high stands and all those people smoking —and, of course, the shadows. . . . It takes at least one series to get accustomed to the Stadium and even then you're not sure." Yet his lifetime batting average there was .340, only four points under his median average.

from him. A bout of flu had laid him low in September. He emerged from his cave in the Hotel Somerset haggard but irresistible; he hit four successive pinch-hit home runs. "I feel terrible," he confessed, "but every time I take a swing at the ball it goes out of the park." He ended the season with thirty-eight home runs and an average of .388, the highest in either league since his own .406, and, coming from a decrepit man of thirty-nine, an even more supernal figure. With eight or so of the "leg hits" that a younger man would have beaten out, it would have been .400. And the next year, Williams, who in 1949 and 1953 had lost batting championships by decimal whiskers to George Kell and Mickey Vernon, sneaked in behind his teammate Pete Runnels and filched his sixth title, a bargain at .328.

In 1959, it seemed all over. The dinosaur thrashed around in the .200 swamp for the first half of the season, and was even benched ("rested," Manager Mike Higgins tactfully said). Old foes like the late Bill Cunningham began to offer batting tips. Cunningham thought Williams was jiggling his elbows;[10] in truth, Williams' neck was so stiff he could hardly turn his head to look at the pitcher. When he swung, it looked like a Calder mobile with one thread cut; it reminded you that since 1954 Williams' shoulders had been wired together. A solicitous pall settled over the sports pages. In the two decades since Williams had come to Boston, his status had imperceptibly shifted from that of a naughty prodigy to that of a municipal monument. As his shadow in the record books lengthened, the Red Sox teams around him declined, and the entire American League seemed to be losing life and color to the National. The inconsistency of the new super-stars—Mantle, Colavito, and Kaline—served to make Williams appear all the more singular. And off the field, his private philanthropy—in particular, his zealous chairmanship of the Jimmy Fund, a charity for children with cancer—gave him a civic presence matched only by that of Richard Cardinal Cushing. In religion, Williams appears to be a humanist, and

10. It was Cunningham who, when Williams first appeared in a Red Sox uniform at the 1938 spring training camp, wrote with melodious prescience: "The Sox seem to think Williams is just cocky enough and gabby enough to make a great and colorful outfielder, possibly the Babe Herman type. Me? I don't like the way he stands at the plate. He bends his front knee inward and moves his foot just before he takes a swing. That's exactly what I do just before I drive a golf ball and knowing what happens to the golf balls I drive, I don't believe this kid will ever hit half a singer midget's weight in a bathing suit."

a selective one at that, but he and the abrasive-voiced Cardinal, when their good works intersect and they appear in the public eye together, make a handsome pair of seraphim.

Humiliated by his '59 season, Williams determined, once more, to come back. I, as a specimen Williams partisan, was both glad and fearful. All baseball fans believe in miracles; the question is, how *many* do you believe in? He looked liked a ghost in spring training. Manager Jurges warned us ahead of time that if Williams didn't come through he would be benched, just like anybody else. As it turned out, it was Jurges who was benched. Williams entered the 1960 season needing eight home runs to have a lifetime total of 500; after one time at bat in Washington, he needed seven. For a stretch, he was hitting a home run every second game that he played. He passed Lou Gehrig's lifetime total, and finished with 521, thirteen behind Jimmy Foxx, who alone stands between Williams and Babe Ruth's unapproachable 714. The summer was a statistician's picnic. His two-thousandth walk came and went, his eighteen-hundredth run batted in, his sixteenth All-Star Game. At one point, he hit a home run off a pitcher, Don Lee, off whose father, Thornton Lee, he had hit a home run a generation before. The only comparable season for a forty-two-year-old man was Ty Cobb's in 1928. Cobb batted .323 and hit one homer. Williams batted .316 but hit twenty-nine homers.

In sum, though generally conceded to be the greatest hitter of his era, he did not establish himself as "the greatest hitter who ever lived." Cobb, for average, and Ruth, for power, remain supreme. Cobb, Rogers Hornsby, Joe Jackson, and Lefty O'Doul, among players since 1900, have higher lifetime averages than Williams' .344. Unlike Foxx, Gehrig, Hack Wilson, Hank Greenberg, and Ralph Kiner, Williams never came close to matching Babe Ruth's season home-run total of sixty.[11] In the list of major-league batting records, not one is held by Williams. He is second in walks drawn, third in home runs, fifth in lifetime average, sixth in runs batted in, eighth in runs scored and in total bases, fourteenth in doubles, and thirtieth in hits.[12] But if we allow him merely average seasons for the four-plus seasons he lost

11. Written before Roger Maris's fluky, phenomenal sixty-one.
12. Again, as of 1960. Since then, Musial may have surpassed him in some statistical areas.

to two wars, and add another season for the months he lost to injuries, we get a man who in all the power totals would be second, and not a very distant second, to Ruth. And if we further allow that these years would have been not merely average but prime years, if we allow for all the months when Williams was playing in sub-par condition, if we permit his early and later years in baseball to be some sort of index of what the middle years could have been, if we give him a right-field fence that is not, like Fenway's, one of the most distant in the league, and if—the least excusable "if"—we imagine him condescending to outsmart the Williams Shift, we can defensibly assemble, like a colossus induced from the sizable fragments that do remain, a statistical figure not incommensurate with his grandiose ambition. From the statistics that are on the books, a good case can be made that in the *combination* of power and average Williams is first; nobody else ranks so high in both categories. Finally, there is the witness of the eyes; men whose memories go back to Shoeless Joe Jackson—another unlucky natural—rank him and Williams together as the best-looking hitters they have seen. It was for our last look that ten thousand of us had come.

Two girls, one of them with pert buckteeth and eyes as black as vest buttons, the other with white skin and flesh-colored hair, like an underdeveloped photograph of a redhead, came sat on my right. On my other side was one of those frowning chestless young-old men who can frequently be seen, often wearing sailor hats, attending ball games alone. He did not once open his program but instead tapped it, rolled up, on his knee as he gave the game his disconsolate attention. A young lady, with freckles, and a depressed dainty nose that by an optical illusion seemed to thrust her lips forward for a kiss, sauntered down into the box seat right behind the roof of the Oriole dugout. She wore a blue coat with a Northeastern University emblem sewed to it. The girls beside me took it into their heads that this was Williams' daughter. She looked too old to me, and why would she be sitting behind the visitors' dugout? On the other hand, from the way she sat there, staring at the sky and French-inhaling, she clearly was *somebody*. Other fans came and eclipsed her from view. The crowd looked less like a weekday ballpark crowd than like the folks you might find in Yellowstone National Park, or emerging from automobiles at the top of scenic Mount Mansfield. There were a lot of competitively well-dressed couples of tourist age, and not a few babes in arms. A row of five seats in front of me was abruptly filled with a woman and four children, the youngest of them two years old, if that. Someday, presumably, he could tell his grandchildren that he saw Williams play. Along with these tots and second-honeymooners, there were Harvard freshmen, giving off that peculiar nervous glow created when a sufficient quantity of insouciance is saturated with enough insecurity; thick-necked Army officers with brass on their shoulders and steel in their stares; pepperings of priests; perfumed bouquets of Roxbury Fabian fans; shiny salesmen from Albany and Fall River; and those gray, hoarse men—taxi drivers, slaughterers, and bartenders—who will continue to click through the turnstiles long after everyone else has deserted to television and tramporamas. Behind me, two young male voices blossomed, cracking a joke about God's five proofs that Thomas Aquinas exists—typical Boston College levity.

The batting cage was trundled away. The Orioles fluttered to the sidelines. Diagonally across the field, by the Red Sox dugout, a cluster of men in overcoats were festering like maggots. I could see a splinter of white uniform, and Williams' head, held at a self-deprecating and evasive tilt. Williams' conversational stance is that of a six-foot-three-inch man under a six-foot ceiling. He moved away to the patter of flash bulbs, and began playing catch with a young Negro outfielder named Willie Tasby. His arm, never very powerful, had grown lax with the years, and his throwing motion was a kind of muscular drawl. To catch the ball, he flicked his glove hand onto his left shoulder (he batted left but threw right, as every schoolboy ought to know) and let the ball plop into it comically. The catch session with Tasby was the only time all afternoon I saw him grin.

A tight little flock of human sparrows who, from the lambent and pampered pink of their faces, could only have been Boston politicians moved toward the plate. The loudspeakers mammothly coughed as someone huffed on the microphone. The ceremonies began. Curt Gowdy, the Red Sox radio and television announcer, who sounds like everybody's brother-in-law, delivered a brief sermon, taking the two words "pride" and "champion" as his text. It began. "Twenty-one years ago, a skinny kid from San Diego, California . . ." and ended, "I don't think we'll ever see another like him." Robert Tibolt, chairman of the board of the Greater Boston Chamber of Commerce, presented

Williams with a big Paul Revere silver bowl. Harry Carlson, a member of the sports committee of the Boston Chamber, gave him a plaque, whose inscription he did not read in its entirety, out of deference to Williams' distaste for this sort of fuss. Mayor Collins, seated in a wheelchair, presented the Jimmy Fund with a thousand-dollar check.

Then the occasion himself stooped to the microphone, and his voice sounded, after the others, very Californian; it seemed to be coming, excellently amplified, from a great distance, adolescently young and as smooth as a butternut. His thanks for the gifts had not died from our ears before he glided, as if helplessly, into "In spite of all the terrible things that have been said about me by the knights of the keyboard up there. . . ." He glanced up at the press rows suspended behind home plate. The crowd tittered, appalled. A frightful vision flashed upon me, of the press gallery pelting Williams with erasers, of Williams clambering up the foul screen to slug journalists, of a riot, of Mayor Collins being crushed. ". . . And they *were* terrible things," Williams insisted, with level melancholy, into the mike. "I'd like to forget them, but I can't." He paused, swallowed his memories, and went on, "I want to say that my years in Boston have been the greatest thing in my life." The crowd, like an immense sail going limp in a change of wind, sighed with relief. Taking all the parts himself, Williams then acted out a vivacious little morality drama in which an imaginary tempter came to him at the beginning of his career and said, "Ted, you can play anywhere you like." Leaping nimbly into the role of his younger self (who in biographical actuality had yearned to be a Yankee), Williams gallantly chose Boston over all the other cities, and told us that Tom Yawkey was the greatest owner in baseball and we were the greatest fans. We applauded ourselves lustily. The umpire came out and dusted the plate. The voice of doom announced over the loudspeakers that after Williams' retirement his uniform number 9, would be permanently retired—the first time the Red Sox had so honored a player. We cheered. The national anthem was played. We cheered. The game began.

Williams was third in the batting order, so he came up in the bottom of the first inning, and Steve Barber, a young pitcher born two months before Williams began playing in the major leagues, offered him four pitches, at all of which he disdained to swing, since none of them were within the strike zone. This demonstrated simultaneously that Williams' eyes were razor-sharp and that Barber's control wasn't. Shortly, the bases were full, with Williams on second. "Oh, I hope he gets held up at third! That would be wonderful," the girl beside me moaned, and, sure enough, the man at bat walked and Williams was delivered into our foreground. He struck the pose of Donatello's David, the third-base bag being Goliath's head. Fiddling with his cap, swapping small talk with the Oriole third basemen (who seemed delighted to have him drop in), swinging his arms with a sort of prancing nervousness, he looked fine—flexible, hard, and not unbecomingly substantial through the middle. The long neck, the small head, the knickers whose cuffs were worn down near his ankles—all these clichés of sports cartoon iconography were rendered in the flesh.

With each pitch, Williams danced down the baseline, waving his arms and stirring dust, ponderous but menacing, like an attacking goose. It occurred to about a dozen humorists at once to shout "Steal home! Go, go!" Williams' speed afoot was never legendary. Lou Clinton, a young Sox outfielder, hit a fairly deep fly to center field. Williams tagged up and ran home. As he slid across the plate, the ball, thrown with unusual heft by Jackie Brandt, the Oriole center fielder, hit him on the back.

"Boy, he was really loafing, wasn't he?" one of the collegiate voices behind me said.

"It's cold," the other voice explained. "He doesn't play well when it's cold. He likes heat. He's a hedonist."

The run that Williams scored was the second and last of the inning. Gus Triandos, of the Orioles, quickly evened the score by plunking a home run over the handy left-field wall. Williams, who had had this wall at his back for twenty years,[13] played the ball flawlessly. He didn't budge. He just stood still, in the center of the little patch of grass that his patient footsteps had worn brown, and, limp with lack of interest, watched the ball pass overhead. It was not a very interesting game. Mike Higgins, the Red Sox manager, with nothing to lose, had restricted his major-league players to the leftfield line—along with Williams, Frank Malzone, a first-rate third baseman, played the

13. In his second season (1940) he was switched to left field, to protect his eyes from the right-field sun.

game—and had peopled the rest of the terrain with unpredictable youngsters fresh, or not so fresh, off the farms. Other than Williams' recurrent appearances at the plate, the *maladresse* of the Sox infield was the sole focus of suspense; the second baseman turned every grounder into a juggling act, while the shortstop did a breathtaking impersonation of an open window. With this sort of assistance, the Orioles wheedled their way into a 4-2 lead. They had early replaced Barber with another young pitcher, Jack Fisher. Fortunately (as it turned out), Fisher is no cutie; he is willing to burn the ball through the strike zone, and inning after inning this tactic punctured Higgins' string of test balloons.

Whenever Williams appeared at the plate—pounding the dirt from his cleats, gouging a pit in the batter's box with his left foot, wringing resin out of the bat handle with his vehement grip, switching the stick at the pitcher with an electric ferocity—it was like having a familar Leonardo appear in a shuffle of *Saturday Evening Post* covers. This man, you realized—and here, perhaps, was the difference, greater than any difference in gifts—really desired to hit the ball. In the third inning, he hoisted a high fly ball to deep center. In the fifth, we thought he had it; he smacked the ball hard and high into the heart of his power zone, but the deep right field in Fenway and the heavy air and a casual east wind defeated him. The ball died. Al Pilarcik leaned his back against the big "380" painted on the rightfield wall and caught it. On another day, in another park, it would have been gone. (After the game, Williams said, "I didn't think I could hit any harder than that. The conditions weren't good.")

The afternoon grew so glowering that in the sixth inning the arc lights were turned on—always a wan sight in the day-time, like the burning headlights of a funeral procession. Aided by the gloom, Fisher was slicing through the Sox rookies, and Williams did not come to bat in the seventh. He was second up in the eighth. This was almost certainly his last time to come to the plate in Fenway Park, and instead of merely cheering, as we had at his three previous appearances, we stood, all of us, and applauded. I had never before heard pure applause in a ballpark. No calling, no whistling, just an ocean of handclaps, minute after minute, burst after burst, crowding and running together in continuous succession like the pushes of surf at the edge of the sand. It was a sombre and considered tumult. There was not a boo in it. It seemed to renew itself out of a shifting set of memories as the Kid, the Marine, the veteran of feuds and failures and injuries, the friend of children, and the enduring old pro evolved down the bright tunnel of twenty-two summers toward this moment. At last, the umpire signalled for Fisher to pitch; with the other players, he had been frozen in position. Only Williams had moved during the ovation, switching his bat impatiently, ignoring everything except his cherished task. Fisher wound up, and the applause sank into a hush.

Understand that we were a crowd of rational people. We knew that a home run cannot be produced at will; the right pitch must be perfectly met and luck must ride with the ball. Three innings before, we had seen a brave effort fail. The air was soggy, the season was exhausted. Nevertheless, there will always lurk, around the corner in a pocket of our knowledge of the odds, an indefensible hope, and this was one of the times, which you now and then find in sports, when a density of expectation hangs in the air and plucks an event out of the future.

Fisher, after his unsettling wait, was low with the first pitch. He put the second one over, and Williams swung mightily and missed. The crowd grunted, seeing that classic swing, so long and smooth and quick, exposed. Fisher threw the third time, Williams swung again, and there it was. The ball climbed on a diagonal line into the vast volume of air over center field. From my angle, behind third base, the ball seemed less an object in flight than the tip of a towering, motionless construct, like the Eiffel Tower or the Tappan Zee Bridge. It was in the books while it was still in the sky. Brandt ran back to the deepest corner of the outfield grass, the ball descended beyond his reach and struck in the crotch where the bullpen met the wall, bounced chunkily, and vanished.

Like a feather caught in a vortex, Williams ran around the square of bases at the center of our beseeching screaming. He ran as he always ran out home runs—hurriedly, unsmiling, head down, as if our praise were a storm of rain to get out of. He didn't tip his cap. Though we thumped, wept, and chanted "We want Ted" for minutes after he hid in the dugout, he did not come back. Our noise for some seconds passed beyond excitement into a kind of immense open anguish, a wailing, a cry to be saved. But immortality is nontransferable. The papers said that the other players, and even the umpires on the field, begged him to come out and acknowledge us in some way, but he refused. Gods do not answer letters.

Every true story has an anticlimax. The men on the field refused to disappear, as would have seemed decent, in the smoke of Williams' miracle. Fisher continued to pitch, and escaped further harm. At the end of the inning, Higgins sent Williams out to his left-field position, then instantly replaced him with Carrol Hardy, so we had a long last look at Williams as he ran out there and then back, his uniform jogging, his eyes steadfast on the ground. It was nice, and we were grateful, but it left a funny taste.

One of the scholasticists behind me said, "Let's go. We've seen everything. I don't want to spoil it." This seemed a sound aesthetic decision. Williams' last word had been so exquisitely chosen, such a perfect fusion of expectation, intention, and execution, that already it felt a little unreal in my head, and I wanted to get out before the castle collapsed. But the game, though played by clumsy midgets under the feeble glow of the arc lights, began to tug at my attention, and I loitered in the runway until it was over. Williams' homer had, quite incidentally, made the score 4-3. In the bottom of the ninth inning, with one out, Marlin Coughtry, the secondbase juggler, singled. Vic Wertz, pinch-hitting, doubled off the left-field wall, Coughtry advancing to third. Pumpsie Green walked, to load the bases. Willie Tasby hit a double-play ball to the third baseman, but in making the pivot throw Billy Klaus, an ex-Red Sox infielder, reverted to form and threw the ball past the first baseman and into the Red Sox dugout. The Sox won, 5-4. On the car radio as I drove home I heard that Williams, his own man to the end, had decided not to accompany the team to New York. He had met the little death that awaits athletes. He had quit.

SELECTED BIBLIOGRAPHY

ANTHOLOGIES

Dunning, Eric. *Sport: Readings from a Sociological Perspective.* Toronto: University of Toronto Press, 1972.

Hart, M. Marie. *Sport in the Socio-Cultural Process.* Dubuque, Iowa: Wm. C. Brown, 1972.

Stone, Gregory, ed. *Games, Sport and Power.* New Brunswick, N.J.: E. P. Dutton, 1972.

Talamini, John T., and Page, Charles H. *Sport and Society, an Anthology.* Boston: Little, Brown, 1973.

Wind, Herbert Warren, ed. *The Realm of Sport.* New York: Simon & Schuster, 1966.

NONFICTION

Angell, Roger. *The Summer Game.* New York: Popular Library, 1972.

Asinof, Eliot. *Eight Men Out.* New York: Ace, 1963.

Axthelm, Pete. *The City Game.* New York: Harper's Magazine Press, 1970.

Bouton, Jim. *Ball Four.* New York: World, 1970.

———. *I'm Glad You Didn't Take It Personally.* New York: William Morrow, 1971.

Boyle, Robert H. *Sport: Mirror of American Life.* Boston: Little, Brown, 1963.

Brasch, Rudolph. *How Did Sports Begin?* New York: David McKay, 1970.

Coffin, Tristram Potter. *The Old Ball Game: Baseball in Folklore and Fiction.* New York: Herder & Herder, 1971.

Collins, Larry, and Lapierre, Dominique. *Or I'll Dress You in Mourning.* New York: Simon & Schuster, 1968.

Edwards, Harry. *The Revolt of the Black Athlete.* New York: Free Press, 1969.

———. *Sociology of Sport.* Homewood, Ill.: Dorsey Press, 1973.

Flood, Curt. *The Way It Is.* New York: Trident, 1971.

Hemingway, Ernest. *Death in the Afternoon.* New York: Scribner's, 1932.

Herrigel, Eugen. *Zen in the Art of Archery.* New York: Pantheon, 1953.

Huizinga, Johan. *Homo Ludens: A Study of the Play Element in Culture.* Boston: Beacon, 1950.

Jordan, Pat. *Black Coach.* New York: Dodd Mead, 1971.

———. *A False Spring.* New York: Dodd Mead, 1975.

———. *The Suitors of Spring.* New York: Dodd Mead, 1973

Kahn, Roger. *The Boys of Summer.* New York: Harper & Row, 1972.

Kaufman, Louis; Fitzgerald, Barbara; and Sewell, Tom. *Moe Berg: Athlete, Scholar, Spy.* Boston: Little, Brown, 1974.

Koppett, Leonard. *A Thinking Man's Guide to Baseball.* New York: E. P. Dutton, 1967.

Kramer, Jerry. *Farewell to Football.* New York: World, 1969.

———. *Instant Replay.* New York: World, 1969.

Liebling, A. J. *The Sweet Science.* New York: Viking, 1958.

McPhee, John. *Levels of the Game.* New York: Farrar, Straus & Giroux, 1969.

———. *A Sense of Where You Are.* New York: Farrar, Straus & Giroux, 1965.

Meggysey, Dave. *Out of Their League.* Berkeley: Ramparts Press, 1970.

Olsen, Jack. *The Black Athlete: A Shameful Story.* New York: Time-Life Books, 1969.

Orr, Jack. *The Black Athlete.* New York: Lion Press, 1969.

Parrish, Bernie, *They Call It a Game.* New York: Dial Press, 1971.

Peterson, Robert. *Only the Ball Was White.* Englewood Cliffs, N.J.: Prentice-Hall, 1970.

Plimpton, George. *Out of My League.* New York: Harper & Row, 1961.

———. *Paper Lion.* New York: Harper & Row, 1965.

Ritter, Lawrence S. *The Glory of Their Times.* New York: Macmillan, 1966.

Schecter, Leonard. *The Jocks.* New York: Bobbs-Merrill, 1969.

Schollander, Don, and Savage, Duke. *Deep Water.* New York: Ballantine, 1972.

Schulberg, Budd. *Loser and Still Champion: Muhammad Ali.* New York: Doubleday, 1967.

Scott, Jack. *The Athletic Revolution.* New York: Free Press, 1971.

Scott, Martha B. *The Artist and the Sportsman.* New York: Renaissance Editions, 1968.

Shaw, Gary. *Meat on the Hoof.* New York: Dell, 1972.

Slusher, Howard. *Man, Sport and Existence.* Philadelphia: Lea & Febiger, 1967.

Smith, Robert. *Baseball: A Historical Narrative of the Game, the Men Who Have Played, and Its Place in American Life.* New York: Simon & Schuster, 1947.

Torres, José. *Sting Like a Bee.* New York: Abelard-Schumann, 1971.

Wallop, Douglass. *Baseball: An Informal History.* New York: Norton, 1969.

Walton, Izaak. *The Compleat Angler.* New York: J. M. Dent, 1906.

Weiss, Paul. *Sport: A Philosophic Inquiry.* Carbondale: Southern Illinois University Press, 1969.

Wolf, David, *Foul! The Connie Hawkins Story.* New York: Holt, Rinehart & Winston, 1972.

Wooden, John. *They Call Me Coach.* New York: Bantam, 1972.

Zimmerman, Paul. *A Thinking Man's Guide to Pro Football.* New York: E. P. Dutton, 1972.

POETRY AND DRAMA

Koch, Kenneth. *Ko, or a Season on Earth*. New York: Grove Press, 1959.

Mersand, Joseph. *Three Dramas of American Individualism*. New York: Washington Square Press, 1961. (Includes *Golden Boy* by Clifford Odets.)

Miller, Arthur. *Death of a Salesman*. New York: Viking, 1949.

Miller, Jason. *That Championship Season*. New York: Atheneum, 1972.

Morrison, Lillian. *Sprints and Distances: Sports in Poetry and the Poetry in Sport*. New York: Thomas Y. Crowell, 1965.

Sackler, Howard. *The Great White Hope*. New York: Dial, 1968.

Thurber, James, and Nugent, Elliot. *The Male Animal*. New York: Samuel French, 1941.

FICTION

Asinof, Eliot. *Man on Spikes*. New York: Popular Library, 1955.

Coover, Robert. *The Universal Baseball Association, Inc., J. Henry Waugh, Prop.* New York: Random House, 1968.

DeLillo, Don. *End Zone*. Boston: Houghton Mifflin, 1972.

Dickey, James. *Deliverance*. Boston: Houghton Mifflin, 1970.

Faulkner, William. *The Bear*. New York: Random House, 1942.

Gardner, Leonard. *Fat City*. New York: Farrar, Straus & Giroux, 1969.

Gent, Pete. *North Dallas Forty*. New York: Morrow, 1973.

Harris, Mark. *Bang the Drum Slowly*. New York: Knopf, 1956.

———. *The Southpaw*. Indianapolis: Bobbs-Merrill, 1953.

Hemingway, Ernest. *In Our Time*. New York: Scribner's, 1925.

———. *The Old Man and the Sea*. New York: Scribner's, 1952.

———. *The Snows of Kilimanjaro and Other Stories*. New York: Scribner's, 1927.

Jenkins, Dan. *Semi-Tough*. New York: Atheneum, 1972.

Lardner, Ring. *Haircut and Other Stories*. New York: Scribner's, 1926.

———. *You Know Me Al*. New York: Scribner's, 1916.

Larner, Jeremy. *Drive, He Said*. New York: Bantam, 1971.

Malamud, Bernard. *The Natural*. New York: Farrar, Straus & Giroux, 1952.

Roth, Philip. *The Great American Novel*. New York: Holt, Rinehart & Winston, 1973.

Schulberg, Budd. *The Harder They Fall*. London: Sphere Books, 1971.

Sillitoe, Alan. *The Loneliness of the Long-Distance Runner*. New York: Knopf, 1959.

Updike, John. *Rabbit, Run*. New York: 1960.